About the Author

Edward A. Wynne is professor of education at the University of Illinois at Chicago. He is a sociologist specializing in the analysis of institutions that shape human values and conduct. He is the author and editor of six books including *Character Policy: An Emerging Issue; Social Security: A Reciprocity System Under Stress; Looking at Schools: Good, Bad, and Indifferent;* and *Growing Up Suburban.*

TRADITIONAL CATHOLIC
RELIGIOUS ORDERS

TRADITIONAL CATHOLIC RELIGIOUS ORDERS

LIVING IN COMMUNITY

Edward A. Wynne

Transaction Books
New Brunswick (U.S.A) and Oxford (U.K.)

Library of Congress Catalog Number: 86-30861

ISBN: 0-88738-129-4

Printed in the United States of America

Library of Congress Cataloging in Publication Data

Wynne, Edward.
    Traditional Catholic Religious Orders.

    1. Monasticism and religious orders. I. Title.
BX2432.W96 1987   271   86-30861
ISBN 0-88738-129-4

BX
2432
.W96
1988

Contents

Introduction   1

1. The First Seeds: The Desert Fathers   5

2. Coming Together: Early Monasteries   31

3. Monasticism Spreads: Growth and Adaptation   61

4. A Landmark: St. Benedict's Rule   95

5. Monasticism At Its Crest   119

6. Into the Secular World   157

7. Helping to Revive the Church   187

8. Confronting Modernity   237

Epilogue   274

INTRODUCTION

There is not, and never was on this earth, a work of human policy so well deserving of examination as the Catholic Church.
　　　　　—Thomas B. Macaulay, *Works*, "Review of Ranke's *History of the Popes*".

Catholic religious orders are probably the most long-lived *voluntary institutions* in Western society. And, by *voluntary institution*, I mean an institution where members deliberately choose to join or remain affiliated. The Catholic church itself antedates the development of such orders. But for most Catholics, the church is only a semivoluntary institution: most believers have inherited their membership, for they became members at birth. Conversely, orders to a large degree are comprised of men and women who have made deliberate decisions to enroll and remain enrolled.

This book is a history and interpretation of the lives of men and women who lived in such orders—as monks, sisters, brothers and priests—and their earlier precursors beginning in the first century A.D. It is also an interpretation of the organizational and intellectual structures that gave these institutions their remarkable vitality. The text will cover developments up to the middle of this century, when complex and dramatic events began to occur in religious life. These changes are important, but will only be summarily treated in

1

this book. Giving fullsome attention to both the past and relative present would overly extend this endeavor.

The text's material will be of interest to any person—layperson or scholar, within the church or without—pursuing a better understanding of these unique institutions. It may especially interest readers concerned with the management or planning of voluntary institutions of all types: colleges and schools, businesses, social clubs, military organizations, and church groups. It would be wrong to argue that such institutions should or can manage themselves as if they were religious orders. But it would be even more simplistic to ignore the insights that the rich history of religious life provides.

The text may also engage Americans concerned with the general history of our country and the special role religious orders have played in advancing the social and educational welfare of many classes of citizens, especially our immigrant populations.

Many limitations have been accepted in treating this vast topic in one volume, and there are some noteworthy justifications for my attempt. True, there is already an enormous literature on religious life, including many histories of particular orders. However, there is no one volume work to which thoughtful laypersons or scholars can turn for a survey of the subject. Interested persons must either do without or absorb an a huge body of material. Furthermore, our immediate era has developed assumptions that significantly handicap our attempts to evaluate institutions (and their members) that have dedicated themselves to the principles of communal living, poverty, chastity, and obedience. And much of existing literature on religious orders takes such commitments for granted; as a result, it loses some credibility for many contemporary readers. Conversely, some of the literature is hostile to such vows and regards their implications as unnatural, and assumes that religious life is unworthy of sympathetic analysis. I have assayed an alternative approach. Apparently unusual forms of human organization which persistently reoccur—such as traditional religious life—have a unique potential. They can tell us special things about ourselves. But their characteristics must be predigested and shaped into appropriate units. Otherwise, readers will treat unfamiliar · facts, portrayed without appropriate context, as encumbering and grotesque and, as a result, will be deprived of access to the precious resources that the past can supply.

One personal word of introduction should be added. Thoreau, in one of his typically cogent observations, said the first rule for every author is to tell his readers who he is, and why he wrote a particular book. I am a sociologist and a Roman Catholic. One day I realized that the church serving my community is staffed by members of a religious order. A variety of order members live together in the parish priests' residence. Gradually, I saw that these members comprise a relatively disparate group. I wondered how they manage to live in relative amicability—if they really do. I tried to answer my question via library research. I discovered that the information available was not conveniently organized, that the problem was more complex than I expected, and that the basic concepts involved would be of interest to many thoughtful persons. I decided to write this book for a broad audience and to share my wonderings and discoveries with them.

It is gratifying to see America approaching her 200th birthday as a formally created nation. However, assume that we hope our country will eventually attain, let us say, double that age. Our innumerable voluntary institutions, a critical ingredient of our society, will undoubtedly be an important resource in our reaching that 400th year. Over our next 200 years, however, it is certain that many of the existing taken-for-granted patterns in our voluntary institutions will become obsolete or maladaptive; thus we must be regularly concerned with evaluating and improving our present institutions. In this process it is important to understand one form of Western voluntary institution that has persisted for many centuries. After acquiring such information, we can make wiser decisions about our own present and future.

1
The First Seeds:
The Desert Fathers

The monk proposed to himself no greater or systemic work beyond that of saving his soul. What he did that was more than this was the accident of the hour.
—Cardinal Newman, *Historical Sketches*

We must begin with some simple definitional material. Formally, the word *religious* designates men and women living in what are popularly called *orders*, and who have made commitments to common living and to observe poverty, chastity and obedience. Religious are priests, lay brothers, or sisters (nuns). Perhaps half the persons now serving as Catholic priests are not religious. Instead, they are diocesan (or so-called secular) priests, committed to serving in a particular diocese under the supervision of its bishop. Secular priests are obligated to chastity and obedience to their bishop and may, or may not, reside in a common residence.

The seeds of religious life appeared during the early Christian era, in the first century A.D. Christian life at that time was affected by two separate but related concepts: that of shared community living, and of individual withdrawal from a corrupt and corrupting world. Both concepts—partly affected by the Jewish traditions carried forward into Christianity—strongly shaped the development of religious orders.

The Acts of the Apostles, a section of the New Testament, is a history of early Christianity written in the first century A.D. It vigorously articulates the concept of communal life. The Acts emphasize that the early Christians lived together and shielded themselves from an immoral, external society:

5

> The faithful all lived together and owned everything in community; they sold their goods and possessions and shared out the proceeds among themselves according to what each needed. They went in a body to the Temple every day, but met in their houses for the breaking of bread; they shared their food gladly and generously . . .[1]

Communal life was a significant element of Christian urban life in the Roman Empire during the first and second centuries. Undoubtedly it was an important cause for the steady enlargement of the church. Converts were attracted by the vitality and cohesion of such groups and the groups would provide members with support to resist temptation and persecution. This does not mean, as Christianity spread and persisted, that "selling all one's goods" became a common element of affiliation with the ordinary congregation. Such a totalist approach occurred only in the earliest period of church development. While the concept of communal life was lauded, the conflicting concepts of isolation and withdrawal also eventually found support with other Christians. Withdrawal, too, was related to precedents in New Testament texts. Christ, before beginning his public mission, went into the desert to fast and pray and prepare for his arduous effort. And, during his public life, he withdrew to meditate and pray on other occasions. John the Baptist, the harbinger of Jesus, spent indefinite periods in the desert to escape the temptations of a decadent environment.

Neither of the two themes was original to Christianity. The withdrawal practiced by Christ and John was consistent with similar patterns displayed by some Old Testament prophets, and the Jews had a long history of being a group-oriented people. However, it is significant that Christianity took these Hebraic themes and transformed them into principles of broader applicability—Christianity had a mission to reach the Gentiles.

Gradually, early Christianity increased its appeal. By the fourth century, it became the official religion of the Roman Empire. The uniqueness of Christian urban life then became diluted: a large proportion of the population was Christian and the religion had government sanction. The idea of isolated groupings in a city became incongruous. At the same time, other changes were associated with the triumph of Christianity. These changes caused some believers to conclude that their official religion lacked much of the power and austerity of its persecuted antecedent. Marcellinus, a Roman writer, cynically described some of the temptations arising from the triumph when he portrayed the dispute over the succession to the Roman bishopric (the successor was formally the *Pope*) in 366. A bloody fight ensued between Christian factions supporting different candidates. Marcellinus felt the divisive conflict was warranted; after all, "the successful candidate is sure to be enriched by the wealth of nations; of riding about in carriages through the streets of Rome, as soon as his dress is composed with becoming care and elegance; and of giving banquets so profuse and luxurious that their entertainments shall surpass the Imperial tables."[2] Christians offended by such luxury and quarrels over spoils were attracted to the theme of withdrawal—at the very moment their formal religion attained its central objective.

Into the Desert

The concept of withdrawal did not start as the battle cry of a deliberate movement. Instead, individual believers pursued their salvation via personal choice. Egypt became the first site of these withdrawals.[3] The early deserters were persons from this area, partly influenced by preexisting hermetic traditions prevailing in Egypt. Saint Anthony of Egypt (251-356) was prominently identified with the withdrawal. The deserters aimed to attain salvation by directing their isolated lives towards prayer, fasting, mortification, humility and meditation. Collectively, the hermits were called the Desert Fathers. The term *father* was accorded to them as a mark of dignity and respect. They were also called *monks*, derived from the Greek—one who lives alone. Eventually the Fathers were designated *anchorites*, the Greek word for "one who withdraws." Over time, two forms of monks evolved: anchorites and cenobites, monks who led communal lives. Cenobitic is rooted in the Greek word for "community." Through most of later history, Roman Catholic monks have largely been cenobitic.

The Fathers had a dual influence on the development of religious life. An immediate effect of their evident sanctity, in a time of religious stress, caused other persons to either adopt their example or explore other means of pursuing sanctity away from decadent environments. Furthermore, other aspiring hermits sought the counsel, or mentorship, of prominent Fathers, and this help was often provided. In addition, the Fathers had a long term effect: various contemporary writings about the day-to-day events in their lives were extraordinarily influential in sharpening religious life, even up into our own times. Among such significant writings were *The Life of St. Anthony*, by Saint Athanasius (ca. 295?-373), the *Institutes*, by Cassian (ca. 340?-432), and the *Lausiac Histories*, by Palladius (ca. 363?-411).

The Fathers had also historic importance. For, while the individual isolation central to their lives did not become the long-term focus of Western Christian religious life, it was coupled with the practice of poverty, chastity, and obedience. And this practice persisted and grew in influence. Different historic eras and religious orders gave varied interpretations to practice of the three virtues; nonetheless, the precedents of the Fathers were often cited to justify the interpretations. Thus the Fathers are identified with themes which still affect religious life, and we must directly consider the ramifications.

In the past, many devout Christians carried out their religious beliefs in ways dramatically different from current American—and even Christian—norms. That statement seems abstractly simple. But it assumes more complexity when we are told that Origen (184?-?253), a prominent scholar in the early Egyptian Christian church, castrated himself to confirm his continuence,[4] or that religious hermits, in the fourth and fifth centuries, engaged in implicit competitions to see who could endure the greatest levels of isolation, starvation, or self-flagellation. Later in this book, we may be similarly amazed—or distressed—at the fortitude displayed by missionaries and other religious. These evangelists accepted incredible hardships and awesomely cruel martyrdom to pursue religious goals. True, such instances of fortitude or self-abnegation usually affected only devout, self-selected volunteers;

a small proportion of the population in most environments. Still, there is no doubt that the amount of suffering pursued, or tolerated voluntarily, by these religious was far higher than we can imagine people deliberately accepting in our era. Readers may intuitively withdraw from considering persons and institutions associated with these patterns of conduct. If they do withdraw, they deprive themselves of one of the major contributions which history and scholarship can make to our lives. Therefore, before continuing any chronological treatment of early religious life, it is necessary to frankly discuss and interpret some of the typical practices of dedicated believers in the early church. The matter is not only of historical interest. Even in our own era, there are religious orders which follow similar practices—practices which have displayed powerful persistence and revitalization.

All cultures persist through suppressing or controlling large components of human potential and expression. Speaking explicitly, the culture of our era has narrowed the role of transcendent or powerful emotional experiences, of sacrifice and of the pursuit of high attainment in human life. Conversely, considerable emotional and personal energy is expended, in our times, in pursuit of goals which many contemporary persons themselves would admit are only of modest salience. Given the prevalence of such trivial contemporary goals, it is understandable that we are troubled to see (via historical writings) people who made immense sacrifices, or seriously harmed others, to strive for superordinate goals. We are not sure that superordinate goals—salvation, obeying the commands of the Lord, or achieving the conversion of one or many unbelievers—justified the distress incident to the pursuit.

Regardless of such opinions, it is still enlightening to see how vigorously men and women formerly pursued the transcendent. That pursuit generates grave dangers. But such patterns of pursuit may cause readers to wonder: Given previous human tendencies to engage in this pursuit, how does one comprehend a culture—our own society—where only a small amount of energy is spent in that effort? Such a society may appear relatively tranquil or mundane. Still, an apparently typical social pattern (i.e., tranquility) may contain important elements of instability. In any event, we can better appreciate the content of such complex issues if we deliberately examine the nature of traditional religious life. It is an alternative pattern of human conduct tied to Western traditions that have persisted for many centuries.

Poverty

In the New Testament, Christ empathetically spoke about the obstacles to a moral life that affluence generated. He never flatly condemned wealthy people to damnation,[5] but he frequently contended that the pursuit and maintenance of wealth might distract his followers from wholesome conduct.

His cautions make good psychological sense. We acquire wealth through gratifying the demands and wants of others. Oftentimes those demands and desires are not morally founded. Gratifying them may lead us to wrongdoing. Furthermore, when Christianity existed in a largely hostile environment, the pursuit of wealth could stimulate Christians to accede to the requests of hostile nonbelievers. Another aspect of wealth—or savings, or possessions—is that capital permits a person to live free from dependence on his immediate surroundings. But Christ recommended such dependency—in an appropriate context. He sent out the twelve Apostles as missionaries, saying, "Provide yourselves with no silver or gold, not even with a few coppers for your purses, with no haversack for the journey or spare tunic or footwear or a staff, for the workman is worthy of his keep. Whatever village or town you go into, ask for someone trustworthy and stay with him until you leave."[6] The inevitable need for the away-from-home Apostles to find food and shelter was thus transformed into a stimulant to the evangelic process. If the Apostles did not actively reach out, they would starve.

The prescription of poverty meant that the dedicated believer was turned from the pursuit of wealth and stimulated to become involved with the proximate community, to earn the right to charity. Speaking colloquially, such principles favor the development of a lean organization.

For the Desert Fathers, poverty was not a virtue pursued to assist institutional needs. Rather, the acceptance of poverty enabled them to personally lead lives in comparative isolation. It meant they did not need to concentrate on buying, selling, or efficient production—activities which would bring them into close contact with irreligious persons and disruptive institutions. To satisfy their physical needs, the Fathers lived in simple shelters, or caves, and secured their livelihood by gathering desert fruits and seeds, by simple gardening and weaving, and by exchanging or selling baskets. A typical story told of the Fathers illustrates the significance they assigned to poverty:

> An old man was asked by a brother the question "How shall I live?" Then the old man took off his garment, and used it to gird up his loins. He then lifted up his hands like a wrestler on guard and said, "It is meet for a monk to be as naked in respect of this world's goods as I am of clothing. And in his striving against his thoughts he must stand as upright as a vigorous athlete, and when the athlete contendeth he also standeth up naked, and when he is anointed with oil he is quite naked, and hath nothing upon him; and he learneth from him that traineth him how to contend, and when the enemy cometh against him he throweth dust upon him, which is a matter of this world, that he may be able to grasp him easily. In thyself, then, O monk, thou must see the athlete, and he who sheweth thee how to contend is God, for it is He Who giveth the victory, and Who conquereth for us; and those who contend are ourselves, and the striving is [our] opponent, and the dust is the affairs of the world. And since thou hast seen the cunning of the Adversary, stand thou up and oppose him in thy nakedness, being free from any care which belongeth to this world, and thou shalt overcome [him]. For when the mind is weighted down with the care of the world it cannot receive the holy word of God."[7]

Chastity

Jesus, the ultimate model for Christians, was unmarried. His first prominent followers, the twelve Apostles, were portrayed with almost no reference to their family—or married—life. The apostle Paul, the first great convert and missionary, was apparently unmarried. The separation of these founders and early leaders from domestic life is consistent with the unique sense of dedication associated with their missionary conduct. Furthermore, there is a particular emotional attraction to leaders who have so totally committed their lives to a holy purpose. In other words, celibacy is consistent with the most prominent models presented to Catholic males, and with the tradition of dedication which the Church tried to maintain and enhance.

The matter of female chastity is more complex. In the unstable world of the time, individual females would not be asked or encouraged to undertake isolated journeys as were undertaken by the Apostles. But innumerable proximate responsibilities arose in sustaining early Christian communities. At that time, there were no formal, government-funded welfare services. The communities had to develop institutions which served as the equivalents of hospitals, orphanages, and hotels. These communities also had the high levels of death, illness and hunger typical of the period. Needy Christians—frequently widows, with their children—turned to the community for help, while the community tried to recruit other believers to assist in providing service. Widows, individually or collectively, were often assigned such responsibilities. In "exchange," they were often supported by the community. Sometimes unmarried young women deliberately associated themselves with these helping groups and, in order to emphasize the seriousness of their association, concurrently committed themselves to virginity. This virginity was essentially similar to the inhibitions accepted by males who chose to become priests. While females were not expected to live hermetic lives in the desert some few, following the principles demonstrated by the Fathers, did pursue lives of isolation, meditating and praying in walled enclosures.

The virtue of chastity was tied to both doctrinal and institutional themes. Virgins were be characterized as Brides of Christ. Parallels were drawn between the chastity of Christ and the chastity of his later ministers. Attempts by Roman persecutors to tempt and threaten consecrated Christian virgins gave a special status to these women and their successors. The many services rendered the Christian community by such persons gave them unique prestige. And the public signs of the virgins' dedication to chastity—their conduct and their dress—clarified and simplified their roles when they worked in disorderly environments.

The commitment to celibacy and chastity was encouraged not only by rational discourse. High praise was given to women who were virgins, tendencies towards sexual expression were sharply criticized, and the "corrupting" effect of sexuality was strongly condemned. For example, St. Jerome (ca. 345-?419), a prominent early Christian ecclesiastic, wrote prolifically on behalf of virginity in a tone that sympathetic modern commentators call "extreme."[8] And I have already mentioned Origen's self-mutilation.

As an institution, the church gradually developed prohibitions against self-injury and adopted more sympathetic attitudes towards conjugal life. However, it was also dedicated to the principle of free will. And over the centuries it saw many important institutional benefits derived from the requirement of chastity. Thus, the church persistently maintained the right of its members to choose a life of chastity in religious orders or in other limiting commitments. Furthermore, the church maintained a belief in the superiority of commitment to the religious life over commitment to domestic and sexual life.

Obedience

In many instances the Fathers acted as masters to individual disciples. The Fathers also recognized that their own persistence in their vocations depended on the sublimation of their will to the perceived dictates of God. This caused the Fathers to strongly stress the trait of obedience—to the will of God in particular, and to legitimate authority in general.

A typical story attributed to the Fathers illustrates the virtue of acceding to authority:

> Abbot John used to tell this story: Once there was a disciple of a Greek philosopher who was commanded by his Master for three years to give money to everyone who insulted him. When this period of trial was over, the Master said to him: "Go to Athens and learn wisdom." When the disciple was entering Athens he met a certain wise man who sat at the gate insulting everybody who came and went. He also insulted the disciple who immediately burst out laughing. "Why do you laugh when I insult you?" said the wise man. "Because," said the disciple, "for three years I have been paying for this kind of thing and now you give it to me for nothing." "Enter the city," said the wise man, "it is all yours." Abbot John then said: "This is the door of God by which our fathers, rejoicing in many tribulations, enter into the City of Heaven."[9]

It is also important to recognize that the obedience "up," which the Fathers expected of subordinates, was coupled with a strong concern for charity, which should be practiced "down" by superiors. While the master could make strong demands on disciples, such demands should be presented with insight and be moderated by the master's own humility.

The Life of the Fathers

The Fathers fasted, practiced other austerities (flagellation, sleeping in uncomfortable situations, living without shelter), engaged in minimal gardening and simple handicrafts, sometimes conversed with each other on holy topics, read scriptures, occasionally participated in religious services (e.g., they received the Holy Eucharist), prayed, and meditated. *Meditation* meant they tried to put themselves into immediate communion with God through reflection and internal dialogues.

Their activities were affected with certain disruptions: Many Fathers reported they received direct, powerful visitations from the devil, his manifestations, or associates. Such temptations were seen by the Fathers as a logical outgrowth of their activities: If one strove to become closer to God, and voluntarily accepted extreme deprivation, it was logical that the devil might intervene to prevent such activities and to proffer temptations. The forces of evil could be as equally personified as those of God. Disruptions also occurred because a certain prestige, in the eyes of visiting pilgrims, became attached to Fathers who carried out the most rigorous mortifications. The mortifications included extraordinary fasts; living for years in small, walled, single rooms with only a slot for passing food; and living atop a tall pillar erected in the wilderness, where food was pulled up with a rope—as Simeon Stylites did for thirty-seven years. Sometimes, certain Fathers deliberately engaged in striving to surpass their competitors' conspicuous mortifications. Undoubtedly, such competitions distracted many persons from the contemplative element of the Fathers' isolation. Another less colorful problem was the distress of accadie. *Accadie* was the Fathers' term for tedium, or disengagement from active religious pursuits. And it is understandable why many Fathers and disciples might find the demands associated with anchorite life too severe.

By the early fourth century, some monks pursuing religous life in the desert began the practice of living in communities—monastaries, homes for monks—as compared to the alternative of anchorite life. One of the first monastaries was founded by Saint Pachomius (ca. 290-346) in Egypt in about 320. The monks living in monasteries eventually were termed cenobites.

Monastic life provided cenobites with certain benefits denied to anchorites; it offered them some degree of physical security. Ill or disabled monks might be cared for by the community. Better organized and larger scale systems of housing and food production could provide cenobites with somewhat greater comfort. Some forms of religious observance might be facilitated: priests, who were also monks, were present to provide Communion; and collections of religious writings were available in a monastery library. Reading of sacred writings was facilitated because every monastery would include one or more persons who could read to the group, for not all monks were literate. In this environment, the more extreme—and competitive—elements of mortification could be constrained, for cenobic life required its members to subject their conduct, even their mortification, to the principles established by the collective. Finally, cenobites participating in religious activities could receive emotional support from proximate co-believers and thus be less subject to the accadie associated with isolation.

The shift to communal, cenobic life was not presented as an absolute rejection of anchorite principles. Poverty, chastity, and obedience were still accepted as vital norms—and even heightened by some elements of collective life. The "sayings," and general tone of anchorite life, were regarded as admirable and held out to cenobites as ideals. It was even suggested that some cenobites should view monastic life as preparation for eventual solitary anchorite life.

The evolution of anchorite life became an important point of distinction between the Latin (or Roman Catholic) and Orthodox churches. In the early Christian centuries, no formal distinctions existed between these two patterns of belief. But, as distinctions gradually developed, then differences in norms of religious life became one important source of contrast. Speaking generally, over many centuries, the Orthodox churches gradually evolved religious patterns that gave lesser emphasis to cenobic life, and more to individualistic anchorite life, than did the Latin church. In the interest of necessary historic focus, however, the rich and important topic of the Orthodox religious tradition will not be further considered in this book.

The most important anchorite principle that the cenobites in the Latin church still honored was that of isolation. For anchorites, isolation meant withdrawal of the believer into the desert to escape contact with all other persons. For the cenobite, the believer became part of a community of believers who collectively withdrew from contact with nonbelievers or from believers who did not share their devotion. And this concept of separation—either individual or collective—has remained a permanent theme in religious life. In a sense, the theme is a recognition of the inevitable heterogeneity of human life: not all persons are, or will be, Christians; not all Christians are, or will be, of a highly devout temper; and not all devout Christians are, or will be, suitable as members of a segregated religious community. Furthermore, the concept assumes that more intense believers can better fulfill their roles through isolation from worldly affairs. It is true that the converse concept of a deeply devout person vitally engaged in worldly activities may hold a certain attraction. Christians might like to believe that presidents, corporation officers and generals can be profoundly devout. But the monks—both anchorites and cenobites—would typically hold such a concept unrealistic, or dangerous to one's religious commitment. Saint Basil (330-379) expressed some of the virtues of such isolation in a letter to a colleague, Saint Gregory of Nazianzus (ca. 330-390). His thoughts are worth quoting at some length:

> We must strive after a quiet mind. As well might the eye ascertain an object put before it, while it is wandering restless up and down, and sideways, without fixing a steady gaze upon it, as a mind, distracted by a thousand worldly cares, be able clearly to apprehend the truth. He who is not yet yoked in the bonds of matrimony is harassed by frenzied cravings, and rebellious impulses, and hopeless attachments; he who has found his mate is encompassed with his own tumult of cares: if he is childless, there is desire of children; has he children, anxiety about their education; attention to his wife, care of his house, oversight of his servants, misfortunes in trade, quarrels with his neighbours, lawsuits, the risks of the merchant, the toil of the farmer. Each day, as it comes, darkens the soul in its own way; and night after night takes up the day's anxieties, and cheats the mind with corresponding illusions. Now, one way of escaping all this is separation from the whole world; that is, not bodily separation, but the severance of the soul's sympathy with the body, and to live so

without city, home, goods, society, possessions, means of life, business, engagements, human learning, that the heart may readily receive every impress of divine teaching. Preparation of heart is unlearning the prejudices developed by evil converse. It is the smoothing of the waxen tablet before attempting to write on it. Now, solitude is of the greatest use for this purpose, inasmuch as it stills our passions, and gives opportunity to cut them out of the soul. Let there, then, be a place such as ours, separate from intercourse with men, that the tenor of our exercises be not interrupted from without. Such pious exercises nourish the soul with divine thoughts. [10]

The Message of the Desert Fathers

The Fathers epitomized the themes of poverty, chastity, obedience, and isolation or withdrawal. In addition, there was a more general approach, or *way*, which the lives of the Fathers typified. That way became an important ingredient in traditional religous life and must be generally considered. However, we should first reflect on how we can now know of, and describe, a way which was practiced by hermits living about sixteen centuries ago. Obviously, such knowledge must largely come through writing—especially since the Fathers consciously avoided constructing significant churches or homes.

Some of the Fathers were literate, but many others were illiterate—a common phenomenon in their era—and the traditions of the Fathers did not place high value on written communications. Thus, much of the message of the Fathers comes to us from the writings of contemporary pilgrims and other observers. The writings about the Fathers have been influential. They have been regularly read by (and to) religious since the sixth century up into our own era. The literal topic of "writing" reveals one cause for the influence of such works. In the third and fourth centuries educated Roman citizens were steeped in a body of classic literature drawn from both Latin and Greek sources. This training caused many early Christians to be extremely able writers, who produced literary works of permanent importance. Consider, for instance, Cassian's discussion of the complex psychological concept of accadie:

> Our sixth combat is with what the Greeks call accadie, which we may term weariness or distress of heart. This is akin to dejection, and is especially trying to solitaries, and a dangerous and frequent foe to dwellers in the desert; and especially disturbing to a monk about the sixth hour [of the day], like some fever which seizes him at stated times, bringing the burning heat of its attacks on the sick man at usual and regular hours. Lastly, there are some of the elders who declare that this is the "midday demon" spoken of in the nineteenth Psalm. . . .

> And when this has taken possession of some unhappy soul, it produces dislike of the place, disgust with the cell, and disdain and contempt of the brethren who dwell with him or at a little distance, as if they were careless or unspiritual. It also makes the man lazy and sluggish about all manner of work which has to be done within the enclosure of his dormitory. It does not suffer him to stay in his cell, or to take any pains about reading, and he often groans because he can do no good while he stays there; and he complains that he is cut off from spiritual gain, and is of no use in the place, as if he were one who, though he could govern others and be useful to a great number of people, yet was edifying none, nor profiting anyone by his teaching and doctrine. He cries up distant monasteries and those which are a long way off, and describes such places as more profitable and better suited for salvation; and besides this he paints the intercourse with the brethren there as sweet and full of spiritual life. On the other hand, . . .11

But the message of the Fathers has more than a fine literary quality. Much of the information transmitted by their lives is presented in anecdotes or proverbial stories written by visitors. The stories display the techniques used by the Fathers to instruct disciples and visitors. The stories often present approaches that demonstrate great insight and that portray the Fathers with persuasive accuracy. The reader tends to believe that these people were real and that we know something about their lives—and what they thought. One may have reservations about the demons they reported to have confronted, or the wilderness animals they had befriended. But one can simultaneously conclude that the Fathers understood the nature of the human heart and of the core of Christian doctrine. Their counsel communicates over the centuries:

> Father Isaac used to say that Father Pambo said, "The manner of the apparel which a monk ought to wear should be such that if it were cast outside the cell for three days no one would carry it away." . . .

> A brother asked of Father Sisoes saying, "Tell me a word whereby I may live." The old man said unto him, "Why does thou urge me, O brother, to speak a useless word? Whatsoever thou seest me do, that do thyself. . . ."

> I have heard that there were two old men who dwelt together for many years, and who never quarrelled, and that one said to the other, "Let us also pick a quarrel with each other, even as other men do." Then his companion answered and said unto him, "I know not how a quarrel cometh," and the older man answered and said unto him, "Behold, I will set a brick in the midst, and will say, 'This is mine,' and do thou say, 'It is not thine, but mine;' and from this quarrelling will ensue." And they placed a brick in the midst, and one of them said, "This is mine," and his companion answered and said after him "This is not so, for it is mine"; and straightway the other replied and said unto him, "If it be so, and the brick be thine, take it and go." Thus they were not able to make a quarrel.[12]

The sayings and conduct of the Fathers present a number of psychological principles: rules for interpreting the operation of the human mind. These principles have persisting vitality, due in part to the relationship between them and religious life—indeed, to human life in general. One principle is the Fathers' stress on teaching by example. Their stories are about what people *did*. They also emphasized the centrality of charity in human relations—this would be especially appropriate in religious life, where affiliation is a deliberate choice; if charity did not prevail, many persons would refuse to join or would leave. Temptation, as personified by the literal wiles of the Devil, was, to the Fathers, a pervasive reality. It had to be actively recognized and confronted. Conversely, virtuous conduct was the outcome of an arduous and persistent pursuit. Few good deeds naturally and easily happened. Physical mortification was an important means of stimulating good conduct. The simplistic acceptance of bodily drives would encourage human beings to engage in selfish and antireligious conduct; disciplining the body and its desires was a means of attaining great fulfillment. It was important that both masters and disciples practice humility. That practice did not come easily, but it was a consistent desideratum. Finally, considerable suspicion was directed against ordinary human conversation. It was likely to lead participants into temptation, or at least, take them away from concern about the divine. Furthermore, the person talking could not be listening, and listening—an act of charity and humility—was a prime obligation.

These principles are not the sole property of the Fathers. Some of them are found in elements of earlier religions. And some later religions, and psychological systems, have adopted such principles from evidently independent searches. Furthermore, some of the principles are related to material in the Old and New Testaments. Still, it seems the circumstance of the Fathers' desert life served to give their insights a particular focus and tone.

As part of the preparation for this book, I had some contacts with contemporary Catholic order members living traditional modes of life. Two typical anecdotes drawn from these contacts suggest ways the spirit of the Desert Fathers still affects the shape of religious life.

One male order member told me about an especially charitable co-member. To portray the nature of such charity he said, "If someone came to him to complain about the deficiencies of another member, he would say, 'Why, that's too bad. We must now stop and pray that he changes such conduct, shouldn't we?'" In another instance, two senior sisters agreed to allow me to interview one of the novices then in training. It was evident that they had mutually agreed who my interviewee would be. Several days later when I arrived for the interview I was introduced to all of the novices. The sister in charge then openly directed a particular novice to meet with me and act as interviewee. It was evident that this was the first occasion the novice had heard about her interview—though the decision had been made many days ago. The novice was a thoughtful woman, with a master's degree in special education. In almost all other work or community environments, such a person would have been informed in advance of the interview by her superiors. I am sure the interview was conducted without notice because the order typically stressed to its members the themes of obedience and simplicity.

It should be noted that one cannot talk about the truth—or falsehood—of the Fathers' psychological principles. Of course some readers may wonder about the probability of demons, but no one has ever seen a superego or an id either. Many principles of all important psychologies are necessarily at high levels of generality and are not easily susceptible to formal scientific tests. Sometimes it is proposed that such untestable principles should not be allowed to serve as guides for human conduct. But such contentions quickly become ridiculous in the world of everyday affairs. It is essential that humans develop fairly clear and persisting principles to guide their routine relationships. Such principles constitute an implicit psychology. There are empiric limits to such semiarbitrary approaches and they contain inevitable imperfections. But all psychologies are imperfect. We just have to decide which less imperfect system to apply in comprehending the world around us. As for the imperfections of more modern and scientific psychologies, one

660 page outline of psychological research findings concluded with the following remarks:

> The image of man presented is as yet incomplete, just as the behavioral sciences themselves, from any historical perspective, are still near their starting point. . . . as one reviews this set of findings, he may well be impressed by another omission more striking still. As one lives life or observes it around him (or within himself) or finds it in a work of art, he sees a richness that somehow has fallen through the present screen of behavioral science. This book, for example, has rather little to say about general human concerns: nobility, moral courage, ethical torments, the delicate relation of father and son or of the marriage state, life's way of corrupting innocence, the rightness or wrongness of acts, evil, happiness, love and hate, death, even sex. . . .
>
> Not yet, anyway, do behavioral sciences see life steadily and see it whole.[13]

The vitality of any particular psychological approach is also affected by the beliefs that practitioners and subjects bring to it, beliefs partly based on the prevailing symbol system. Since symbol systems are especially the province of religious orders, the matter of psychology and symbolism requires explication. Take, for example, one contemporary psychology for treating alcoholism. In our time, one disposition is to view alcoholism as a "disease." That disposition is based on a particular psychology: it implies the affliction of alcoholism is largely due to matters outside of the control of the alcoholic. As a result, curing alcoholism depends on external forces and persons correcting some troubling "cause." The psychology of alcoholism-as-disease is symbolically supported by legislative declarations, court decisions, and resolutions passed by professional associations. These community forces are trying to popularize an allegedly scientific premise by giving it the status of an approved doctrine. After all, it is impossible to "prove" alcoholism is a disease—unless we radically redefine the word disease. The real hope is that if we "believe" hard enough, it will be as if alcoholism is a disease; research will be carried out, curative approaches will be tried with more persistence, and members of society will change their ways of relating to alcoholics.

The difficulty is that the alcoholism-as-disease approach lowers the responsibility of the afflicted person. The approach recognizes that a diseased person should help in effecting his cure; however, prime responsibility for the cure is put on agents outside the sufferer. Thus, the psychology of alcoholism-as-disease diminishes the viability of cures focusing on the personal responsibility of the alcoholic.

Whether the disease approach or the personal responsibility approach is the better way to correct alcoholism is problematic. All we can be sure of is that either approach will be more effective in an environment of strong belief, and that they are somewhat antithetical to each other. Similarly, the psychology of the Fathers may oftentimes be more effective—for many purposes—than more modern psychologies. However, as in the case of all complex psychologies, belief is an important component. As we have seen, and will see, the Fathers and their successors worked hard to maintain a climate of belief.

The Challenge of Living Together

When the monks collected into monasteries, a novel problem arose: What principles or rules should determine how they lived together? A solitary anchorite could develop his own set of habits, shaped partly by the directions of his master, the necessities of his situation, and principles drawn from the Scriptures. Oftentimes, individual Fathers applied different approaches or developed contrasting habits, but those differences had little effect on the other Fathers. A group of people living in common, however, had an innumerable number of decisions that had to be integrated into a coordinated whole. Consider some of the questions which would probably arise:

1.   How should the group ensure its isolation?

2. Who should be permitted to join the group, and how should "joining" occur?
3. What relationships should be maintained between members and non-members, and, especially, between members and their former families?
4. Should equivalent institutions be developed for females? How should they be similar—and different—than those maintained for males?
5. How should the necessary productive activities of the group be conducted?
6. What should be the role of art (e.g., literature, music, architecture) in advancing the purposes of the group?
7. What sort of sleeping arrangements should be maintained?
8. What sort of eating arrangements should be maintained?
9. How should members of the group dress?
10. What provisions should be made for sick, injured or aged members of the group?
11. What, if any, charitable activities should the group undertake? How should they be managed?
12. What persons, if any, should have special authority in the group? What should the nature of the authority be?
13. How should discipline be maintained in the group?
14. How should decisions about novel issues be made?
15. How should the wealth of the community—its land, buildings, tools, any income it earns or receives—be controlled and owned?
16. What relationship, if any, should be maintained among physically separate religious communities applying generally similar policies?
17. What relationship should the group maintain with other agencies of the Church?
18. How can the organization develop an institutional memory, which should persist beyond the lives of individual members?

Obviously, such a list can be even further enlarged. If we reflect, we can see that most of the questions only reiterate concerns that arise in all persisting human relationships—particularly, in our era, in nuclear families. And persisting nuclear families, on the whole, solve such concerns, but rarely via developing highly original, deliberate answers. Instead they apply solutions learned from other models—especially the families of procreation of the two spouses. In other words, our own family life often replicates many of the principles learned from our parents. Families are also helped to solve their organizational problems because they are relatively small units: they start off as two adults, and then gradually may add some children, who, incidentally, are not able to directly challenge parental authority for a number of years. Furthermore, many of the complex concerns listed above are handled, in society, outside of the family unit, for example, at the job site, or by a local church. And other concerns—such as the principle of monogamous family life—are settled by preexisting norms articulated by the whole society.

Developing a vital mode of cenobic life was an immensely more complicated matter than the practices of the anchorites. There was a good sense to the idea that collective religious life, for most devout believers, provided a more wholesome environment than solitary isolation. But designing collective life generated many questions. Furthermore, if an individual anchorite's activities were flawed, only that individual might be damaged. But, if a community was improperly regulated, many persons might be afflicted, even individuals who themselves had no deliberate bad judgments. Thus, considerable responsibilities were generated for religious communities and their systems of governance. Finally, large-scale community life by persons of the same sex—not simply agglomerations of nuclear families—was, historically, a relatively novel human problem. There were few, or no, convenient role models to adopt—apart from the general principles articulated by the Fathers, or derived from the language of the Scripture. The first monasteries triggered a process of experiment and analysis which has continued into our own time.

One can see parallels between the governance problems of monasteries and those of traditional political units, such as nations or cities. These political units must persist through time. As in monasteries, deliberate, formal governance decisions are routinely made, put into writing, and applied on a regular basis. Political systems often governed larger bodies of persons than monasteries; but, after about the tenth century, some particular monastic and religious organizations, existing in many different countries, encompassed tens of thousands of religious. Monastic units also accepted many more responsibilities towards "citizens" than most political entities. It is evident the parallel between political and religious organizations should not be overextended. Still, it is correct to say that the monastic system is an early, important, and novel example of political organization, which has shown great persistence and adaptability.

Notes

1. Jerusalem Bible, Acts 3:44-47.

2. Quoted in Herbert Workman, *The Evolution of the Monastic Ideal* (Boston, MA: Beacon Press, 1962), p. 8.

3. W. H. Mackean, *Christian Monasticism in Egypt* (London: Society for Propogation of Christian Education, 1920).

4. *New Catholic Encyclopedia* (Washington, DC: Catholic University, 1967), vol. 10, p. 767.

5. Christ's famous pronouncement about it being easier for a camel to pass through the "eye of the needle" than for a rich man to enter heaven was not taken literally by his listeners. The "Eye of the Needle" is and was a door in the wall of Jerusalem. It was opened to admit visitors when the main gate was closed for security reasons. That doorway was narrow to insure that it could not be assaulted by enemy attackers if the main gate was closed to them— —hence, its name "the Needle." But presumably a camel could manage to enter.

6. Jerusalem Bible, Matt. 10:5-11.

7. Ernest W. Wallis, ed. and trans., *The Paradise of the Desert Fathers* (New York: Duffield, 1909), p. 36.

8. *New Catholic*, vol. 7, p. 873.

9. Thomas Merton, *The Wisdom of the Desert* (New York: New Directions, 1960), p. 39.

10. Quoted in Ann Freemantle, *A Treasury of Early Christianity* (New York: Viking, 1953), p. 491.

11. Freemantle, *Treasury*, p. 522.

12. Wallis, *Paradise*, p. 66.

13.   Bernard Berelson and Gary A. Becker, *Human Behavior* (New York: Harcourt, Brace and World, 1964), p. 666.

14.   For some discussion of these complex issues, see Workman, *Evolution,* and David Knowles, *From Pachomius to Ignatius* (Oxford: Clarendon Press, 1966).

2
Coming Together:
Early Monasteries

The sacrifices of the monk included also the neglect of his family, for the "remembrance of kinsfolk" was the work of evil spirits. So the address at the admission of a new monk bade him to remember nothing of his kinsfolk . . .
— Herbert Workman, *The Evolution of the Monastic Ideal*

From the founding of the first monasteries in Egypt in the fourth century, religious orders have been governed by written procedures. Several factors have brought about the development and persistence of these formal written structures. Many Christians who joined the first monasteries were already accustomed to using written materials—the Scriptures—as guides for conduct. The study of Scripture also established the habit of looking for precedents to resolve immediate concerns: it implied that some answers had already been discovered in the past, and we should pursue those discoveries. Finally there is the probability that any effective system for governing numerous bodies of people deliberately brought together for prolonged, common activities, should be put into writing.

The basic documents which govern religions are termed *Rules*, or *the Rule*. *Rule*, in this context, is similar to our word *constitution*. In other words, a religious rule may state broad principles, as well as specific, concrete details. In later stages of religious development, the Rule of an order was usually supplemented with other, more explicit, and transitory guidelines, adapted to local circumstances. Thus, there is a form of regulatory hierarchy, just as Americans have a federal constitution, laws, rules of regulatory agencies, court decisions, and bodies of state and local laws. But, in the early history of religious life, the differentation between such levels was less precise: rules included both general, as well as minute, principles and prescriptions.

A distinction should be noted between the *rules* of particular religious orders, and the general laws, or rules, governing the entire contemporary Catholic church. The rules of the church are codified into *canon law.* The Rules of religious orders are subject to canon law, but that law provides considerable room for discretion in the development of particular rules. Readers should also know that, under contemporary canon law, religious groups can be formed into different associations called *orders, congregations,* or *institutes.* These designations signify different obligations and privileges allocated to their members by the church. In early religious life, such distinctions among orders were not drawn, but evolved over time. The distinctions can sometimes be significant, but it would unduly burden readers to clearly articulate them throughout this book. Thus, the word *order* will be applied indiscriminately, unless the context makes a more precise usage constructive.

In particular orders, at different times in history, the fidelity of order members to the Rule—and its "right" interpretation—became subjects of great controversy. It was rare for order members to reject or radically change a Rule. But it is true that, on occasion, Rules were ignored, or interpreted in problematic fashions. Some of these controversies will be discussed later in this book.

Rules are typically designated by the names of prominent religious figures—often saints—who first wrote or promulgated them, and otherwise "founded" the order. The first Christian monasteries in Egypt were governed by the Rule of Saint Pachomius. This form of designation is significant. (Some of the significance can be appreciated if we recall that James Madison was probably the individual with the greatest direct influence on the text of the U.S. Constitution. Suppose we called it the Constitution of Madison?) The form of designation used for Rules reveals an important characteristic of traditional religious life. In the eyes of later order members, the founder of their order is a person of great prominence. (In early periods, religious orders of women often had a male designated as "founder," although females were also identified with the founding process. In many instances, the male was simultaneously engaged in founding a parallel order for males. Later religious orders of women may—or may not—have had females designated as founders, depending on circumstances.)

It is understood that the founder rarely acted solely on his own. But it is routinely emphasized that the creation of the order was largely due to the founder. We will see later some of the procedures used by orders to heighten their members' sense of the role of the founder—and the principles he articulated. But, at this moment, the point is to emphasize that religious perceive the development of their order as the outcome of a personal act. In a sense, there are parallels between the role of Christ, and that of the founder. Each represents an individual who accepted great responsibility, and wielded great authority.

As a practical matter, founders usually did not draft Rules in solitude. Drafters used previous documents and precedents as resources; researchers can identify phrases and concepts derived from earlier sources. Furthermore, Rules were often vague on many issues. They were often more like essays, or homilies, than legislative enactments.

The designation of a Rule by the founder's name makes it likely members will personify the characteristics and virtues of the individual founder. The identification of an order with a single individual is a strength—and a liability. It is a strength since one prominent role model is put before members. Thus, the order's iconographic and commemorative resources can be directed, to honor the founder and his principles, in a unified fashion. It is a liability because the group is not provided with alternative models to follow when changes arise that require adaptability. The single person identification also emphasizes the focus on hierarchy and obedience typical of religious life: if the original Rule is presented as written by one individual, it is logical that the order defined by the Rule be governed by an individual, compared to some highly consensual or legislative process.

The Form of Rules

An important characteristic of most rules is their emphasis on biblical quotations, and the iteration of homilectic themes. A typical example is found in the following quotation from one of the Pachomian Rules (ca. 340):

> . . . this coming together of ours, and the community in which we are joined is a work of God. For the Apostle teaches us when he says "Do not forget good works and sharing: God is pleased by sacrifices of that kind" [Hebrews 13:16]. And then we read in the *Acts of the Apostles.* "The multitude of believers was of one heart and soul, and no one called anything his own; rather, everything was in common. The Apostles gave witness to the Resurrection of the Lord Jesus with great power" [Acts 4:32-37]. The Psalmist agrees with these words when he says: "Behold how good and pleasant it is for brothers to dwell as one" [Ps 132:1]. So let us live in cenobia and be joined with one another in mutual love. We should be zealous for discovering how, in this life, we may have fellowship with the [saints in Heaven] so that in the future life we may share their lot; knowing that the Cross is the source of our doctrine, and that we must suffer along with Christ [Rom 8:17] and experience the fact without tribulations and sufferings no one attains the victory.[1]

The next quotation is from the preliminary Rule of a female religious Roman Catholic order in the process of being developed and defined in the early 1980s:

> A religious community is primarily God's work. His love is first offered to the individual as an attraction to a specific community; personal responses to love bring the Sisters together; oneness in response is constantly being made through worship, through the observance of the common life, through sacrifice. Together the Sisters are unceasingly being built into a house where God lives in Spirit.[2]

Such Rules—whether modern or ancient—reiterate biblical themes about the principles of communal living. The Rules help order members relate their lives to the values of early Christianity, whether those values are supported by either the New or Old Testament. Most biblical themes, incidentally, were originally developed and tested by the Jewish people in the crucible of common living. The themes describe how people and their leaders worked together to confront problems. Their approaches and solutions often had theocratic elements. However, working with God is part of the problem-solving pattern disclosed by the Bible. In a sense the Bible is simply a history book. It was used by religions as a resource for handling immediate community problems. And the long history of Judaism and Christianity indicates that biblical advice has a certain vitality: it is based on significant insights into human nature.

The pattern of biblical citation typical in rules also meant that Rules were relatively similar in tone to religious writings with which members were familiar. The patterns also meant the Rules were constrained to take their themes from Scriptures. In effect, the authors of the various Rules had to adapt scriptural principles to the operation of their orders.

It is notorious that the contents of the Bible can be cited to support diverse contentions. Still, the themes of the Bible dealing with community life are more constrained than its total contents. And the New Testament themes relating to community life are even more restrictive than those found throughout the whole Bible. Thus, in a somewhat literal sense, persons who draft Rules for religious orders—and who must accept such parameters—are held to tighter boundaries than drafters of other principled documents. To be explicit, take some key phrases from basic American documents: "equal protection of the laws," or "the right to the pursuit of happiness." Such phrases have less precision than most biblical injunctions. Religious orders, engaged in carrying out the intent of the Scriptures regarding community living, probably receive more precise guidance about principles from the Bible than Americans do from their basic documents. These traditions of biblical guidance may be one means of inhibiting the extraordinary authority granted to persons who develop and direct religious orders.

Voluntarism and the Catholic Church

The topic of authority invites some general remarks about the governance of orders. The degree of member obedience demanded by orders varied in different orders and countries, and at different periods in church history. Generalizations about religious obedience should be regarded as just that: generalizations. But, when this qualification is recognized, it is still accurate to say that religious, throughout most order history, have been subject to more constraints toward obedience than are typical for contemporary laypersons. Furthermore, some constraints have been very severe. One Desert Father story which has been included in the readings for potential members for some orders (up to, and including, our own era) was of the master who directed his disciple to plant a broomstick handle in the sand, and water it daily for several years to make it grow. Religious obedience often extended to matters that would seem to include, to many laypersons, the ridiculous. If a novice could not accept such strictures, he was informed he was not called to religious life.

The implications of such constraints can be better appreciated if we examine the contexts in which they were applied. Most orders comprise members who chose to join as young adults, or adults. (The topic of age of joiners at recruitment is complex and will be considered in more detail later.) Such recruits, during the joining process, were deliberately informed about the obligations and restrictions associated with membership. One way of receiving such information was to study matters such as the "plant the broomstick" story. Thus, the real focus on member participation in order governance was more the decision to join, rather than involvement in making or changing existing rules. In contrast, Americans usually do not choose their country; we are rather born into it. Thus, we may be entitled to more say in governance, since we never had a formal right to enlist, or to refuse to join.

The voluntary element of religious orders is somewhat unusual when compared to mainstream Catholic tradition. For most of the history of the church, its membership largely comprised persons born into the religion. They were born of Catholic parents and reared in largely Catholic countries, or in Catholic local or ethnic groups. Due to such factors, their Catholicism could be taken for granted. This pattern of involuntary enrollment seems self-evident. But it contrasts with the norms of some Protestant sects (which restrict enrollment, or baptism, to adults), and with the history of the early Christian church in the first and second centuries. In the early period, church members are adults who deliberately chose to join. The difference between situations where members were created through infant baptism, compared to enlisting adults, has significant implications for Catholic doctrine and "style." Those implications have affected order history—since orders essentially comprise adults who have chosen to join.

The early Catholic church was an unpopular minority religion without great power or economic resources. It could only survive if it recruited— and held—significant numbers of adults. There are obviously reasons why such a handicapped institution might expire. However, if it did persist and grow, one can deduce certain traits which successful religions of this sort would possess. Such a religion would make people who did choose to join it feel very supported, and emotionally enhanced. New members would be required to carry out significant responsibilities to help a comparatively poor institution. Many of these members would need to be people of considerable determination, to withstand the pressures of a hostile external environment. The religion would stress after-life rewards to make up for the sufferings now inflicted on members. While the religion might make strong demands on members, it would more motivate people by promises of reward, instead of the threat of immediate punishment: punishment would be relatively implausible if members could easily leave the church and reaffiliate with majority society.

While I have just characterized the early Catholic church as a church for adults, one should not assume that a adult church would make special intellectual demands on its members.

It is true that many early Christians—and later, members of
religious orders—displayed significant intellectual capabilities
(as evinced by their writings). But the difference between
adults and children and adolescents is not so much a matter of
intellect as of emotional depth. Adults are capable of more
profound and persisting feelings than children and adolescents,
and a that which recruits them has to respond to that
capability. Similarly, religious orders should make more
profound emotional demands on members than ordinary church
life. Adult churches (and orders) must also provide their
members with higher levels of emotional gratification. The
basic adult demand of the early church, and of religious orders,
was that doctrine be taken with consistent seriousness.

Much of the spirit just attributed to early Christianity is
articulated in the Acts of the Apostles and the Epistles. These
portions of the New Testament are a history of Christian life
during the first century A.D. A typical expression of the theme
of supportive community is articulated in these writings is found
in Saint Paul's (A.D. 10-?67) first epistle, or letter of counsel, to
his congregation in Corinth:

> Though I speak with the tongues of men and of
>   angels, and have not charity,
> I am become as a sounding brass, or a tinkling
>   cymbal.
> And though I have the gift of prophecy, and
>   understand all mysteries, and
> All knowledge; and though I have all faith, so that I
>   could move mountains, and have not charity,
>   I am nothing.
> And though I bestow all my goods to feed the poor,
> And though I give my body to be burned, and have
>   not charity, it profiteth me nothing.
> Charity suffereth long, and is kind; charity envieth
>   not; charity vaunteth not itself, is not puffed
>   up . . .
> And now abideth faith, hope and charity, these
>   three; but the greatest of these is charity.[3]

Greedy Institutions, Greedy Members

Louis Coser analyzed diverse institutions that made high-level demands on members. His catalogue included typical religious orders along with other apparently powerful institutions, such as, certain military groups and religious sects. The title of his book is *Greedy Institutions.*[4] Its theme is self-evident and encompasses a plausible truth. Some institutions make greater demands on members than do many others, and there are certain common characteristics to such institutions. Of course, his book—and its title—goes farther than mere description. *Greedy* is a pejorative word. Greedy institutions are implicitly undesirable and bad.

Coser's analysis has a limitation. It does not clearly separate voluntary and involuntary institutions: institutions members choose to join and can (sometimes) choose to leave without physical danger, compared to institutions people are thrust into, and perhaps cannot leave. His analysis is also flawed because he sees the relationships involved as largely between the member and "institution." But, especially in voluntary institutions, the members largely relate to other members—who are, in effect, *the institution.* And, in *strong* institutions—to use a less pejorative term than greedy—the quality of member-to-member relationships is different than in weak institutions. In strong institutions (compared to weak ones), member-to-member relationships are likely to more (a) predictable, (b) engaged, and (c) generally supportive. They will follow this pattern because strong institutions have the *power* to cause members to act routinely in such a manner. Furthermore, if a relatively voluntary institution is truly greedy, in the worst sense, members will be prone to leave, and fewer persons will choose to be recruits. And there have been periods when people frequently left religious orders, and times when the numbers of recruits were low. Conversely, weak institutions have more varied patterns of member-to-member conduct: many members may have slight relations with their peers, and some few may have gratifying and exciting (or very painful) contacts. But strong institutions should develop policies hostile to members forming extraordinarily close relationships. The small group or clique loyalties developed in such relationships may be inconsistent with the principle of obedience and with group coherence.

The matter of member/institution relations can be stated in another direct fashion: We might imagine that an institution whose members join as adults should make low demands so as not to drive away potential recruits and to retain the members who have joined. Conversely, an institution that enrolls everyone in an area by virtue of birth might be demanding, since no competition exists. Such assumptions may be incorrect. If the institution that enlists members keeps its demands too low, there will be no particular incentive for people to choose to join and stay: the undemanding relationships among members will not be very rich nor worth much trouble to acquire or maintain. If the universal (member-from-birth) institution makes its demands too stressful, the very variety of personalities that comprise its membership means that many unselected members will display resistance, noncompliance, and cynicism. (This partially explains the frequent alcoholism and political withdrawal commentators find in modern Soviet life: the Soviets are trying to maintain a generally demanding universal institution.) Universal institutions can only sustain high-level demands on members during periods of grave outside threat or other external stress.

Evidently, at one time in Catholic history a certain proportion of persons chose to affiliate with "greedy" institutions—or, at least, some of those recruits got what they bargained for. They wanted an institution to provide them with certain supports and demands and to place those demands in a transcendent framework. It is interesting to wonder whether, in our own era, there are enough strong institutions to supply the needs of potential recruits. If there are an insufficient number of such institutions, a problem may exist. Potential members cannot easily form new religious orders or similar agencies. Such institutions are the product of severe travail and stressful conflict; they often challenge, in dramatic fashion, many existing policies and institutions. As a result, their births often generate considerable tension for their founders and the members of challenged agencies.

Obedience and Good Decisions

Numerous decisions had to be made in the management of traditional religious orders. However, given the stress on obedience in such institutions, could wise decision making occur? Did not the emphasis on discipline stifle creativity and debate and lead to poor decisions? (As we will see, religious principles often laid stress on consultative and deliberative elements. Still, the theme of unquestioning obedience received greater emphasis in traditional religious life than in other complex institutions.)

The sociologist George Homans made some telling observations about efficiency in decision making. He noted that many experiments have been conducted about the effects of different systems of group management on the quality of decisions. The experiments compared decisions made by democratic groups, autocratic groups, and single individuals. Generally, they found that the democratic decisions were of better "quality" (according to plausible criteria) than the decisions of the other groups. But Homans asserted it would be simplistic to contend from such data that democratic decision making was always—or usually—the best technique. The research did not analyze the amount of participant time used by the different techniques. And it is obvious that it usually takes a small group longer (in man hours) to reach a collective decision than it does one person. If a group of people has a large amount of time available, democratic decision making is better—but we rarely have that much time. Homans contended that given limited time, one may often get better decisions from designated individuals than from groups. And all of us can identify situations where groups made foolish decisions because they did not have or take the time to collectively work the issue through. His analysis means that decisions in "autocratic" groups are not necessarily worse, and may often be better, than decisions made in more democratic contexts. Democratic decision making is only theoretically superior if great amounts of time are available for collective deliberation.

Even if autocratic decision making is intellectually adequate, it has another limitation. Democratic decision making helps give group members an emotional stake in carrying out decisions. Thus, democratically made decisions of low intellectual rigor may work, due to member support, while autocratically made good decisions may fail due to member alienation. This proposition has some plausibility. And there is evidence that religious orders have worked to handle the implicit problem. One measure is the concept of voluntary enlistment, which generates member stakes in the institution and its policies. But beyond the matter of choice, there is an immense stress in religious life on the theme of benevolent leadership. This matter will be amplified throughout the book. It is only mentioned in passing here. However, one of the creative themes of traditional religious discipline was the obligation of love and affection (for subordinates) placed on religious superiors, and which subordinates were also supposed to attribute to their superiors. This theme of benevolent leadership intensifies the ties between members and leaders—and the decisions of leaders.

An interesting piece of contemporary research illustrates many of the preceding themes. The researchers studied a relatively cloistered Catholic monastery which operated a farm. The most respected community member was its abbot, who received his position due to election. His work assignment was driving a dump truck. Several other monks held positions of formal managerial authority (e.g., comptroller). The community respected these persons and accepted their necessary authority. Ultimately, however, it chose a leader who possessed highly benign qualities.[5]

Another aspect of member stake is the persisting concern in orders with the maintenance of leader legitimacy: leaders are treated as people who deserve, and have earned, great respect. Members should not feel uncomfortable carrying out the directions of such persons. The relationship between the order and the founder, and, implicitly, between the founder's successors and the order is often emphasized. The founder was a great person (and saint?) due to the founding of the order. As a result, successive leaders are also entitled to reverence. And leaders were given forms of address that demonstrated status: "Mother," "Mother Superior," or "Abbot," meaning father.

The Pachomian System

Saint Pachomius founded about ten monasteries, the first beginning in about 320. His average monastery contained about 300 monks, while the largest had about 1,000. The rule applied in the system has been derived from the written reports of pilgrims, surviving writings of the monks, and archeological research.[6] The system he founded is recognized as relatively complete, and anticipates many succeeding patterns in monastic life. Its effect on later monastic development was moderate, however, since information about the system was transmitted to possible users in incomplete and sporadic patterns. Furthermore, while the system survived for about 100 years, its life did not significantly overlap the appearance of the important elements of European monastic movements. Still, due to the system's relative completeness and archetypal nature, it deserves detailed consideration.

Pachomius had been a Roman soldier, and his experience undoubtedly influenced his plan of organization. All governance of the system was in the hands of one person—in the beginning, Saint Pachomius—and he appointed subordinate supervisors and designated his successor. The monasteries were each surrounded by a wall and were relatively complete microcosmic societies. They were usually located in remote areas. Each site included a church, place of assembly, refectory (the common eating hall of a monastery), library, kitchen, larder (a place for food storage), infirmary (for sick members), workshops (e.g., forge, tannery), and houses where the community members lived. Outside the wall, but near the door of the monastery, was a house for the reception of strangers and friends of the monks; women were also admitted as religious, but in locations separated from male members. Each monastery also had its own garden for growing food.

All who came and were willing to obey the Rule were admitted as members. A few of the recruits were priests, but the majority of them were laymen. Some recruits were evidently aged fourteen and fifteen, while others were considerably older. There were regulations providing for the care of younger children on the premises. Newcomers asking admission as members had to remain outside the doors of the monastery for some days while the doorkeeper taught them prayers, psalms, and the rule. All members were obligated to practice poverty, chastity and obedience. One section of the Rule provided that recruits be instructed that henceforth—if they chose to join—they would live lives emotionally and physically separate from their relatives. Monks were subdivided into living groups comprising members doing the same work and were under the charge of immediate superiors. The dress of monks was precisely prescribed and was simple, similar to lower class dress of the era. When monks were not wearing particular garments (assigned to them), the garments were left in the possession of the assistant head of the group. Thus, in one sense, a monk did not actually possess his own wardrobe.

Monks were expected to regularly engage in productive work, both to support the community and to prevent accadie. Many of the monks were assigned to work to help maintain and feed the monastery, while others worked at weaving rushes into baskets and mats for sale. Monks necessarily practiced a variety of skills, since the aim was to make the monastery a self-contained unit, isolated from the world: Their skills included carpentry, shoemaking, blacksmithing, milling, herding, and agriculture.

The monks, in addition to their work assignments, gathered together several times a day in church, and once in the middle of the night, to pray aloud and sing hymns and psalms set to music. These periodic collective prayers were analogous to a practice that became common to many other (at times, nearly all) later monasteries and became called the Divine Office. The word *office* is derived from the Latin, meaning work or responsibility. The signal for monks to assemble for the office was given by the persons assigned to that duty for the week.

Twice a week monks received instruction in Christian doctrine. Great emphasis was placed on the study and memorization of the Scriptures, and monks also frequently participated in regular discussions of a spiritual character. Monks ordinarily ate together in the refectory. Meals were taken in silence—to avoid the distraction from religious thought provoked by conversation. Requests for food were made by hand signals. Two days a week were dedicated to all day fasts during which very little food was taken. During the weeks of Lent only uncooked food was eaten, and some monks ate only every two or five days. Monks slept in individual cells, and their doors were left open. After retirement for the night, they could not speak to others or leave their cells (except to participate in the night office).

A system of punishment for violations of the rules was established. They ranged from private reproofs, to public corrections, to brief periods of imprisonment, and finally, expulsion. Considering the harsh nature of the times, several authorities have characterized the punishment system as relatively mild.

Was the Rule Followed?

A recital of the main elements of the Pachomian system will not give readers an adequate appreciation of the system's fuller implications. And those implications are important. Some explication is necessary. But before the explication, another basic and complex question arises: To what extent did the monks actually observe the system's Rule and policies, including practicing poverty, chastity and obedience? After all, we are all familar with laws and social prohibitions which were—and are—widely avoided: the Prohibition amendment to the U.S. Constitution; laws against adultery, which exist in almost every American state; laws against the use of illegal drugs; and so forth.

The question of member compliance with religious Rules is a complex and widely controverted issue. Part of the complexity is due to a central principle of religious life: members live removed from the world. One effect of this isolation is that the world cannot easily tell what members are doing. Furthermore, religions have a tendency, common to members of all significant private organizations, to try to conceal from the public the deficiencies of their institutions. The seclusion inherent in religious life assists this tendency. The issue of member rule compliance will be discussed intermittently throughout this book. At this point, a direct answer will be presented and briefy justified.

From the written reports of contemporary visitors, it seems the monks of Pachomius regularly observed the Rule. And we must recognize that visitors inside the monastery (the written reports indicate that guests were admitted, after a brief wait) could effectively observe its main operations: They could see and hear the monks chant their office, see the food served, "hear" the practice of silence, observe the sleeping and dress procedures, and evaluate the quality of discipline. It may be remarked that such evaluations were necessarily incomplete: female "visitors" to monks might be kept in secret, extra food might be hoarded and eaten in concealed places, and other improper practices could be followed in a covert manner. This issue of compliance is relatively important. Similar charges of widespread Rule avoidance have been levelled regarding later monasteries and religious institutions.[7] There is no doubt that avoidance and manipulation of religious Rules were common in some places and eras. Thus, the claim may be made that much of religious history is essentially a fraud: The study of religious Rules and policies is a formalistic exercise; the Rules were sometimes disregarded in a semipublic fashion (this is true) and at most other times generally disregarded in covert fashion. How do we know this was not the case in the monasteries of Saint Pachomius, as well as in later religious life?

An effective response to this charge is awkward. It is a little akin to proving the nonexistence of some alleged conspiracy. Every piece of evidence against the existence may only prove the deviousness and skill of the conspirators. Still, there is substantial and plausible evidence that many religious orders, over sixteen centuries of order history, have had high apparent levels of rule compliance for long periods of time. Such evidence does not prove there were no important secret violations in the monasteries of Pachomius. However, it does increase the likelihood that what people reported they saw was not a deception, but actually there. Some of the historic evidence adduced over many centuries follows.

First, in later eras of the Catholic church, bishops were expected to visit residences of religious orders in their dioceses and write reports and recommendations (based on the visit) for internal church purposes. The procedures recommended for developing the reports were relatively elaborate (e.g., individual members of the order were questioned in private by the bishop or his representative) and followed in many instances. Some of these reports have been recovered, made public, and studied. In some situations, reports criticized or praised different residences with considerable specificity. The residences praised were praised for observing the Rule. If the visitors were willing to direct serious and plausible criticisim at malefactors, it seems likely that their specific praise was sincere and well-founded.[8]

Second, there are numerous instances of religious leaving their orders or strongly criticizing existing policies because of ignorance of the Rule by most order members.[9] The dissenters sometimes founded new residences, or even new orders, to apply the Rule more literally. Or sometimes they suceeded, with the help of others, in reforming their orders.[10] In such circumstances, the great public attention to the principle of following the original Rule would probably generate internal pressure for similar fealty in orders or monasteries led by reformers and their immediate successors.

Third, there is a vast body of uncontrovertable evidence about the remarkable hardships and sufferings which many order members voluntarily accepted on behalf of the church and their orders. Compared to such deliberately accepted stress and death, the deprivation due to observing the Rule would only be minor. For example, it strains credulity to believe that the Franciscan missionaries who travelled from Spain (in the seventeenth century) to live in the wilderness of New Mexico did not simultaneously generally follow the Franciscan Rule—which was part of the rationale for their trip.[11]

Fourth, diverse information about day-to-day life in many (nearly contemporary) traditional religious orders has been made public in our era, for a variety of reasons. Some information has come from pro-order sources, and some even from former order members who are comparatively critical of the general themes of order life.[12] In this whole literature there is little or no criticism of direct, significant violations of the letter of the orders' Rules. Instead, when charges are made, it is said that the Rules are irrelevant, or that they are applied with excessive literality, or that their spirit is evaded. Even charges about lesbianism among sisters emphasize the effective suppression of such conduct and relevant emotions among order members.[13] Thus, regardless of the merits of such charges, one can conclude that in the recent past (most of the evidence runs up to about 1970) traditional Catholic orders maintained a relatively high level of formal Rule observance. This evidence has important implications for other eras in religious life.

Fifth, probably, throughout history, most substantial patterns of Rule avoidance came to public attention.[14] Naturally, many avoiders sought to conceal such breaches, and the structure of orders, with their stress on isolation, did abet efforts at concealment. But there was always some interaction between orders and the world (and the interaction often increased as, and if, an order became decadent). Thus some contacts were maintained with relatives; new members had to be informed and recruited; if order members did misspend funds, the money went to outsiders, to buy goods and services; if illicit heterosexual conduct occurred, nonmembers (of the other sex) were informed; finally, some members of decadent orders often objected to rule violations and carried their complaints into diverse arenas. Sometimes the public tolerated such malfeasance for diverse reasons—and sometimes resisted it, as in the Protestant Reformation. But in any case, the evidence suggests that most malfeasance did not stay secret and, conversely, when religious orders had good reputations for observance, they deserved it.

The Significance of the Pachomian System

The comparatively absolute principle of leader designation prescribed by Saint Pachomius (he appointed the heads of subordinate monasteries, and his own successor) was not followed in later monastic systems. Perhaps one cause for the decline of the system of Saint Pachomius, despite its careful general design, was the narrow base of its principle of leadership succession. It is hard to identify any persisting leadership system that has rested on the principle of each individual leader designating his successor. The principle has a certain degree of appealing simplicity. Nevertheless, it evidently has other inherent defects.

The self-sufficiency and isolation of monastic life helped the Pachomian monks to maintain a relatively high degree of solitude: they could avoid engaging in barter or traveling to acquire goods, and incidental contacts with the world were infrequent. The self-contained arrangements of the monasteries were somewhat similar to the subsistence farming that many farmers might practice in traditional society. But the monks acted to greatly increase their potential for self-sufficiency. A monastery with several hundred members could train members to high levels of specialization (and increase the institution's self-sufficiency). Such comparatively large living units required monastic managers to become seriously concerned with questions of planning, scheduling, organizing resources, assessing members' peculiar abilities, and allocating authority. It is no coincidence that some of the earliest timekeeping devices used in post-Roman society, such as waterclocks, were developed and applied in monasteries—where uniform timekeeping was important in scheduling group activities. Each monastery was also responsible for monitoring and sheltering each inhabitant for twenty-four hours every day. Persons managing successful Pachomian monasteries necessarily had, or developed, substantial administrative skills.

The matter of early monks being largely laymen is significant. Priests necessarily were literate and had at least rudimentary educations. Under the class distinctions that prevailed through most of preindustrial history, educated persons were not expected to engage in manual labor. They would instead apply their skills to clerical matters—hence the parallel between the words *clerk* and *cleric.* If a few monastery members were priests, they could be expected to perform religious and clerical functions, while other members engaged in manual labor. If the proportion of priests in a monastery became large, however, such arrangements became more cumbersome. We will see how such complications eventually arose and were handled.

The sometimes age of joining—fourteen or fifteen—may seem to us to be too young for applicants to make an informed decision, but it must be considered in context. In traditional societies, to cite Hobbes, "man's life was *short.*" Perhaps for this reason, and also the generally low level of resources, young persons—especially males—oftentimes left their nuclear families for mature pursuits at earlier ages than are typical in our era. Boys were put out for apprenticeship or to live and work with relatives at ages between thirteen and fifteen. There is also some evidence that such boys were in many ways more emotionally mature that their counterparts in our era. This maturity was partly due to the more emotionally stressful demands that traditional life made on them. Due to such patterns, enrollment in a monastery at the age of fourteen or fifteen was not inconsistent with persons making deliberate decisions to join religious orders. Or, at least, the amount of deliberation surrounding such decisions was about the same as that surrounding other life decisions being made by youths in the same culture. The existence of child-care procedures implied that children were regularly on the premises. It is possible that some Pachomian monasteries included schools or orphanages—some later monasteries followed this practice. Sometimes, "graduates" of such an institution for the young were routinely enrolled as monks. In later eras the wisdom of such systems of child care and succeeding recruitment were questioned by religious leaders for many reasons. Those issues will later be discussed in more detail.

The proposition that recruits must be prepared to separate their lives from their families may seem extreme. But it is consistent with some of the sayings of the Desert Fathers. Religious recruits join a "new family"—and, in the process, become detached from their earlier family. The concept is not without biblical precedents. In sending his disciples forth as missionaries, Christ said:

> I have come to set a man against his father, a daughter against her mother, a daughter-in-law against her mother-in-law. A man's enemies will be those of his own household. Anyone who prefers father or mother to me is not worthy of me. . . .

Anyone who does not take up his cross and follow
my footsteps is not worthy of me.[15]

In a much later era, Saint Vincent de Paul (1595-1660)
was a noteworthy founder of two separate religious orders in
France. His widowed mother and siblings lived in a remote part
of the country, and as a mature adult and priest, he went back
home for a final visit. After the visit he transmitted the
following reflections, in writing, to a close companion.

> I had seen good priests who accomplished much
> good when far away and I noticed that after
> visiting their relations they came back quite altered
> and of no use to their flocks. . . . I, too, was afraid
> of becomming too attached to my family . . . [after
> the visit] I was so deeply grieved at parting with
> my poor brothers and sisters and relatives that I
> did nothing but weep and sob all along the road . . .
> [the temptation to use my status to advance my
> family persisted for three months]. God gave me
> the grace to leave them to his Fatherly care and to
> regard them as better off than if they had every
> comfort, though indeed they still had to receive
> public charity.[16]

The precise and uniform dress requirements were
undoubtedly partly to stress the members' commonality: they
looked alike. The requirements also simplified the manufacture
of clothes, since only limited kinds of materials, and particular
patterns were then needed. This simplicity is consistent with
the theme of poverty and a focus on the transcendent—and
immaterial. Uniformity also diminished potential sources of
envy and competition among members. The subject of dress
requirements has been one of recurrent controversy in religious
life. The founder usually prescribed the typical lower class,
peasant dress of the era. If an order persisted, such a garment
often became anachronistic. But to many order members such
anachronism was one means of separating order life from that
of the transitory temporal world—reminding them of the
founder and the order's sources. Furthermore, more
anachronistic or conspicuous dress directed attention towards

order members in public places and subjected them to surveillance.

The requirement of productive work brought an element of worldliness into the monastery. Members might well develop some emotional investment in their work—as craftsmen, or simply producers. This might be especially true in collective activities, where members might assess each other's competency or exchange technical advice. As we will see, this issue of religious working at secular activities became increasingly complex as the centuries proceeded.

The Divine Office

Frequent, routine collective prayer was prescribed in the Pachomian monasteries in the fourth century. By the sixth century, such practice had developed into the recitation of the *office*, a relatively elaborate system of prayer. Monastic prayer is a matter of doctrinal and psychological importance. Much of the office was sung: that is how Gregorian chant evolved. Furthermore, the contents of the office varied from day to day.

We do not have clear information as to the forms of prayer variation in Pachomian monasteries. But, Christianity—the Catholic and Protestant churches—eventually developed an annual cyclic sequence of religious events (or performances). The events comprise the church year. They are congruent with the central feasts of the church—namely, Christmas and Easter. Through such occasions the faithful are annually invited to sequentially reconsider the central episodes in the life of Christ. Interspersed with these cyclic biblical events are other memorable events in church history, for example, commemorations of individual saints, all of who came after the death of Jesus. The texts of the Divine Offices and Mass presented daily in the church vary according to the events celebrated each day. Such patterns of commemoration may be roughly analogized to cyclic holiday patterns in our national secular life, such as the Fourth of July. Major church events, however, are not celebrated in the isolation of one day. They are surrounded with preliminary and postliminary activities, which frame and highlight the occasion. Thus, before Christmas there is Advent; and, between Easter and Ascension Thursday, there is a special sequence of activities observed. All of these variations are reflected in the daily offices or Mass.

In addition to the day-to-day variations during Mass or other sacred rites, believers are also invited to pray, or meditate, at regular times during each day on topics appropriate to that "hour." These times were eventually called the canonical hours. In our era, the Catholic church has designated eight canonical hours during each twenty-four hour cycle; these comprise the different times of the office. One of the hours is celebrated during the dark hours of the night.[17] The Pachomian monasteries did not observe such a full pattern of office observance; some later monasteries, however, did engage in relatively complete observance.

In sum, the office has a schedule of day-to-day variations, plus different parts for different occasions (technically called the *hours*) during the day. As the office evolved, there were five separate chants sung during each hour. Almost all parts of the office were sung in Latin in the major elements of the Roman Catholic church. Obviously, depending on the rule of the order or the practices of a monastery, the performance of the office by all, or almost all monks was an activity of considerable significance.

During later church history the complete daily office was performed only by members of what are called the contemplative orders—male or female orders deliberately isolated from the secular world and largely dedicating their lives to prayer. Members of many other orders not so formally isolated (termed active orders) perform abbreviated portions of the office. The following excerpt is from a relatively contemporary autobiographical essay on the practice of the Divine Office, written by a contemplative sister. The essay was published in 1964. Naturally, the sister is sympathetic to this practice, which is an important part of her life. One can hardly be, however, both an informed and neutral observer about such matters:

[When the community is in the chapel], Mother Abbess begins the short morning prayer which precedes Prime [the first part of the office occurring during daylight]. All the intentions of friends and benefactors and the needs of the whole world are offered up like a chalice of tears to a compassionate God. Prime itself is sheer poetry, from the glorious cadences of its opening hymn through the tremendous plea: "O Christ, Son of the living God, have mercy on us!" to the final petition that God will show quick mercy to the souls in Purgatory and bring them into the rest which He is.

In the midst of Prime, the versicular [the sister designated to read special passages aloud] leaves her stall and goes to the lectern to call the roll of the saints of the next day. It is a kind of liturgical preview of the next showing, but has a thunder and a glory all its own. On the greatest solemnities, two candlebearer novices stand beside the versicular, and the announcement of the next feast is chanted with all possible solemnity.

There is a half hour of meditation after Prime, followed by Terce [another "hour"], that part of the Office which summons the Holy Spirit upon the new day, and is our immediate preparation for the holy sacrifice of the Mass. Mass has an entirely new significance for the heart which has been prepared for it by the Divine Office. Beginning with the night Office of Matins, you have gradually become saturated with the spiritual joy of the day's feast or the grave beauty of the feria [a day when no special feast is celebrated]. Now comes the great and climactic sacrifice for which your soul has been well briefed. The conventual Mass is the great event in the monastic day. To it all things lead, and from it all others progress.[18]

The matter of singing—or chanting—is, in itself, quite relevant. Contemporary Americans probably grossly underestimate the important role played in everyday tradition/ life by typical citizens performing music as amateurs. In c time music largely comes to us over radio, television, or records, or at concerts (with paid, professional perform Most of these ways of receiving music are historically u/ e. Even fifty years ago, most music—instrumental or vocal· was performed in homes or at other informal occasions. Today the technical level of most performances we hear is much high. than in the past. But the pool of performers is infinitely narrower. The pool has shrunk in part because technology has lessened the incentives for people to learn to perform—they can hear better quality performances through the media. Also, the spread of urbanization has heightened the diversity of music forms performed in any geographic area, such as a neighborhood. Members of a casually defined group are unlikely to know songs in common—so they cannot easily begin to sing together.

Observers of more traditional environments have often remarked on the pervasive role of informal music in the life of citizens.[19] The performances occurred because almost everyone knew the same material. Technology has moderated the incentives for people to learn how to perform, and for listeners to accept a certain level of amateur imperfection. A typical instance of traditional music making is disclosed in a social history—developed through interviews of older persons—of rural life in early twentieth-century England. One respondent observed that much of his young life had been hard:

> But I have forgotten to mention one thing—the singing. There was a lot of singing in the villages then, and this was my pleasure, too. Boys sang in the fields, and at night we all met at the pub and sang. The chapels were full of singing. When World War I came, it was singing, singing, all the time. So I lie; I have had pleasure. I have had singing.[20]

Readers of nineteenth century novels may recall another instance of musical self-entertainment. Young ladies from better-off families were often expected to play an instrument or sing for guests during social occasions at home. In novels such activities sometimes were portrayed in a semihumorous perspective. But the more basic point is that on many occasions, the performances were perceived by the guests as considerate acts of entertainment, for they otherwise could not easily hear music performed. Guests often made such incidents occasions for group singing, too.

From the prevalence of music in preindustrial societies, we might infer that many people have an inherent need to participate in the performance (and creation) of music. Our current unmusical situation—where we are largely passive listeners—is an historic anomaly. If this inference is correct, the frequent musical activity of the monks (and often of other religious, too) probably provided them with important gratification. Perhaps many people in our society would like to often be called on regularly to gather with others to practice and perform significant music which symbolizes important group values.

Dining and Sleeping

The significance of the common meals practiced by the monks seems evident. It is notable, however, that in contemporary society, it is not uncommon for people working in some collective enterprises to eat lunch in groups which exclude many coworkers (or, in some situations, to frequently eat alone). Furthermore, many American nuclear families have difficulty arranging to eat together regularly at home.

The monasteries applied two principles: people were regularly brought together to eat, and they were constrained to practice silence during these meals (the policy of silence at meals was often applied in later religious orders as well). Undoubtedly, one aim of the meal was to heighten social control: to discourage engagement in wrongdoing through conversation (since most of the injury done to others is by uttering particular words). The practice of silence at meals is incidentally congruent with the Desert Fathers' emphasis on silence. Another virtue of common meals was that the enforcement of dietary rules—fasts, abstinence from meat—was simplified.

Monks could also be discouraged from excessive and self-destructive (or competitive) fasts.

The sleeping arrangements, in light of later monastic experience and practice, were probably designed to discourage homosexual (or heterosexual) activity. Each monk was alone in his room, but doors were kept open.

Readers may muse about the considerable suspicion (of potential misconduct) evinced by some of these policies. Still, such musing should keep in mind that the order placed more emphasis on members internalizing values, as compared to intrusive rule enforcement. After all, members had voluntarily joined, and each member spent several hours a day in collective prayer, plus diverse scriptural studies. These patterns of self selection and religious involvement probably more influenced members' values than the constraints in their sleeping arrangements. Still, there is no doubt that many order practices assumed that serious temptations will arise in collective life. The Devil of the Desert Fathers could penetrate monastery walls. These assumptions are not inconsistent with many elements in the Roman Catholic doctrine, for example, man's propensity for sin as revealed in Adam and Eve's fall. The assumptions were supported by the evident disorder that reigned in the late Roman Empire. Furthermore, many persons became monks because they perceived the norms of the world as sinful. They hoped to escape such temptation and misconduct. Given those beliefs, it would be natural for the monastery to take rigorous measures to inhibit the potential sinfulness of its members. Finally, as a historical fact, religious often did find occasions to break the Rules of their orders. Thus, the human propensity for wrongdoing (which Pacomius assumed) was later demonstrated by notorious events.

Some people may contend that the display of institutional suspicion (of members) tends to generate countervailing member hostility and stimulate wrongdoing. Others may contend that institutions that display unqualified trust in their members are naive. Of course, intermediate intellectual positions can be taken. As this book proceeds we will see some instances of application of policies of trust—and mistrust—and where these policies apparently led.

Notes

1. Francis Martin, "Monastic Community and the Summary Statement of the Acts," in *Contemplative Community*, ed. Basil Pennington (Washington, DC: Cisterian Publication, Consortium Publications, 1972), p. 35.

2. The rule quoted was provided to me by members of a prospective contemporary order on my commitment to maintain anonymity.

3. The Holy Bible, King James Version, 1, Cor. 13:1-13. (On aesthetic and philosophic grounds, I prefer the King James translation of this statement.)

4. Lewis Coser, *Greedy Institutions* (New York: Free Press, 1974).

5. Richard Hella Fave and George A. Hillery, Jr., "Status Inequality in Religious Community," *Social Forces* 59, no. 1 (September 1980): 62-84.

6. For a careful discussion of the sources of information about Pachomian monasteries, see W. H. Mackean, *Christian Monasticism in Egypt* (London: Society for Propogation of Christian Education, 1920).

7. For strong statements of the charges of frequent rule violations, see G. G. Coulton, *Five Centuries of Religion* (Oxford: Cambridge University Press, 1950), vols.; and Henry Charles Lea, *A History of Sacredotal Celibacy* (London: Watts, 1932). For a more temperate statement, see Eileen Powers, *Medieval English Nunneries* (New York: Bilbo and Tannen, 1964). For a more dramatic, fictionalized work, see Denis Diderot, *The Nun* (Los Angeles: Holloway House, 1964), written in 1760.

8. For extracts from written visitation reports of bishops in the thirteenth and fifteenth centuries, see Powers, *Medieval*, App. 2 and 3, pp. 645-84.

9. For examples of the effects of reformers and order
    founders, consider the histories of orders, such as John
    Moorman, *A History of the Franciscan Order, From Its
    Origins to 1517* (New York: Oxford University Press,
    1968).

10. For examples of the effects of dissenters, both as
    reformers and order founders, see Fr. Cuthbert, *The
    Capuchins* (Port Washington, NY: Kenikat Press, 1971),
    2 vols.; Louis J. Lekai, *The Cistercians: Ideals and
    Realities* (Kent, OH: Kent State University Press, 1977);
    and Moorman, *History*. For a broad discussion of internal
    Catholic reform activities, see Jean Delumeau,
    Catholicism Between Luther and Voltaire (Philadelphia:
    Westminister Press, 1977).

11. For information on the Franciscans in early New Mexico,
    see F. A. Dominguez, *Missions in New Mexico*
    (Albuquerque: University of New Mexico Press, 1956).

12. For instances of critical or mixed descriptions of
    semicontemporary traditional religious life, see Helen
    Rose Fuchs Baugh, *Out of the Cloister* (Austin, TX:
    University of Texas Press, 1977); Nancy Henderson, *Out
    of the Curtained World* (Garden City, NY: Doubleday,
    1972); Geoffrey Moorhouse, *Against All Reason* (London:
    Widenfeld and Nicholson, 1969). For more sympathetic
    descriptions, see Monica Baldwin, *I Leap Over the Wall*
    (New York: Rinehart and Co., 1950); Bro. Bernard, ed.,
    Contemplative Nuns Speak (Baltimore: Helicon Press,
    1964); Suzanne Campbell-Jones, *In Habit* (New York:
    Pantheon Books, 1978); Suzanne Cita—Milard, *Religious
    Orders of Women* (London: Burns and Oates, 1964); Joan
    Leaux, ed., *Convent Life* (New York: Dial Press, 1964);
    Rosemary Howard-Bennett, *I Choose the Cloister* (London:
    Hodder and Stoughton, 1956); Gerard McGinley, *A
    Trappist Writes Home* (Milwaukee, WI: Bruce Publishing
    Co., 1960); and Barbara and Grey Villet, *Those Whom
    God Chooses* (New York: Viking, 1963), which includes
    many striking photographs.

13. Rosemary Curb and Nancy Monahan (eds.), *Lesbian Nuns Speak* (New York: Warner, 1985).

14. For examples of popular complaints about rule avoidance, see Giovanni Boccaccio, *The Decameron*, trans. Mark Muso and Peter Bondanella (New York: Norton, 1982), written in 1350, and filled with ribald tales of erring monks and nuns; or, for a more recent, nonfictional, and less sensational expose, Joseph McCabe, *Life in a Modern Monastery* (London: Grant Richards, 1898).

15. Jerusalem Bible, Matt. 10:34-39.

16. Mary Purcell, *The World of Monsieur Vincent* (New York: Charles Scribner and Sons, 1963), p. 85.

17. *New Catholic Encyclopedia* (Washington, DC: Catholic University, 1967), vol. 4, p. 920. The current Roman Liturgy for the Divine Office includes matins (or nocturns), lauds, the minor hours (prime, terce, sext, nonce) vespers, and compline.

18. Sr. Mary Francis, "What Do They Do All Day?" in Leaux, *Convent Life*, p. 104.

19. For some references to the role of music in traditional environments, see J. R. S. DeHoney, *Tom Brown's Universe* (New York: Quadrangle, 1977), p. 139; and Benjamin Zablocki, *The Joyful Community* (Baltimore: Penguin Press, 1971), p. 47.

20. Ronald Blythe, *Akenfield* (New York: Dell Publishing, 1969), p. 51.

3

Monasticism Spreads:
Growth and Adaptation

Monasticism spread gradually and sporadically as a plant
spreads from seeds that are blown abroad.
— David Knowles, *Christian Monasticism*

In the late fourth century, patterns of monastic life began
to appear in parts of Europe encompassed by the decaying
Roman Empire.[1] These appearances began perhaps fifty years
after the first monasteries of Saint Pachomius occurred in
Egypt. The founders and saints associated with the new
European monasteries were partly inspired by precedents set by
the Desert Fathers: they had either visited the Fathers, or read
about them. A variety of themes, however, beyond the example
of the Fathers, was associated with the developments. One
theme was the tension generated by the transformation of
Christianity from a minority to a majority religion. The
withdrawal of devout Christians into isolated life in the desert,
which has already been briefly discussed, was a response to
these tensions. Such withdrawal was eventually regularized via
the evolution of cenobitic, or monastic, life. This response
requires further consideration.

Shortly after the conversion of Emperor Constantine in
312, the empire adopted a policy of toleration, and even
favoritism, towards Christianity. This concession offered
obvious advantages for institutional Christianity and for the
advancement of its goals. But cooperation of church and state
confronted individual church members with temptation to
advance self-interest at the cost of basic religious principles.
Many converts were now also partly attracted by the material

61

benefits associated with joining the established church. These temptations contrasted with the chiliastic elements which had only recently pervaded church doctrines (during the eras of isolation and persecution). Due to this contrast, many church members experienced strong disillusionment over the fruits of their institutional success.

Individual Withdrawal Becomes Collective

In sum, the withdrawal evinced by the spread of cenobitic (and anchoritic) life was an implicit criticism of existing church norms. The effects of this criticism were complex. Monks were dedicated to obedience and humility; as a result, the withdrawal was not always associated with explicit criticism of existing church practices. Still, not all dissatisfaction with the status quo was muted. Gregory Nazianzen (330-390), a prominent early church father, wrote, "at this time the person holding the most holy office is likely to become the most contemptible of all. For the chief seat is gained by doing evil, not by virtue, and [bishop's] sees belong, not to the more worthy, but to the more powerful."[2] The climate of dissatisfaction is also demonstrated in the writing of Sulpicius Severus, a Christian traveler in the Middle East. He told of travelling with several friends to visit with an anchorite in the desert. Severus described their host as humble, generous and wise. He then went on to observe:

> By our inquiry into the customs of the inhabitants we learned one notable thing: they neither buy nor sell. What cheating is they have no idea. And gold and silver, which men value highest, they neither have them, nor do they wish to. When I offered our host ten pieces of silver, he recoiled in horror, declaring in his profound wisdom that with silver and gold, one does not build up the Church but, rather, destroys it. . .[3]

Obviously, there were incipient tensions between the early monks and the institutional church. Prolonged, aggravated conflicts between the two forces did not arise, however, and in later church history such tensions occasionally recurred—with diverse effects which will be analyzed.

The muting of hostility between the early church and its monks contrasts, to some degree, with the striking intrareligious conflicts described in the Old Testament. The conflicts occasionally occurred between the Hebrew Prophets and the Jewish people (or the formal leaders of the Jews). Such disputes sometimes reached a intense pitch. And it is significant that the early monks—both anchorites and cenobites—saw parallels between their own conduct and that of the Prophets. These parallels did not lead to equivalent controversies. Several possible reasons for the contrast between the Prophets' disputes and the relative cooperation associated with monks come to mind. The reasons are worth discussion. Their ramifications may even be significant in our era, where one can imagine themes of withdrawal and criticism arising from current religious disputes.

The Christian anchorites partly found their inspiration in the Acts of The Apostles, and the life of Christ as described in the New Testament. The themes of obedience and abnegation were important in such works. Furthermore, monks did not hold formal church office—they were typically not priests and were separated from administrative church activities. One pronouncement from Pope Gregory I (540-604) even forbade monks from becoming priests, or priests from enrolling in monasteries.[4] These patterns of separation had important ramifications for the early monks. Under Catholic norms, only ordained priests could administer the sacraments which were a key element of Catholic life. This made it difficult for monks to adopt positions of unqualified hostility to the institutional church; such hostility might deprive them of sacramental access. Conversely, in Judaism, there was no equivalent ordained clergy who "controlled" the religious rites. Throughout most of history Jews have probably been held together by external pressure—the forces of discrimination and segregation. And, where that pressure has been moderated or extinguished (as in America), the cohesion of the group has diminished. Catholicism has persisted, and resisted centrifugal forces, even it was unthreatened, through central control of its sacraments.

The early Christian monks also moved from the sporadic, individual pursuit of isolation—like the Prophets—to routinized, institutional, segregated collective living. This shift probably heightened the stability of individual monks, and also made them more vulnerable to collective and institutional pressures. Due to such routinized living, monasteries often became the residences of disciplined, competent people. This regularization probably made monks more understanding of the needs of the institutional church. The church gradually discovered ways to use this potential resource. Over time a variety of different relationships arose between the church and religious orders, and the church and particular monasteries.

It is true that conflicts sometimes occurred from order/church or monastery/church differences. But usually the overall benefits of mutual cooperation and shared religious beliefs mitigated such problems. Still, it is important to recognize that during many centuries of church history few—or no?—orders were founded by the deliberate initiative of the institutional church. Orders were founded by individuals, and small groups of men or women, who wanted to accomplish some personal or collective religious purpose and could not easily find support in the church and its existing orders and institutions. Most monasteries were founded by equivalent groups or by religious who left their own monastery to colonize another site. Eventually all persisting orders and monasteries entered into routine and frequently fruitful relations with the institutional church. New orders have, however, sometimes represented a form of institutionalized innovation or dis-ease. And, thus, periods of religious or social disorder have often also been times in which new orders have appeared. In many ways the history of Catholic religious life might be contrasted with the traditions of Protestantism. Dissatisfied Protestants secede from their congregation and form new religions or sects. Many dissatisfied Roman Catholics, or extra-activists, have formed or participated in new orders or monasteries.

This pattern of order/church relations might bring to mind the much overworked sociological term *cooptation*.[5] The word characterizes certain relationships between institutions and assertive external groups. Cooptive relationships occur when the institution brings such outsiders into the institution and, in the process, persuades the new group members to accede to many of the institution's traditional goals. In many contexts cooptation is considered as equivalent to a sell-out, or goal abandonment by the outsiders; it also tends to cast doubt on the motives of the affected institution. Persons more sympathetic to particular cooptive situations, however, might be prone to substitute—for the word cooptation—terms like compromise, adaptation, or symbiotic relationship. Oftentimes the negative connotations connected with the word cooptation largely reflect a listener's (or speaker's) personal and polarized views about which of two conflicting positions is ultimately correct.

The Matter of Asceticism

Cenobitic life regularized the ascetic activities of the anchorites. And this regularized asceticism encompassed a variety of activities: fasting, chastity, the acceptance or pursuit of physical pain (e.g., flagellation), the maintenance of discomforting postures, clothing which was inadequate for the climate, and the tolerance of personal humiliation. Regularization meant that efforts were made to make the activities more uniform, collectively monitored (to ensure that they were not institution-threatening or otherwise excessive), rewarding, and oftentimes more rigorous. For example, in the matter of diet, regularization would mean that the person dieting ate prescribed amounts of particular foods at predetermined times, did not eat other foods, made dieting part of a group activity, and saw dieting as part of a process aimed at attaining particular individual and collective goals. Under such circumstances dieting undoubtedly became an easier and more gratifying activity than idiosyncratic, individual dieting carried out to generally improve a person's health. It may seem incongruous that such regularization of deprivation and pain could foster the spread of religious life. But readers must recognize that the concept of mortifying the flesh (mortification is rooted in the word *death*) has a long historic and intellectual tradition. It would be naive to cavalierly dismiss such a powerful tradition without a careful discussion.

Throughout most of human history physical discomfiture has been an ordinary fact of life. Human beings typically have had relatively inefficient means of moderating excessive heat, cold, or humidity, and of regularly acquiring adequate, varied, well-prepared food. Furthermore, the techniques for treating innumerable ailments and injuries—decaying teeth, cuts, sprains and strains, parasites, infections—were extremely inadequate. These patterns are demonstrated by the brief life spans typical for primitive peoples.[6] Finally, while humans probably have an inherent need for comforting emotional intimacy, it is evident to any student of social history that large proportions of people have lived long periods of their lives without such gratification. None of this is to contend that such forms of suffering are objectively good. But the prevalence of this suffering is evidence that a tolerance for discomfiture is a highly adaptive human trait. Such tolerance will enable sufferers to keep their focus on survival or achievement goals despite the distractions which surround them. Conversely, less hardy persons may be unable to concentrate their energies on survival issues. Individuals who genetically possess a tolerance for hardships will pass on a precious resource to their descendants, and they (and their descendants) will be more likely to have future descendants. Probably in many human beings there is even a drive towards self-expression via testing and exercising this tolerance. Such an instinct would enhance the cultural vitality of groups placing a high value on displaying personal endurance.

The preceding references to adaptive individual and group patterns invite some incidental general remarks about adaptive patterns which will be relevant throughout this book.

Authorities ranging from Aristotle[7] through B. F. Skinner[8] and Edward O. Wilson[9] make a distinction between individual and institutional adaptation. Individual genetic adaptations can affect the survival chances of a species, whereas institutional adaptations can affect the survival chances of an institution, or social system. A species survives if its members have genetic traits that make it more likely that they will have descendants and that those descendants will have similar traits. Thus, imagine that a genetically inherited tolerance for discomfort makes it more likely that certain people will live to adulthood and bear children. Then, over thousands of years, such a tolerance will be bred into their descendants. But institutions do not have genes: institutional survival rests on different principles. Suppose a particular institution cultivates its members' genetic tolerance for discomfort. Such an institution is more likely to persist, or revive if it temporarily declines, since it is catering to a strong human propensity.

Something must also be said about the concept of individuals or institutions maintaining persisting tendencies. Individuals maintain tendencies over generations through our genetic memory, which is a biologic form of recall. A genetic tendency—such as tolerance of extreme heat or cold—can be transmitted across several generations even if the persons transmitting the tendency never themselves experience extreme heat or cold. But an "institutional memory" must be a more active force. Theoretically, institutions can remember by relying solely on documents and physical artifacts. Thus, practice or policy may become extinct within a particular institution and be revived based on documents. And means such as documents are important bases of institutional memory. For example, religious orders emphasized that members should study the Bible: this was because orders were intended to revive and carry forward biblical traditions. Still, there are limitations to relying solely on such formal resources as documents for transmitting traditions. It would be very difficult for us to recreate the cultural environment of ancient Egypt based solely on papyrus scrolls and architecture such as the Pyramids. Ideally, an institution's memory must include both formal materials and an active tradition of practice, to which observers can turn for information and reassurance. In the case of most religious orders, both formal materials and networks of practice were the means by which values and styles were transmitted across generations and among different orders.

Now, it is possible that some genetically transmitted human predispositions are no longer helpful to species survival due to changed circumstances. Perhaps the race would be better off if we assumed that it was undesirable for human beings to be able to bear high levels of discomfiture and tension. We might even conclude that the cultivation of this potential pandered to masochistic and sadistic tendencies. Such logic could lead us to decry institutions which stressed self-control, discipline, sacrifice, and hardihood, and favor institutions whose policies lauded sensitivity and flight from pain and distress. This shift might be to our advantage—maybe.

In passing, it should be noted that our innate drive for self-deprivation is probably concurrently accompanied by a drive for material fulfillment: the attainment of goods and "ease." The drive towards attaining goods and ease probably helps perpetuate our species also. Persons who pursue and attain goods and ease are more likely to have the power to transmit their genetic strain. In sum, there is a matter of balance. Excessive concern for goods and ease may leave us ill-equipped to deal with deprivation; total disinterest in goods and ease may leave us unable to acquire the resources necessary to live in an unpredictable world. Since we are talking about genetic traits, we should recognize that different persons will have different mixes of these tendencies. Furthermore, in different eras and situations, diverse genetic traits will have varied implications for group and individual survival.

Obviously, the matter of moderating or extinguishing innate human drives is extremely complicated. For many of us it may seem that the devil we know—our drives towards exploration, mastery, expression, sexual gratification—may be better than a world in which those drives have been extinguished (or redirected) in uncertain ways. To some extent, traditional religious orders may be perceived as institutions with long-term concerns about the stimulation and focussing of certain basic human drives. Such drives are genetically transmitted (as well as cultivated by many institutions). Many of those drives assisted species survival in the past and may serve such purposes in our time, and in the future. By mobilizing and focussing the drives, the orders often served both institutional and individual purposes.

Seeing Self-Deprivation Through American Eyes

To talk about self-deprivation as an adaptive trait, worthy of cultivation, may seem strange to many contemporary Americans. But we may not adequately appreciate the unique characteristics of our own culture: historically speaking, we are probably the largest important culture (which has ever existed) dedicated to the pursuit of happiness and the attainment of speedy gratification. It is understandable why self-deprivation appears to be for us such an uncomfortable topic.

Americans place a premium on speedy gratification because they are a comparatively wealthy and egalitarian society. Our wealth enables us to afford many gratifications. And our dedication to egalitarianism makes it difficult for us to justify asking (or requiring) particular segments of our society to accept less gratification than others. Furthermore, persons asked to accept lesser gratification may feel more aggrieved (in American society) than equivalent persons elsewhere. Our norms do not provide apparent justification for such literally discriminatory treatment; therefore, such "deprived" persons display a special resentment towards such inequality.

We also cannot ignore the role advertising plays in fostering such American patterns. This pervasive force constantly reminds us of the benefits we miss by not acquiring certain goods, services or experiences. To the contrary, it is hard to identify any prominent group or institution in America that constantly and explicitly reiterates that we would be better off if we had less, or gave up something.

There is an important irony to the usually unuttered argument that many Americans would really be better off with less. The argument is objectively correct and frequently implicitly recited. Sedentary living, overeating, and consuming improper foods and other substances (e.g., alcohol, cigarettes) are important causes of the shortening of our life spans and the weakening of our vitality. Again, many adolescents who bear out-of-wedlock children would be better off practicing delayed sexual gratification. Finally, American society is afflicted with the highest divorce rate ever attained by any known society.[10] It is hard to believe that this extraordinary freedom from the constraints of traditional marriage has increased human happiness. In other words, many of us would benefit from less relaxation, food, stimulants, sex, and freedom to dissolve marital commitments.

In addition to the material sphere, we can also look at the topic of emotional deprivation. It is hard to evaluate levels of happiness or estimate what responses to "happiness surveys" signify. But one can identify tendencies in contemporary America—like our record divorce rate—which imply that many Americans are afflicted with considerable stress. It is also noteworthy that our country is surely the world center for developing new modes of psychiatric treatment. All of this suggests a strong disposition to try to cure or avoid psychic discomfort.[11] Other cultures, apparently, were more prone to accept discomfort as part of the stuff of life: or to offer it up for the souls in purgatory. A reasonable case can be made that institutions that encourage their members to live with stress may actually maintain lower levels of member stress than environments where members are expected to flee from, or be cured of, their tension.

It is also provocative to recognize the widespread contemporary interest in certain forms of self-mortification. Thus, among my (admittedly nonrepresentative) circle of acquaintances, I can identify five persons who have completed twenty-one mile marathon races in the past few years. These races cannot be completed unless the participants submit to arduous training. And the material—and even vocational—rewards of such participation are typically nil. It is likely that the immediate prevalence of "recreational" running is largely a fad—and, surely, many practitioners do not ever show serious dedication. But the considerable appeal of such arduous non-material—and even relatively unsocial—activities in our materialistic society is evidence of my basic point: Many persons have strong, inherent needs to engage in rigorous such self-mortification. Imagine the importance self-mortification could assume in an institution that associated such activity with powerful artistic symbols, the attainment of historic status, a significant social context; and a variety of modes of mortification (so different "talents" were gratified).

Mental Prayer

Mental prayer has been an important responsibility for many religious. Mental prayer encompasses the diverse forms of internal communication with God and his manifestations which were and are practiced by persons in religious life—and incidentally by a variety of other Christians.[12] It should be distinguished from the silent, internal recitation of formally composed prayers, (e.g., the Lord's Prayer). The more elaborate aspects of mental prayer are characterized by the concept of mysticism. There is necessarily some element of spontaneity in *mental prayer*, though such spontaneity is often constrained by particular traditions and conventions.

The topic of mental prayer (and the subtopic of mysticism) is important in understanding life in religious orders. All persons in religious life dedicate portions of their time to some form of mental prayer. Indeed, the practice of mental prayer was almost the sole purpose of some orders. Concern with diverse forms of mental prayer has not been unique to Catholics or Christians in general. Many traditions of belief have given great weight to mental prayer—though such concerns were sometimes phrased in terms of mysticism, meditation, the pursuit of visions, and other psychic practices. Physiological research has even identified particular internal symptoms associated with forms of mental prayer practiced by (adept persons associated with) different religious traditions. One oriental scholar, E. G. Browne, made thoughtful remarks about the widespread prevalence of mental prayer:

> There is hardly any soil, be it ever so barren, where Mysticism will not strike root; hardly any creed, however formal, round which it will not twine itself. It is, indeed, the eternal cry of the human soul for rest; the insatiable longing of a being wherein infinite ideals are fettered and cramped by a miserable actuality; and so long as man is less than an angel and more than a beast, this cry will not for a moment fail to make itself heard. Wonderfully uniform, too, is its tenor; in all ages, in all countries, in all creeds, whether it come from the Brahmin sage, the Persian poet, or the Christian quietist, it is in essence an enunciation more or less clear, more or less eloquent, of the aspiration of the soul to cease altogether from self and to be at one with God.[13]

In the Catholic church distinctions gradually evolved among different forms of mental prayer: meditation, contemplation, and what is called "affective prayer." The distinctions are understandable. When able people dedicate attention to any complex topic, they gradually identify distinctions which are pertinent to understanding the topic.

Individual members of religious orders who appropriately practiced mental prayer might receive precious insights and reassurance, and could have their religious practices hearteningly confirmed. After such communion with the divine, everyday travails might lose much of their significance. It is understandable why persons who accept the restraints inherent in much religious life frequently turn to mental prayer. However, while religious institutions have encouraged members to practice mental prayer (by making it part of their members' schedules), the institutions have recognized the complexity of that process. This recognition has affected the procedures and expectations of orders regarding mental prayer. Furthermore, many prominent religious have carefully considered the topic of mental prayer and written about their practices and analyses.[14] These writings have affected the opinions and conduct of all Catholics (and Christians) about this complex topic.

Most order procedures and writings have stressed the cooperative element of individual mental prayer.[15] Even adept practioners were expected to have spiritual advisors. Early concern with the matter of spiritual advisement is disclosed in the writings of Saint Ambrose (339-397) and Saint Jerome. This is not to deny that occasional individuals may have attained special insights without such mentorship. To apply religious perspectives, however, either the devil or God may come to people who pursue mental prayer. And the guises of the devil are innumerable. So perspective—in the form of counsel—is recommended for persons who practice intense mental prayer. To put the matter in secular terms, persons practicing such introspection are liable to develop fantasies or imaginings which are ambiguous, sterile, or even destructive. There needs be an interpreter, or intellectual anchor. (The ubiquitous and overworked word *guru* is simply the Hindu term for such a spiritual advisor.)

Something of the nature of the advisement process is indicated by the following remarks, written by Friar Domingo Banes in 1575, about the spiritual devotions of Saint Teresa of Avila. Saint Teresa (1515-1580), an enclosed sister, particularly requested advice because she was affected by unique spiritual experiences. One advisor requested the saint to write a narrative of her life to help the church assess her perceptions. Friar Banes, an experienced spiritual advisor, was asked to evaluate the text and the significance of its revelations. He said:

> [This book, in which Sister Teresa] gives a plain account of her soul, in order to be taught and directed by her confessors, has been examined by me, and with much attention, and I have not found anywhere in it anything which, in my opinion, is erroneous in doctrine. On the contrary, there are many things in it highly edifying and instructive for those who give themselves to prayer. The great experience of this religious, her discretion and also her humility, which has made her always seek for light and learning in her confessors, enabled her to speak with an accuracy on the subject of prayer that the most learned men, through their want of experience, have not always attained. [Only one thing about the book must be carefully examined] . . . it contains many visions and revelations, matters to be afraid of, especially in women who are ready to believe of them that they come from God, and to look at them as proofs of sanctity, though sanctity does not lie in them. . . I have always proceeded carefully in the examination of the prayer and life of this nun, and no one has been more incredulous than myself as to her visions and revelations—not so, however, as to her goodness and good desires, for herein I have had great experience . . . [in conclusion I believe her] visions, revelations and ecstasies . . . to be the work of God, as they have been in others who were Saints.[16]

In addition to the value of advice or counsel, mental prayer is also facilitated by making use of a variety of practices and other aids. Using such materials properly requires learning and discipline. Gradually, an elaborated lore has evolved on the topic of mental prayer. Different bodies of knowledge were provided for persons with diverse dispositions or experience, or in different life situations (or in religious orders with different missions). These developments allowed for diversity among orders, or among members of a particular order, and affected the form of training (or socialization) of potential order members. Persons practicing different forms of mental prayer needed appropriate bodies of iconographic knowledge, personal counsel, and an appreciation of the particular mental prayer techniques encouraged in their environment. As mentioned above, systems of mental prayer, which developed in particular orders, oftentimes diffused outside their boundaries and affected the practices of other orders, diocesan priests (or *parish* clergy), and devout laypersons.

Many Americans, living in a relatively secular society, may have uncertainty about the perspective to apply to the topic of mental prayer. For this reason some general remarks are appropriate: All human beings spend some part of the time with their brains, as it were, shifted into neutral. There are no external demands absorbing their attention. During that time our minds inevitably turn towards certain forms of reflection, reverie, or fantasy. The proportion of energy dedicated to such activities is probably a product of personal disposition and the external environment surrounding the individual. The matter of variations in disposition is evident. As to environment, we can imagine environments that deliberately, or accidentally, cause people to ignore, or suppress, such psychic life. Such environments cut down the time for reverie or channel reflection along highly constrained courses. Conversely, other environments may cultivate such potential and enlist it for various purposes. Understandably, such cultivating environments may have a special attraction—or utility—for persons predisposed in this direction due to genetic factors or early socialization.

Environments which encourage reflection will set time aside for it; "say" in many ways that they believe it is important; instruct (and socialize) new members in how to practice it; provide counsel for practioners; use such forms of reflection as a ways of attacking life challenges and decisions; and develop a literature on such matters and encourage members to read it.

Obviously, contemporary American society on the whole either suppresses such reflection, or encourages its focus on material (the concept of a "dream house") or problematic (the glorification of romantic love, or raw erotic desire) goals. It is arguable whether such patterns are wise. It is surely unfortunate that significant portions of our psychic lives—especially those of young people—are focused on many trivial, even harmful ends. As for the American tendency to suppress such intrapsychic life, such suppression has evidently worked for certain people in all societies. But one might muse that, for many people, the world would be a better place if they were assisted to dedicate more time to purposeful, directed reverie—essentially, something akin to mental prayer. Unfortunately, such a prescription is meaningless unless there is an appropriate infrastructure of socialization, and supporting institutions. And, whether readers see my pro-mental prayer suggestion as good or bad, we all must agree that such an infrastructure does not exist at this time.

Charismatic Leaders

Charisma is derived from the Greek. It means a gift freely given, a favor. It has been applied in the Catholic church to signify a beneficial or special attribute given to individual persons by God. It implies the "beneficiary" acquires some grace, or authority, due to the gift. Often, in a religious context, such a gift is the outcome of prayer.

The term has been adopted by modern social science to designate persons who attain special influence or authority due to unique personal characteristics.[17] Thus, charismatic leadership (by such gifted people) has often been contrasted with routinized, or traditional hierarchal administration. The contrast is not always intended to be simply critical of traditional administration—each of the two forms of providing groups with direction has inherent strengths and drawbacks. But it is true that founders of religious orders often displayed what social science calls charismatic leadership—and the church, similarly, may say that such persons had unique charismas. The more precise elements of charisma require amplification, to help us better understand important aspects of order formation, including the founding of new monasteries.

Charismatic people have special talents for communicating new insights to others. These insights then help stimulate receivers to important and decisive action. The sequence underlying such communication involves original perceptions by the leader; development of powerful communication techniques; and persisting interaction between the leader and his evolving and interacting group of followers. Because of such communication talents, followers of charismatic leaders often acquire a sense of personal mission and determination. They may pursue that mission despite the absence of traditional forms of organizational support, or in the face of great resistance. But we should not assume that charismatic leaders can communicate whatever they choose to their followers: followers are predisposed to receive and act on only certain messages. Charismatic leaders know, or learn, what to do to communicate vital messages to people. One of the most important of such communication techniques is to *live* the message one wishes to transmit. If one hopes to excite people to devotion to God, then one must practice such devotion in one's own life. If one wishes to preach the importance of humility or sacrifice, then one must live humility. And so on. In other words, charismatic people practice, with great determination, the values and ideas they preach. Then their message has a special power.

Secondarily, charismatic people must have talent for dramatizing the ideas that they vigorously practice. Not all forms of humility or devotion are visible. Thus, imagination is needed to determine how to make some internal disposition into something visibly evident. One must usually couple determination with imagination, since dramatic acts are usually carried out in the face of resistance. Furthermore, extreme forms of determination are easier to dramatize. Sometimes the dramatization (into visibility) may occur through writing or oratory. But it can just as readily occur by means of a visual event.

Charismatic people *persuade* because we believe messages that are founded on determination and imagination: We are prone to give trust to persons who display such traits, unless we find their conduct especially abhorent. Undoubtedly, the focus in Christianity on conduct as a mode of communication is immensely heightened by the status of Jesus Christ as a role model: the New Testament portrays him voluntarily dying a humiliating and painful death. Descriptions of such a remarkable action communicated a great deal to his followers. A typical instance of charismatic transmission via conduct in religious life is found in the description of the death of the anchorite Saint Anthony, in the book attributed to Saint Athanasius. The moment of death is a special occasion for important messages, since the dying person—under evident pressure—can communicate much to us by the poise or disorder he betrays:

> It is meet that we should call to rememberance his death, and should relate how it took place, and in what manner he finished his life, for I know you will be exceedingly pleased therewith. He was accustomed to go out and visit the memorial stones of the brethren on the outer mountain. Now, the matter of his death was not hidden from him, and he went forth to visit the stones even when he knew his departure was high. After he had spoken to the brethren according to his wont, he said unto them "This act which I have just performed in the end of all my acts; and I marvel at this world. It is time for me to die." And he was about one hundred and five years old.
>
> And when the brethren heard these things, they wept bitter tears, and each of them began to embrace and kiss him, and the old man, like unto

a man from a strange country who is about to
depart thereto, with great gladness besought them
to be quiet, and exhorted them, saying, Be not ye in
despair by reason of your tribulations, and be not
lax in your lives and works, but even as men who
are dying daily, prepare ye for [eternal] life, and,
as I have said, be watchful ever . . . take good heed
of the good doctrine of our fathers, and to the
preaching of the truth of our Lord Jesus Christ,
which ye have received from the Scriptures.[18]

Religious and Missionary Activities

A noteworthy characteristic of Christianity is its
missionary orientation. Christians were directed to invite and
persuade non-Christians to join their religion. Indeed, many
Christians believed they were obligated to accept stress and
suffering to transmit this message. During the late Roman
Empire, missionary concern was a unique characteristic of the
Christian religion. Most other religions of that time were
confined within ethnic groups. The Greeks had their gods; the
Romans theirs; the Jews, Yahweh; and so on. Members of each
group were expected to be loyal to their peculiar faiths, but
usually had no procedure for recruiting or enrolling members of
other ethnic groups as new believers. In contrast, in the first
century Saint Paul said, in writing to a Christian community,
"there is no room for distinction between Greek and Jew,
between the circumcised or the uncircumcised, or between
barbarian and Scythian, slave and free man. There is only
Christ: He is everything, and in everything."[19]

This contrast between Christianity and the ethnic
religions was of immense importance. It meant that Christian
doctrine, to a remarkable degree, would strive to lessen
distinctions among races, nations, classes, and sexes. And it
meant that Christians would strive to carry this message
throughout the world.

The principle thrust tremendous responsibility on strongly
committed Christians. They were obligated to abandon their
local associations, accept the hardships of travel, live in foreign

lands, learn other languages and customs, develop doctrines that reconciled Christianity to complex purposes, accept intolerance, and possibly, torture and death. On the other hand, the missionaries were invited to undertake important tasks, visit strange places, and observe novel events. In all of these activities the members of religious orders played a central role.

It is also significant that Christian missionary doctrine generated obligations for those staying at home: to pray for the success of the missions, and, if possible, to provide them with material help. Thus, the missionaries, in a psychological sense, were never really alone.

Perhaps some of the roots of Christian missionary doctrine evolved from the concept of Roman citizenship. As the Epistles of Paul reveal, early Christians were highly cognizant of the significance of that status.[20] Briefly put, the concept of Roman citizenship evolved through the development of the Imperial Empire. During its early stages, Roman citizens were simply persons born in the city of Rome. Such persons were entitled to a special legal status throughout the Empire—with unique privileges—compared to other persons governed by the Empire. Gradually, for reasons of policy, the privilege of being designated a Roman citizen was extended to selected individuals and groups not born in Rome. The benefit apparently had a low cost to the Empire, and gave the beneficiaries powerful incentives to support and extend systems of Roman control over other groups. Or, to put the matter more sympathetically, the grant of Roman citizenship was an act of tolerance that helped stimulate the spread of a superior civilization via pacific means. In any event, the development of this status fostered the spread of a class of international citizens. Similarly, Christianity spurred the evolution of an international group of religious believers.

The first identified Christian missionaries after the Ascension of Jesus included some of the twelve apostles and Saint Paul of Tarsus. These men accepted the charge to "go out to the whole world; proclaim the Good News to all creation."[21] And, remarkably enough, they were relatively successful. By the end of the first century, Christian groups existed throughout many parts of the Roman Empire. Each newly developed local group of Christians, as a *diocese*, developed its own bishop and pool of local priests. But such communities were designed to persist in one place. They could not easily assist proselytization in remote areas. Sometimes, it is true, Christian belief could be transmitted from a diocese to some nearby site; the transmission of Christianity across long distances, however, was more complex. True, the Apostles accepted such missionary tasks on a semispontaneous basis. But there gradually arose a need to regularize missionary activities. Concern arose over questions such as: which persons should go on a mission; where should they go; how could stay-at-home Christians help them; if some foreign group wanted a missionary, to whom should they direct their request; how should the church relate to newly formed groups of believers; what body of doctrine should be transmitted by missionaries; and how could the translation of written materials be facilitated.

The concept of religions performing missionary work is not solely associated with Christianity. Other religions have had equivalent activities (particularly Islam—which was influenced by preexisting Christian patterns). But there is no doubt that the Christian missionary tradition has vitally influenced many aspects of secular Western culture. It is true that sometimes even Westerners have assessed missionary activities as intrusive and meddlesome. Such conclusions, however, are partly based on an observer's opinion about the doctrines carried by missionaries. One can imagine persons who look critically on missionaries, while they simultaneously applaud the "dedicated" work of Peace Corps volunteers, agricultural extension workers, or union organizers. True, some missionary approaches in foreign countries have sometimes been associated with imperial expansion. But they still constitute a unique form of expansion. Missionary approaches, whether they finally transmit religious or secular doctrine, aim to convert the natives to a new doctrine. In other words, the goal is not to exterminate, or even directly rule the natives. Instead, missionaries, through communicating their doctrine, hope to move relationships between natives and the intruders onto a new plane. And it is not always self-evident that the preferred new plane will subject the natives to economic exploitation. In sum, the influence of Western culture within the West, and throughout the world, has been powerfully fostered by persons (including communists) whose styles and basic values have been affected by the basic missionary tradition of Christianity—go forth, and teach to all nations. For persons who recognize this important theme of Western civilization, the issue is not pro- or antimissionary: the issue is, what doctrines should missionaries transmit?

Cenobitic monks, living in monasteries, were the first religious involved in the Christian missionary process, which still proceeds in our era. Theoretically, such monks were affiliated with particular monasteries. But, in early Western monastic life, individual commitment and stabilization (in one monastery) was not a firm pattern. As a result, monks, singly and in small groups, occasionally left their home monasteries to beg, escape unpleasant conditions, go on pilgrimages, found new monasteries, or explore and exploit believers. There are numerous recorded complaints about the patterns of such vagabond monks.[22] These itinerant practices also created the concept of the monastery as a base of operations: a residence of devout persons, unattached to families and living under a formal leader—persons who might provide assistance to the church within their neighborhood. As this potential as a base became evident, the founding of monasteries became a key mode of evangelization in Western Europe. A founder—a missionary—would convert and collect a group of converts in a non-Christian environment. Some of these males and females would choose to go into monastic life. And, in many cases, they (especially the males) would then engage in evangelization throughout their area. Sometimes the founder would continue to remain at the founded monastery, and sometimes he would eventually go on to other missionary endeavors. The group of religious in the monastery would have their own means of livelihood (agriculture), while their concentration would enable them to support each other's new faith.[23]

In some areas of Western Europe (e.g., Ireland, England, France), conversion of non-Latin natives to Christianity was carried out largely through the process just described. In other instances (e.g., Germany), emphasis was given to the development of local dioceses, although such efforts were supplemented with various forms of monastic activities. These diverse conversions occurred between about the second and eighth centuries. The missionary activities were carried out by male saints such as Saint Martin (316-397), Saint Patrick (389-461), Saint Augustine of Canterbury (d. 604) and Saint Boniface (672-754). The circumstances of these missionaries varied, but certain common patterns marked their lives: They first affected potential converts through their devotion and dedication. They had great initiative and energy. They often displayed political acumen in negotiating and compromising among diverse groups. To try to put it in a word, they were saints. These precious traits were partly due to the rigors of their monastic training, and their own self-selection into the role of missionaries.

A variety of forces undoubtedly assisted their remarkably successful efforts.[24] And many of such forces also affected later missionary activities. The missionaries were representative of an institution based in the capital of the Roman Empire—or its last remains. Despite such decay, the prestige and achievements of the Empire undoubtedly heightened the curiosity and interest of potential converts. The missionaries' conduct also represented an apparent and novel act: each missionary demonstrated by his presence that he had determined to live among foreigners, and possibly die in a strange land. Even in our era, such an act would be noteworthy. Among primitive peoples, whose sense of place and tribe would be strong, such an act of abandonment would be extraordinary. Throughout missionary history, there are reiterated examples of the respect won by missionaries simply because of the act of travel. It was a symbol of dedication and charity. Thus, during the early nineteenth century, one French missionary in the southwest Pacific reported that natives wondered about their visitors and asked questions such as "Why do they come from such a distance?" and "Are not their mothers and relations intensely grieved at seeing themselves separated for life from them?"[25]

Christianity also provided tribe members with an intellectual bridge into a broader environment. The Christian convert could choose to leave his tribe, participate in the larger

Christian world, and (perhaps) learn to read its literature. In addition, the missionary represented forces outside of the ethnic community. Thus, community leaders often sought to use their own conversion to Christianity to develop new, and favorable inter- and intra-tribal relationships. Because of Christianity's interethnic aspects, a tribe could be converted without necessarily changing its existing political structure. This helped persuade some tribal leaders to support—or even compel—the conversion of their peoples. (Although we should realize that compulsory baptism, at the behest of tribal leaders, was not as repressive as it might seem in our era. Tribal peoples often assumed that they would adopt the religion—new or old—practiced by their chief.) Sometimes the missionaries had technical knowledge—about agriculture or architecture—which gave them status in the eyes of locals.

It should be separately noted that missions were ideally a self-liquidating process. The aim was not to leave a foreign people indefinitely under the direction of alien religious. Instead, missionaries would eventually be replaced by local ethnic Christian clergy. Undoubtedly, this ideal was sometimes delayed, and sometimes the delays were due to bad faith. But, comparatively speaking, the historic record of Christian missions has largely demonstrated the sincerity of the goal of native control. Thus, in almost all regions of the contemporary world, long established Catholic (or Christian) churches are typically under the control of ethnically local peoples.

In the early period of the missionary process basic policies developed that powerfully colored church history and later missionary practices. These policies also shaped the missionary activities of many orders. One policy involved the attitude missionaries should adopt towards local non-Christian religious practices. Putting it directly, how sharply should the church highlight or confront the differences between Christian doctrine and existing native norms? This question affected Saint Augustine of Canterbury, who was engaged in evangelizing the Anglo-Saxons in England. A letter to him from Pope Gregory I in 601 advised him about this topic:

The idol temples of [the Anglo-Saxon] race should
by no means be destroyed, but only the idols in
them. Take holy water and sprinkle it in these
shrines, build altars and place relics in them, for if
the shrines are well built, it is essential that they
should be changed from the worship of the devils to
service of the true God. When the people see that
their shrines are not destroyed they will be able to
banish error from their hearts and be more ready
to come to the places they are familar with, but
now recognizing and worshipping the true God.
And because they are in the habit of slaughtering
much cattle as sacrifices to devils, some solemnity
ought to be given in exchange for this. So on the
day of dedication, or the festivals of the holy
martyrs, whose relics are deposited there, let them
make themselves huts from the branches of trees
round the churches which have been converted into
shrines, and let them celebrate the solemnity with
religious feasts. Do not let them sacrifice animals
to the devil, but let them slaughter animals for food
in praise of God, and let them give thanks to the
Giver of all things for His bountiful provision . . . It
is doubtless impossible to cut out everything at once
from their stubborn minds; just as a man who is
attempting to climb to the highest places rises by
steps and degrees and not by leaps.[26]

Another concern was the relationship between the
developing institution of the papacy and the wide-ranging
activities of the missionaries. Saint Boniface travelled from
England to act as a missionary in Germany. Excerpts from a
letter to him, in Germany, from Pope Gregory III (pontificate,
731-741) illustrate the evolving principles of support, counsel,
and direction. The letter is quoted at some length, since it
illustrates the spirit animating many missionary activities:

Gregory, servant of the servants of God, to
Boniface, his reverend and holy brother and fellow
bishop.

The teacher of all nations, the eminent Apostle Paul spoke, saying: "All things work together for good to them that love God." When we learned from your report that God in His mercy had deigned to set free so many in Germany from the power of the heathen and had brought as many as a hundred thousand souls into the bosom of Mother Church through your efforts and those of Charles, prince of the Franks, and when we heard what you had accomplished in Bavaria, we lifted up our hands to heaven in thanks to the Lord our God, giver of all good, who opened the gates of mercy and loving-kindness in those western lands for the knowledge of the way of salvation and sent his angel to prepare the way before you. Glory be to Him forever and ever!

In all this you have acted well and wisely, my brother, since you have fulfilled the apostolic precepts in our stead and have done as we directed you. Cease not therefore, most reverend brother, to teach them the holy catholic apostolic tradition of the Roman See, that the natives may be enlightened and may follow in the way of salvation and so may gain eternal reward. . . .

In regard to a council which you are to hold in the Danube valley in our stead: we direct Your Fraternity to be present there vested with apostolic authority. In so far as God shall give you strength, cease not to preach the Word of Salvation that the faith of Christ may increase and multiply in the name of God.

You are not at liberty, my brother, to linger in one place when your work there is done; but strengthen the hearts of the brethren and of all the faithful throughout those regions of the West, and wherever God shall open to you a way to save souls, carry on your preaching. Wherever you may find places in need of bishops, ordain them in our stead according to the canonical rule and teach them to observe the apostolic and canonical tradition. For so you will prepare great rewards for yourself, because you will gain for our God Almighty a well-instructed and devout people. Shrink not, beloved brother, from hard and long journeys, that the Christian faith may be spread far and wide through your exertions; for it is written: "Strait and narrow is the way that leadeth unto life." Carry on, therefore, my brother, the good work you have begun, so that in the day of Christ our God you can speak in the assembly of the saints about to be judged saying: "Lo, here am I and the children thou hast given me; I have not lost a single one of them." And again: "Lord thou gavest unto me five talents: behold, I have gained other five also." Then shall you be worthy to hear the voice of God saying: "Well done, thou good and faithful servant: Thou hast been faithful over a few things, I will make thee ruler over many things: Enter thou into the joy of thy Lord."

God keep you in safety, most reverend brother.

Given on the fourth day before the Kalends of November on the twenty-third year of our most pious and august Lord Leo by God crowned emperor, on the twenty-third year of his consulship and the twentieth year of the Emperor Constantine his son, in the eighth indiction.[27]

The Structure of Early Religious Orders

Individual monasteries were the first religious institutions created in Western Europe. On some occasions such institutions actually housed congregations formed solely of females, although they were still historically termed *monasteries*. The information about the forms of governance and organization applied in such early institutions is somewhat incomplete. Still, it is clear that the institutions did not approach the organizational complexity evident in the institutions developed by Saint Pachomius. Several factors militated against the development of such complexity.

Early European monasteries were often comparatively small, with ten to twenty-five members. Smallness made it less necessary for them to develop elaborate formal organizations (or perhaps they were small because they lacked the principles to permit them to become larger). In some cases, where monasteries became larger, preexisting forms of governance were adapted for monastic purposes. Thus, in Ireland, when large-scale religious conversions occurred, local chieftans often became monastic leaders[28] their followers enrolled into their monasteries. Under such circumstances, the previous chief/subordinate relationship could be transferred to monastic life. Sometimes, too, it is evident that considerable confusion reigned in certain monasteries due to the lack of clear, generally applicable principles to direct the activities of a number of persons living and working closely together.[29]

Gradually, efforts occurred to promulgate formal principles (*rules*) to provide necessary structure. One early and still persisting Rule was provided by Saint Augustine of Hippo (354-430) for a group of women desirous of forming a religious congregation. (Authorities also attribute a somewhat similar rule for males to Saint Augustine.)[30] We do not know the circumstances under which Saint Augustine's original rule was implemented. We only know that about a century after his death, the text of the Rule was identified and it was later adopted by various orders. The Rule totals 3,300 words and deals with a variety of principles and practices relevant to community life, including holding property in common; the disregard of distinctions which prevailed before people became members; the procedures for collective prayers and the singing of psalms; the practice of fasts and abstinence; the development of realistic and necessary distinctions among members based on individual characteristics; the appropriate forms of dress, and the maintenance and allotment of clothing; the practice of good conduct both inside and outside the monastery; the monitoring of each other's conduct by religious; the respect due the prioress, and the concern she should have for members' welfare; and the requirement that all members read over the Rule once each week.[31]

The Rule, in some ways, shows a degree of development beyond the so called Pachomian Rule (so-called because that Rule was not stated in a complete, formal text but actually in diverse documents). Saint Augustine's Rule is more precise about the forms of human relations it aims to foster, and of higher literary quality. Yet the Augustian Rule provides less information about institutional structure, partly because it was designed to apply to less elaborate organizations than comparatively large monasteries.

The text of the Saint Augustines's Rule displays considerable psychological insight. In discussing the matter of dress, for example, it provides:

> And whatever may be brought out to you as wearing apparel suitable for the season, regard it, if possible, as a matter of no importance whether each of you receives the very same article of clothing which she had formerly laid aside, or one receive what another formerly wore, provided only that what is necessary be denied to no one. But if contentions and murmurings are occasioned among you by this, and some one of you complains that she has received some article of dress inferior to that which she formerly wore, and thinks it beneath her to be so clothed as her own sister was, by this prove your own selves, and judge how far deficient you must be in the inner holy dress of the heart, when you quarrel with each other about the clothing of the body . . . no one is to work in making any article for clothing or for the couch, or any girdle, veil, or head-dress, for her own private comfort, but that all your works be done for the common good of all with greater zeal and more cheerful perseverance than if you were each working for your individual interest.[32]

The Rule also recites the charitable and doctrinal principle underlying its pronouncements. Thus, the Rule instructs members to restrain their glances towards males, then gives directions to members about what to do if they observe members violating this provision. The tone of these directions is revealing:

> And if you perceive in any one of your number this forwardness of eye, warn her at once, so that the evil which has begun may not go on, but be checked immediately. But if, after this admonition, you see her repeat the offence, or do the same thing on any other subsequent day, whoever may have had the opportunity of seeing this must now report her as one who has been wounded and requires to be healed, but not without pointing her out to another, and perhaps a third sister, so that she may be convicted by the testimony of two or three witnesses, and may be reprimanded with necessary severity. And do not think that in thus informing upon one another you are guilty of malevolence. For the truth rather is that you are not guiltless if by keeping silence you allow sisters to perish, whom you may correct by giving information of their faults. For if your sister had a wound on her person which she wished to conceal through fear of the surgeon's lance, would it not be cruel if you kept silence about it, and true compassion if you made it known?[33]

In Matt. 18:15-18, Jesus gave practically the same counsel about confrontation to his disciples.

The obligation to confront the wrongdoer, and in private, makes excellent sense. It places the obligation of correction squarely on each community member. It diminishes the potential for destructive gossip. It presents correction as a form of affection. And it makes it likely that erring members will receive fast feedback, before they are confirmed in misconduct. Now, none of this is to imply that such Rules are always followed, but simply to remark that the Rule applies inherently sound psychology, and that organizations that cause their members to follow it are likely to persist.

Augustine did not invent his Rule *de novo*. The Rule reaffirmed many biblical themes. In addition, Augustine had earlier read and been greatly impressed by *The Life of St. Anthony*, which influenced his recommendations.

Augustine's Rule contained certain strengths and deficiencies. It was written with style and insight, by a person who was eventually recognized as one of the great minds of the early Catholic church. And it was more inclusive than many Rules evidently being practised. The text left unsettled, however, many matters that might affect religious life: explicit dietary principles, how members might be admitted, the routine activities of the religious (apart from worship), the selection of leaders, and the creation of subordinate offices. This uncertainty meant there was a need for other forms of rules. And that need was eventually fulfilled. Saint Augustine's Rule was never totally eclipsed, however. Its very generality made it adaptable to divergent and even unforseen situations which might arise in future centuries. As a result, in different places and eras, Saint Augustine's Rule has often played a central role for important religious organizations.

Notes

1. David Knowles, *Christian Monasticism* (New York: McGraw-Hill, 1969), Chap. 2.

2. Herbert Workman, *The Evolution of the Monastic Ideal* (Boston, MA: Beacon Press, 1962), p. 9.

3. Ann Freemantle, *A Treasury of Early Christianity* (New York: Viking, 1953), pp. 508-09.

4. Workman, *Evolution*, p. 11.

5. For a classic study of cooption, see Phillip Selznick, *TVA and the Grass Roots* (New York: Harper and Row, 1966).

6. For data about life spans in other eras, see Matilda White Riley, John W. Riley, Jr., and Marilyn Johnson, *An Inventory of Research Findings*, vol. 1: *Aging and Society* (New York: Russell Sage, 1968), p. 25; and Gy. Acsadi and J. Neneskeri, *History of Human Life Span and Morality* (Budapest, Hungary: Akademia Kiado, 1970).

7. Aristotle, *Politics* (Cambridge: Harvard University Press, 1932).

8. B. F. Skinner, *Beyond Freedom and Dignity* (New York: Alfred P. Knopf, 1971).

9. Edward O. Wilson, *Sociobiology: The New Synthesis* (Cambridge: Harvard University Press, 1975).

10. Arland Thornton, "Trends in Marriage and Divorce," *Population Bulletin* 46, no. 4 (Fall 1983), entire issue.

11. Philip Rieff, *The Triumph of the Therapeutic* (New York: Harper and Row, 1966).

12. *New Catholic Encyclopedia* (Washington, DC: Catholic University, 1967), vol. 11, p. 674-77.

13. Edwin G. Browne, *A Year Among the Persians* (London: A. and C. Black, 1959), p. 136.

14. For a classic beginner's guide to mental prayer, see Saint Francis de Sales, *A Guide to the Devout Life* (Garden City, NY: Doubleday, 1964), first published in 1608; for a work directed at more advanced readers, see St. John of the Cross, *The Collected Works* (Garden City, NY: Doubleday, 1964).

15. *New Catholic*, vol. 4, p. 890.

16. Saint Teresa, *Life*, trans. David Lewis (Westminister, MD: Newman Book Shop, 1947), p. XXVII, XXIX.

17. Max Weber, *On Charisma and Institution Building*, ed. S. N. Eisenstadt (Chicago: University of Chicago Press, 1968).

18. Freemantle, *A Treasury*, p. 486.

19. Jerusalem Bible, Col. 3:11.

20. Ibid, Acts 22:26.

21. Ibid, Mark 16:16.

22. Workman, *Evolution*, p. 134 et seq.

23. Knowles, *Christian Monasticism*, Chap. 2.

24. For a thorough consideration of many issues of missionary theory, see Joseph Schmidlin, *Catholic Mission Theory* (Techny, IL: Mission Press, 1931).

25. Lillian Keys, *The Life and Times of Bishop Pompallier* (Christ Church, New Zealand: Pegasus Press, 1957), p. 58.

26. Venerable Bede, *Bede's Ecclesiastical History* (Oxford: Clarendon Press, 1966), p. 107-9.

27. Ephraim Emerton, *The Letters of St. Boniface* (New York: Columbia University Press, 1940), p. 72-73.

28. Knowles, *Christian Monasticism*, p. 31.

29. Workman, *Evolution*, p. 123.

30. *New Catholic*, vol. 1, p. 1059.

31. Freemantle, *A Treasury*, p. 494-503.

32. Ibid, p. 499.

33. Ibid, p. 498.

4
A Landmark:
Saint Benedict's Rule

Hearken, my son, to the precepts of the master and incline the ear of thy heart; freely accept and faithfully fulfill the instructions of a loving father, that by the labor of obedience thou mayest return to him from whom thou hast strayed by the sloth of disobedience. To thee are my words now addressed, whomsoever thou may be that, renouncing thine own will, to fight for the true King, Christ, dost take up the strong and glorious weapons of obedience.

        — Opening of the prologue of Saint Benedict's Rule

Saint Benedict of Nursia (480-547) spent his life in central Italy, during the decline of the Roman Empire. He is a major figure in Catholic history because he authored a rule for religious life which eventually became the predominant—or almost sole—rule followed by Catholic religious for a number of centuries. Saint Benedict's Rule was originally drafted for the governance of male religious; yet from its early stages it was regarded as adaptable to religious orders of women, and was so applied.

Over time, the rule underwent adaptations, and differences in interpretation and application arose.[1] Furthermore, some elements of the rule were general in tone, and this became part of its strength. Such generality meant that local clarifications and supplementary regulations were necessary and permissible in individual monasteries and particular situations. Variations also became necessary since most monasteries in the saint's era had no more than fifteen to twenty five monks enrolled; in later periods, the rule was applied to institutions housing hundreds of religious. But, recognizing such variations, it is still correct to say that the original Rule had a profound and continuing influence.

It is not clear whether Saint Benedict deliberately wrote his Rule for the governance of diverse monasteries. Perhaps he only wanted to provide a rule for the monastery of Monte Cassino, where he was abbot. Whatever his original intentions, the Rule's unique qualities led to its gradual and pervasive diffusion throughout early medieval Europe and, eventually, the whole world. Even when other Rules appeared and gained influence, Saint Benedict's Rule persisted, and oftentimes flourished. Furthermore, many later Rules have been affected by the precedents established by Saint Benedict's Rule.

One device we might apply to more fully understand the significance of the rule is to look at the details of Saint Benedict's life. But we have very little information about this topic. Our only contemporary (or near-contemporary) report about the saint is derived from a biography written nearly fifty years after his death by Pope Gregory the Great.[2] Saint Gregory's biography, included in his *Dialogues*, is important, if not persuasively accurate. Its author's engaging style and notable status gave the *Dialogues* persisting and wide circulation. And the biography articulated strong and plausible praise for the Rule. Thus, the biography played an important role in popularizing the Rule and provided a setting for interpreting its intent.

Beyond such textual information, we can infer other information about Saint Benedict, since we know about the era in which he lived, and some of the monasteries and other activities with which he was associated.

Nevertheless, while Saint Benedict (and his sister, Saint Scholastica, who also founded a women's monastery) as described by Saint Gregory's hagiographic work is engaging, after all is said, we know most about the Saint through his Rule. The Rule is about 19,000 words (subdivided into 73 chapters, of varying length) and is a constitution for the operation of a monastery. There is no doubt that the composition of the Rule was influenced by Saint Benedict's study of other documents, such as the writings about the Desert Fathers, and perhaps another Rule, the Rule of the Master—and, of course, the New and Old Testaments. Considerable scholarly effort has gone into analyzing the relationship between these sources, the contents of the Rule, and Saint Benedict's original contributions. The current consensus is that Benedict's hand was an important and, perhaps, decisive element in regard to both, substance and tone. And, as we will see, the tone of the Rule is very important.

What Monks Were Directed to Do

The Rule's first aim was to enable cenobitic monks to lead lives that would make it likely they attained eternal salvation. The Rule told them how to direct their energies towards this end. In particular, it required monks to spend a considerable proportion of their time in the oratory of the monastery (an oratory is an altar or church designated for private use) performing the Opus Dei—the work done for God. The Opus Dei consisted of chanting and reading the Hours of the Divine Office. Thirteen chapters of the Rule discuss the arrangements for such performance: the texts and other materials to be sung or read, and other aspects of these rites.[3] The Rule specified eight separate occasions daily for the performance of the office, including one in the middle of the night. One authority estimated the typical winter day of a monk in Saint Benedict's monastery would be divided as follows (summer hours would be different, due to more daylight, and increased agricultural responsibilities):[4]

2:00 a.m.	Rise for Office (Matins)
2:10-3:30	Matins
3:30-5:00	Reading
5:00-5:45	Office (Lauds)
5:45-8:15	Reading and Office (Prime)
8:15-2:30	Work, broken by Offices (Terce, Sext, and None)
2:30-3:15	Dinner
3:15-4:15	Reading
4:15-4:45	Office (Vespers), Light meal, Office (Compiline)
5:45 p.m.	Bed

Apart from meals, four, five and six hours, respectively, were dedicated to prayer, reading and work each day.

The Rule made it clear that the performance of office was a serious matter. Thus, it specified how to treat monks who arrived late for the performance of matins, presented in the middle of the night. The text of that provision also discloses something about the general spirit of the Rule:

> If anyone shall come to Matins after the *Gloria* of the ninety-fourth Psalm (which on this account we wish to be said slowly and leisurely) he shall not take his place in the choir, but go last of all, or to some place apart which the abbot may appoint for those that so fail in his sight, until the Divine Office be ended and he shall have done penance and made public satisfaction.

> We have judged it fitting that these [latecomers] should stand last, or in some place apart, in order that, being seen by all, for very shame they may amend. For if they remain outside the oratory someone will, perhaps, return to sleep, or at least sit outside by himself, or setting himself to idle talk give an occasion to the evil one. Let such a one, therefore, come inside, so that he may not lose all, but make amends during the rest of the Office. (chap. 43)

Efforts were made to insure that all members of the community participated in all presentations of the office. Monks who were working at locations remote from the monastery were provided with instructions about how to perform the office away from the oratory (chap. 50).

The Rule observed that "idleness is the enemy of the Soul" (chap. 48). To prevent idleness, monks were expected to engage in the various activities necessary to feed each other and otherwise maintain the monastery. A number of responsible positions were described, and the tasks of the incumbents recited: the cellarer (to maintain the storehouse); kitchen servers; persons to read aloud to the monks at meals; craftsmen; and the porter, or gatekeeper (chaps. 31, 35, 38, 57, 66). The directions given to incumbents stressed themes of service and obedience. The craftsmen were directed to not become excessively proud or possessive of their products (chap. 57). And the porter should be "some wise old monk who knows how to give and receive an answer, and whose age will not allow him to wander from his post" (chap. 66).

One aim of the division of labor was to enable the monastery to be self-sufficient. "If possible, it should be so constructed as to contain within it all necessaries, that is watermill, garden, and places for the various crafts, so there be no occasion for monks to wander abroad, since this is no wise expedient for their souls" (chap. 66).

Technically speaking, early religious communities of women also lived in monasteries. The word is a generic term, and simply means one who lives apart. But eventually such female communities were designated by sex-related terms, such as nunnery. It was not expected that female religious communities should be economically self-sufficient, since their members would lack some of the necessary skills and strength. Thus, such communities regularly received certain resources (e.g., food) from the outside. Such materials came either as gifts from the faithful, through purchase, or barter. Female religious were still usually expected to engage in materially productive labor, such as the embroidery or sewing of sacramental vestments. Sometimes, male and female monasteries were established in physically close conjunction, and monks were expected to assist the female religious in their transactions with the external world. Also, priests who were members of the monastic community could provide sacramental services for the female community.

Over centuries, the division of time—between prayer, work and reading—envisaged by Saint Benedict was often varied by diverse circumstances. In some situations, monasteries developed that were heavily endowed, or given the right to levy taxes or tolls. This permitted them to hire laypersons (or to own serfs) to perform the manual tasks formerly done by monks. And it became common for high

proportions of monks to be ordained priests, as compared to
being *lay* brothers. Thus, many monasteries evolved to the
point where most monks spent high proportions of their waking
hours performing the Divine office—and the contents of the
Office became highly elaborated.[5] Meanwhile, the secular work
was performed by serfs, servants, and lay brothers.

A number of provisions of the Rule described the
organization of meals (chaps. 37, 39, 40). Monks were
prohibited from talking during meals. Readers were designated,
who would read aloud from religious works during dining hours.
Some provisions specified the dietary restrictions which would
be applied to monks (chaps. 40, 49). Community members were
prohibited from engaging in more rigorous fasts without the
permission of their superiors. The Rule's provision about the
consumption of wine provides a revealing example of its
common sense approach:

> Every one hath his proper gift from God, one thus,
> another thus, [For this reason] the amount of other
> people's food cannot be determined without some
> misgiving. Still, having regard for the weak state
> of the sick, we think a pint of wine a day is enough
> for any one. But let those to whom God gives the
> gift of abstinence know they shall receive their
> proper reward. . . . Although we read that "wine is
> not the drink of monks at all," yet, since in our
> days they cannot be persuaded of this, let us at
> least agree not to drink to satiety, but sparingly. . . .
> (chap. 40)

A lengthy chapter of the Rule outlined the hospitality to
be provided to travellers (chap. 53). They were to be cordially
welcomed, and seated at the abbot's table, which was specially
maintained to facilitate hospitality. The text remarked that the
New Testament emphasized that Christians had a special
obligation to shelter wanderers. This provision had a special
significance during the medieval era, when travellers often
journeyed without carrying money or valuables, and hotels and
equivalent facilities were rare or unknown. Furthermore,
travellers were often persons on pilgrimages to religious sites.

Obedience and Authority

The principal officer of the monastery was the abbot. The word is derived from the Greek *abba*, or father. The abbot was elected (or nominated to the local bishop for designation) by all members of the community (chap. 64). He served for life, and could only be removed by the local bishop, or other abbots of the neighborhood, if the monks and their abbot were collectively leading vicious lives. In later eras, the Rule was revised to provide fixed terms for abbots instead of lifetime authority. All members of the community were eligible for designation as abbot.

The Rule continuously emphasized the high degree of obedience that monks owed to their abbot. Three major chapters of the Rule were titled, "On Obedience," "On Silence," and "On Humility" (chap. 4-6). The prologue mentioned the virtue of "holy obedience." On the other hand, the Rule enjoined the abbot to rule with a prudent and loving hand:

> The abbot should ever be mindful that at the dread judgment of God, there will be inquiry both as to his teaching and to the obedience of his disciples.... Let him make no distinctions of persons in the monastery. . . . The abbot in his teaching should always observe that apostolic rule which saith "Reprove, entreat, rebuke". . . . Let him manifest the sternness of a master and the loving affection of a father. He must reprove the undisciplined and restless severely, but he should exhort such as are obedient, quiet and patient . . . thus shall he so shape and adapt himself to the character and intelligence of each [monk], that he not only suffer no loss in the flock entrusted in, but may even rejoice at its good growth . . . let him understand for certain that at the Day of Judgment he will have to give to our Lord an account of all [the monks' souls] as well as his own. (chap. 2)

In deciding any weighty matters, the abbot was directed to solicit the collective advice of the whole community.

> After hearing the advice of the brethren let him consider it in his own mind, and then do what he shall judge most expedient. We ordain that all must be called to council, because the Lord often reveals to a younger member what is best. And let the brethren give their advice with all humble submission, and persume not stiffly to define their own opinion. (chap. 3)

An order of precedence was provided to determine ranking of community members in processions, while standing in choir, and other occasions (chap. 63). In general, a monk's precedence was determined by the time of his profession of vows, not by his age or secular status. The abbot was authorized to vary such precedence if he felt it was in the interest of the whole community.

Several provisions outlined the forms of punishment to be applied to malefactors (chaps. 23-30, 43-46). Some of the punishments were provided for specific violations (e.g., arriving late for Divine Office), while others had general applicability. The punishments included oral reprimands by the abbot, isolation (for varying lengths of time) from other community members, corporal punishment, and finally excommunication —expulsion from the community. The abbot was enjoined to make special efforts to bring about the reformation of wrongdoing monks. He was to assign "older and wise brethren" to work with each "isolated" monk, to win him to make humble satisfaction. "The abbot ought to take the greatest care and to use all prudence and industry to lose none of the sheep entrusted to him. Let him know that he hath undertaken the care of souls that are sick, and not act the tyrant over such as are well" (chap. 27).

The Rule provided for the creation of deans and a provost (chaps. 21, 65). The holders of these offices were designated by the abbot. The deans (the word is derived from the Latin for *ten*) were superiors for designated subgroups of monks. The provost acted as the immediate subordinate of the abbot.

There were explicit provisions about the sleeping arrangements. Monks were to sleep in a large common room and stay dressed while sleeping (chap. 22). The room was lighted throughout the night. Younger monks were to be separated from one another by the beds of older monks. These provisions made it easier for older monks to monitor their juniors and facilitated the monks' rising at 2:00 a.m. for matins. They also probably served to discourage homosexual practices.

Concerns about homosexuality also related to what came to be called "particular friendships."[6] Thus, the Rule prohibited one monk from defending another against criticism or acting to advance the interests of a relative or friend who was also a monk (chap. 69). Essentially, the issue of homosexual pairings was only one element of fears concerning the formation of small groups or cliques in the larger community. Such groups might be based on previous extra-monastic factors—such as family ties or ethnicity—or on bondings—such as homosexual relationships—which evolved during community membership. The Rule saw these groups as a threat to overall community loyalty. In effect, small groups were discouraged to stimulate members to greater affiliation with the whole. The principle is understandable, but it undoubtedly generated diverse problems in practice. But, for many religious orders, fidelity to the principle was persistently stressed.

A major factor in maintaining harmony and obedience in the community was the rule's careful directions about the acceptance of new members (chap. 58). The pertinent chapter is among the longest in the Rule. Potential members were required to remain outside the monastery gate for several days before being allowed to enter the premises. The aim of the policy was to try the spirits of potential members. When recruits were admitted to the premises, each was assigned to the tutelage of a senior monk, "skilled at winning souls." Two times during the year of novicehood, the entire rule was read aloud to the recruit. Each time he was told he might choose to depart if observing the rule seemed too arduous. On the third and final reading, if

> [H]e shall promise to keep all the law and to do
> whatever is commanded of him, let him be received
> into the community, knowing that he is now under
> the law of the *Rule* . . . let him in the oratory, and
> in the presence of all, promise before God and His
> saints, stability, amendment of manners and
> obedience. . . . He shall draw up the form of his
> promise in the name of the saints, whose relics are
> reposing there, and of the abbot there present. Let
> him write out this form himself [or set his mark on
> it]. (chap. 58)

This ceremony was called profession—speaking out. In later
monastic practice, the period of noviceship tended to be
lengthened. The solemn profession required by the Rule,
however, was maintained.

The word "stability" in the vow meant that a monk,
absent extraordinary circumstances, obligated himself to spend
his entire life in the monastery where he professed, as compared
to transferring to another monastery. An inevitable effect of
this restriction would be that monks had to dedicate themselves
to coming to terms with the other members of the community,
and vice versa.

The Age of Profession

The Rule spoke of the profession of applicants who were
obviously adults. Still, it is clear that boys and young men also
resided in monasteries. Thus, the Rule specified different
obligations and punishments to be applied to the young and
discussed receiving grants of funds or property from guardians
as a (sometimes) condition for accepting young enrollees (chaps.
30, 39, 59, 70). A three-pronged system of recruitment existed:
Some young and mature adults made deliberate decisions to
profess. Some children were placed in monasteries by parents,
with the expectation they would be raised to be religious. And
some children were placed in monasteries, either as orphans or
by their guardians, to be reared, and possibly choose to become
religious on attaining adulthood. Often when children were
placed by guardians, their placement was accompanied by a
payment or endowment given to the community.

The provisions for youthful (or child) recruitment served diverse needs. They gave monasteries a simple means of recruitment and enabled them to totally control the socialization of potential members. In some cases, the endowments received from parents with such children were substantial, and increased the total resources of the institution. Families, which felt an obligation to care for all of their children, were provided with another alternative career which could be purchased. And, on some occasions, the system served as a form of care for orphans. It is also pertinent to note that, in the case of females, placement allowed prosperous families to place daughters whom they saw as unmarriageable in secure situations. It should be recognized that in the medieval era (and even somewhat later), not all unmarriageable females were necessarily afflicted or incompetent. *Unmarriageable* could also mean that a substantial family could only afford to subsidize appropriate marriages for certain of its daughters; any other daughters would be placed in nunneries as a form of lesser provision. But youthful recruitment also generated disadvantages.

No matter what the Rule provides, decorum must be tempered in any environment seriously engaged in rearing children. Also, when members are recruited as children, their level of adult aptitude is problematic. The monastery can substantially control their socialization, but it cannot determine their energy, innate intelligence, and so on. Conversely, when a religious community focuses on adult recruits, it can make a more informed assessment of the bundle of abilities it is considering. Indeed, when an adult chooses to profess, in the face of the world's evident temptations, a community can assume that their recruit possesses a certain psychic vitality. But someone who stays in a monastery into adulthood because that is the way he (or she) was reared may only be a person who lacks determination or initiative.

Throughout the history of religious life, the matter of age at profession has remained a vexsome question. Presumably, the ideal novice is someone who has attained substantial maturity before becoming a novice and can make an informed decision about the significance of profession. Many important religious have followed that course. Saint Ignatius Loyola

(1491-1556) served as a military officer before making his commitment to religious life at the age of thirty. The widowed Saint Louise de Marillac (1591-1660) helped to found the Daughters of Charity at the age of forty-two after rearing her son. But there are many exceptions to this pattern. Saint Bede (672-735) was enrolled in a monastery at the age of eight.

The reality is that many pressures stimulated religious orders to engage in early recruiting. The endowments provided by the families of such recruits helped provide economic stability. Again, orders often accepted, during periods of growth, bodies of charitable and missionary responsibilities; an assured flow of recruits was necessary to continue to satisfy such obligations. Finally, many orders accepted duties in fields such as teaching and caring for foundlings; an inevitable effect was to encourage some of the "helped" children to want to enroll in the community.

The question of age of profession is a complex one. If the age is set too soon, undermotivated and uninformed members may be admitted. If it set too "late," many potential members may have been socialized in environments essentially hostile to religious life, or made have commitments (e.g., marriage) inconsistent with taking vows.

The Life of the Mind

The Rule required that monks spend part of their time reading religious literature (chap. 48). In the first Benedictine monasteries, the literature was in Latin, because some form of Latin was the language of the population. But Latin then became the formal language of the church. Thus, as monasteries spread to areas beyond Italy, all monks were placed under practical pressure to learn to read Latin. The readings provided religious with a body of knowledge to (a) assist them in performing the Divine Office, which was partly comprised of Psalms; (b) heighten their understanding of how to acquire and practice virtue; and (c) give them insights (based on biblical texts and the writings of Church Fathers) about how to live in community. The requirement of reading meant that religious in monasteries could not—or should not—live in complete isolation. Reading would put them in touch with experiences and information from the past, and with relevant contemporary thought. But it was assumed that all of these resources would be reviewed by superiors, to insure that disruptive information and concepts did not pollute the environment (chap. 54).[7]

Concern with reading affected several elements of monastic life. It meant that monasteries needed to have libraries. The libraries had to acquire books, which were manuscripts, often expensive or in short supply. Thus, some monks were assigned to act as copyists to enlarge the libraries. Copying gradually became an important part of monks' work. Its importance increased as growing numbers of monks became priests. It was not expected that priests would perform manual labor, but copying was an acceptable form of activity.

Gradually, the focus on text acquisition and copying broadened into an interest in more diverse acquisitions and the critical reading of texts. A concern for literary style (in Latin), per se, emerged. Acquisition policies were directed not only towards religious authors, but on classic Latin and Greek (secular) writers, whose texts might help in interpreting religious materials, or whose style might prove an admirable model. We must also note the relationship between the role of Latin as the formal language of the church, and the access to classical literature that such knowledge provided. Of course, over centuries, a gap arose between the characteristics of classic Latin and the Latin applied by typical churchmen. Still, even such abased usage kept alive an interest in a body of important literature. Eventually, a group of religious evolved whose work solely encompassed scholarship and religious devotions. These scholars read, wrote, copied, communicated with peers, and instructed more untrained religious in religious doctrine and literary matters. Their original writings included commentaries on texts, chronologies, devotional literature, dictionaries (for the use of missionaries), journals, and texts for religious music. Many of these activities served directly the interests of their community, or the whole church. Still, it is evident that the creators often had a natural sense of identification with their products.

Cuthbert Butler has contended that copying (and the scholarship arising from copying) was the "ideal" materially productive work for monks.[8] Copying could be done without establishing schedules which interfered with the Opus Dei, and without extensive engagement with the extramonastic world. Butler observed that the value of copying was extinguished by the invention of the printing press. Since then, the development of appropriate material work for monks has become more complicated—as will be considered in more detail later.

Some of the intellectual spirit of religious scholarship is suggested by the remarks of Saint Bede (i.e., the Venerable Bede, 672-735) about the problems of translating verse into a foreign language. His text quoted certain religious verses he attributed to a famous singer. The original words were sung in Old English. Saint Bede recited the words solely in Latin. After his quote, he went on to note, "This is the sense but not the order of the words which he sang. . . . For it is not possible to translate verse, however well composed, literally from one language to another without some loss of beauty and dignity."[9]

A striking example of the contributions of these intellectuals is provided in a letter written in 710 by an abbot to a king of one of the regions of England. The letter was part of an effort to assist the merger of two disparate segments of the Catholic church on the island.[10] One point of contention was the procedure for establishing the proper calendar system to be used to set the date for celebrating Easter. Undoubtedly, the two competing calendar systems symbolized other differences affected by the proposed merger. The 2,000 word letter was an argument for the virtues of one system. It was an elaborate, clear, and balanced presentation of the whole, complex issue. Any reader would be impressed, not so much by the letter's rightness, but more by its lucidity and thoroughness. And, in fact, the calendar system urged in the letter was eventually designated as the base for computation. In sum, the intellectual training of monks provided an important resource for the church.

It has been recognized that the rigorous pursuit of scholarship can cause scholars to develop relatively individualistic and disputatious temperaments. Still, for religious scholars, the procommunity forces structuring their work unquestionably served as one moderating force. Thus, a twentieth-century academic who was a religious and taught at a Catholic college (affiliated with an order) remarked that sometimes he attended faculty meetings with the expectation of participating while leisurely smoking a pipe. It seemed to him that, on just such occasions, the meetings were opened with the group singing "Vene Sanctus Spiritus," the hymn "Come Holy Spirit."[11] That hymn invokes the Holy Spirit to provide guidance. It would logically be sung before a meeting to consider a divisive and complex topic; the practice might well serve to temper the succeeding discussion—though pipe smoking could still be regarded as out of place in the circumstances.

Undoubtedly, assessing the virtues of traditional religious scholarship is complicated. One can easily recall the forced recantation of Galileo and the general disposition of the church to constrain speculative thought into limited channels. It may be argued, however, that high proportion of scholarship, in all eras, is necessarily overspecialized and often degenerates into tendentious controversy. This may be especially true when the scholars are not bound by some body of overarching rites and beliefs. In any case, it is evident that our era and society has opted for scholarly freedom, with its diverse virtues and drawbacks.

The Matter of Property

Five of the chapters of the Rule explicitly discuss the principle of poverty. Monks were directed, upon profession, to donate all their goods to the poor, or to the monastery (chaps. 33, 34, 54, 55, 58). They were provided with specified and limited amounts of clothing. Every effort was made to have all materials maintained for common use and not identified with any particular user. If monks received any presents while in the monastery, they were directed to surrender them to the abbot, who might distribute them to anyone he designated. The only persons who might be entitled to receive more food or goods than others were elderly or ill monks, who might require special resources.

One effect of the stress on poverty was to heighten each monk's loyalty to the community. No individual monk could acquire enough capital to tempt him to leave the community with his personal possessions. It is evident that rule is colored by the Desert Fathers' hostility to material possessions. Like the Fathers, Saint Benedict saw the desire to possess goods as a source of dissension and envy. It should be noted, however, that the Rule contained no provision against the monastery, itself, owning goods. Indeed, as a practical matter, any functioning and productive community would need to possess material goods to sustain itself. And, over time, some monasteries acquired significant wealth and works of art and architecture. Some of these resources were used for explicitly religious purposes, while other resources were used for purposes that where in evident violation of the spirit of the rule.

The fact that many monasteries were elaborately constructed and decorated is due partly to the restrictions on individual possession: in a more "individualistic" environment, more resources might have been dedicated to personal consumption. On the other hand, there are powerful incentives for monks to dedicate the same resources for collective and religious purposes.

Another problem surrounding the enforcement of poverty stemmed from priority that gradually evolved for the Divine Office. If monasteries acquired significant wealth, more monks could dedicate more time to performing the office. Thus, there might be an evident religious purpose to the monasteries seeking to acquire collective wealth.

Religious Communities as Utopias

A significant body of historical and contemporary thought exists regarding the formation and governance of utopias—ideal human communities.[12] Many concepts developed through such analysis and experience have relevance to traditional religious life, and so deserve amplification.

There is a long history of thoughtful persons who have used the concept of an *ideal state* as a tool for political analysis.

Plato's *Republic*, for example, was an exercise of that nature. Irving Kristol pointed out that, for most of human experience, such utopian thought was of an essentially abstract nature.[13] Plato did not expect anyone to actually try to create his "republic." It was simply an analytic model. Accordingly, when Thomas More (1478-1535) coined the word *utopia*, he used a Greek root meaning "nowhere."

But Kristol contended that, as history moved closer to modernity—and, perhaps, the Industrial Revolution—utopian thought more frequently was perceived as a means of prescribing concrete action. Thus, writings of persons such as Rousseau and Marx were looked upon in part as guides to practical policies, even though Rousseau described his influential "Reflections on the Origins of Inequality" as a "hypothetical history,"[14] and Marx said that a communist society, "makes it possible for me to do one thing today and another tomorrow, to hunt in the morning, fish in the afternoon, rear cattle in the evening, criticize after dinner . . . without ever becoming a hunter, fisherman, shepherd or critic."[15] Historians and sociologists have identified a great many of attempts to form utopian communities—based on principles of perfecting human nature and relationships—over the past two hundred years.[16] A number of these efforts have occurred in the United States, both during the nineteenth century, and during the recent past, as part of the hippy/commune movement of the late 1960s and early 1970s.[17] Some of the attempts lasted for significant periods of time. The great majority, however, were of short duration.

Utopian communities, like traditional orders, usually made efforts to isolate themselves from the world.[18] They were situated on farms, in frontier environments, and (hypothetically?) on islands. The communities, like orders, aimed to develop human relationships that were more humane and cooperative than those that typically prevailed in the larger society. Sometimes the utopias saw their activities as exemplary for the external society; and sometimes there was some element of missionary purpose—as in some orders. Most utopias, like orders, envisaged their members as making a prolonged or lifetime commitment. The economic purposes of utopian-type communities, apart from meeting basic needs, were usually not a high priority—like orders.

On the other hand, most utopias differed from order patterns in several ways. Some utopias had religious concerns, but many others did not. Few utopias were relatively closely tied to an established church, such as the Roman Catholic church. Few utopias had their purposes defined by documents. Even when such documents existed, they had usually been created on an ad hoc basis, as compared to being "inherited" and incrementally developed. Some utopias have not significantly restricted the sexual activities of their member. Religious communities tried to maintain rigorous restrictions on sex. The aim of most utopias was to provide members with fulfillment during their lifetimes. In religious communities, fulfillment could usually be attained only in an afterlife. Many utopias conceived of themselves as potentially enlisting large portions of society as members. Religious communities were professedly elitist; the principle of celibacy necessarily limited the proportion of recruits. And no utopias have endured as long as the most persisting religious orders.

Mention might also be made of what could be called common sense. The alleged lack of common sense has been a classic criticism of utopian efforts. Or, as James Russell Lowell observed about Brook Farm, a nineteenth century New England commune, "Everything was held in common but common sense." Utopian groups usually isolate themselves from typical human concerns, aspire to engage in a dramatic and ambitious experiment, and are prepared to accept significant deprivation. Under such circumstances, a group's values may become highly unrealistic. But religious communities, for a variety of reasons, practiced only limited isolation: members were required to read regularly materials about a different place and time, observe a rule typically developed away from the community, and submit themselves to the sacramental life and overall governance of the worldwide Catholic church. In later centuries, many religious also regularly participated in community-service activities which put them in touch with elements of everyday secular society. To the extent that religious activities could be described as common-sensical, such common sense may be attributed to the ways in which they were only in part utopian.

Whether religious communities are utopian institutions is essentially a matter of definition. Perhaps any utopia that persists is not a utopia. Still, there are notable parallels between religious life and utopian activities. These parallels suggest that, in some eras, many inherent human tendencies towards utopianism found their expression in religious life.

A final problem affecting many utopian movements is the matter of charismatic leadership. Charismatic leaders often played an important role in founding monasteries and other forms of religious communities; they are important in new, relatively unstructured institutions, where members are often under considerable stress. Similarly, many secular utopian activities have been led by charismatic persons. The problem is that charismatic leaders, due to the emotional tone they possess and project, are quite capable of leading groups into disorder and encouraging undesirable forms of anxiety release. Thus, Adolph Hitler, a charismatic leader, persuaded the German people to transform their mild anti-Semitism into brutal genocide. And the American examples of the Reverend James Jones[19] and Charles Manson[20] also come to mind. Speaking in traditional terms, charismatic leaders may become possessed by demonic aspirations.

Various elements in religious life moderated the danger of disordered charismatic leadership. Some forms of religious life, such as monasteries, were deliberately isolated from society. This meant that religious institutions afflicted with disordered leadership could not easily infect other persons. Furthermore, all religious orders were provided eventually with a written *rule* and traditions; this put their organizers under less pressure to invent their own society, and moderated the need for pure charismatic leadership. Finally, religious orders, as part of the institutional structure of the Catholic church, were subject to various forms of external government. This, too, tempered their reliance on purely charismatic leadership. In effect, the structures and traditions of religious life generated a form of institutionalized charisma. In our era, with the spread of secularism and individualism, these constraints have declined in influence. But social problems still arise periodically that invite the application of charismatic approaches.

General Considerations

The basic requirement of celibacy meant that Saint Benedict's ideal community could only be maintained by a minority group: a monastery had to be outside of mainstream society, where the essential social task of procreation would be carried on.

Still, even for a minority group, the Rule placed extraordinary demands on community members. But, at the same time, each stressed member was surrounded by other members who were to assist each other to bear their demanding burdens. The recurrent problem of religious decadence that afflicted monastic communities demonstrates that the system articulated in the rule was not always effective. It is difficult to determine, however, what vantage point should be the base for estimating the value of the rule. And it is central for us to realize how temporal our judgment must be concerning assessment. A short example will nicely illustrate time-bound perspective.

The first sentence of the Rule's prologue, quoted at the beginning of this chapter, invites potential monks to listen to the precepts of the "master," and to hear the voice of a loving "father." In the second sentence, reference is made to the true "King; Christ." It is possible that the words "master" and "father" both refer to Jesus Christ. It is also possible that the two words simply refer to the monastic abbot, or some other human religious master—perhaps simply Saint Benedict. Thus, later in the Rule, there are references to the monastic abbot as a "master."

The alternatve interpretations are significant. Assume Saint Benedict, or an abbot, can properly be called a "master" in the prologue. This implies a vital form of authority that novices should attribute to other mortals. If Christ is the "master" mentioned in the prologue, then the implicit authority of the abbot is diminished. The translations of the text made by Catholic scholars in the eighteenth and early nineteenth centuries assumed that the master was the abbot, or an equivalent person.[21] Thus, in those translations, the *m* in *master* was printed in lower-case type. The most recently published Catholic translation of the Rule prints the word master as "Master."[22] As a result, authority is transferred from identifiable human beings to a benign but diffuse and remote agency. Obviously, the shift in interpretation, whether is right or wrong, signifies an important change in philosophic perspective. There are many different ways of seeing monastic life.

In conclusion, despite such differences, there are some points of departure which must be considered by all evaluators of the rule. The substance of these points can be implicitly derived from the Rule's chapter on the treatment of sick and infirm community members:

> Before all things and above all things care must be taken of the sick, so that they may be served in very deed as Christ himself; for he said: "I was sick and ye visited me;" and, "what ye did to one of these least ones, ye did unto Me." But let the sick on their part consider that they are being served for the honor of God, and not provoke their brethren who are serving them by their unreasonable demands. Yet they should be patiently borne with, because from such as these is gained a more abundant reward. Therefore let the abbot take the greatest care that they suffer no neglect. For these sick brethren let there be assigned a special room and an attendant who is God-fearing, diligent, and careful. Let the use of baths be afforded to the sick as often as may be expedient; but to the healthy, and especially to the young, let them be granted seldom. Moreover, let the use of fleshmeat be granted to the sick who are very weak, for the restoration of their strength; but, as soon as they are better, let all abstain from fleshmeat as usual. Let the abbot take the greatest care that the sick be not neglected by the cellarers and attendants; for he must answer for all the misdeeds of his disciples. (chap. 36)

Notes

1. For examples of the voluminous literature on the Rule, see Cuthbert Butler, *Benedictine Monasticism* (New York: Barnes and Noble, 1924); Paul Delattre, *Commentary on the Rule of Saint Benedict* (Latrobe, PA: Archabbey Press, 1921), trans. Justin McCann; and David Knowles, *Christian Monasticism* (New York: McGraw-Hill, 1969). A useful bibliography can be found in Christopher Brooks, *The Monastic World* (New York: Random House, 1974).

2. Gregorius, *Dialogues* (New York: Fathers of the Church, 1959), trans. Odo John Zimmerman. See also Justin McCann, *Saint Benedict* (Garden City, NY: Doubleday, 1958).

3. Saint Benedict's Rule, chaps. 9-19, 43, 45, 50. Subsequent references to specific chapters of Saint Benedict's Rule will be noted in the text.

4. Knowles, *Christian Monasticism*, p. 213; and Butler *Benedictine Monasticism*, p. 287.

5. Joan Evans, *Monastic Life at Cluny, 910-1157* (Hamden, CT: Acron Books, 1968).

6. Delattre, *Commentary*, p. 476-478.

7. Chapter 54 provided that letters to particular monks could only be received with the explicit permission of the abbot.

8. Butler, *Benedictine Monasticism.*

9. Venerable Bede, *Bede's Ecclesiastical History* (Oxford: Clarendon Press, 1966), p. 417.

10. Ibid., pp. 535-47.

11. Ronald Knox, *Come Holy Spirit* (New Rochelle, NY: Scepter Books, 1961), p. 17.

12.   For an introduction to the analysis of utopias, see Rosabeth M. Kanter, *Commitment and Community* (Cambridge: Harvard University Press, 1972).

13.   Irving Kristol, *Two Cheers for Capitalism* (New York: Basic Books, 1972), pp. 153-70.

14.   Jean Jacques Rousseau, *The First and Second Discourses on the Origins and Foundation of Inequality* (New York: St. Martin's Press, 1964), trans. and ed. Roger D. Master.

15.   Karl Marx, *German Ideology*, quoted in translation in Erich Fromm, *Marx's Concept of Man* (New York: Fredrick Ungar, 1972), p. 206.

16.   For useful surveys, bibliographies, and research on utopias, see Milton Yinger, *Countercultures and Alienation* (New York: Free Press, 1982), and Benjamin Zablocki, *Alienation and Charisma* (New York: Free Press, 1980).

17.   For research on American communes of the 1960s and 1970s, see Yinger, *Countercultures*.

18.   There is an elaborate literature analyzing the emotional and psychological components of religious life. Much of this material does not explicitly mention the potential utopian elements involved. See, for example, Suzanne Cita-Milard, *Religious Orders of Women* (London: Burns and Oates, 1964); Geoffrey Moorhouse, *Against All Reason* (London: Widenfeld and Nicholson, 1969); Suzanne Campbell-Jones, *In Habit* (New York: Pantheon Books, 1978). For an analysis sensitive to the utopian overtones, see Ephraim H. Mizruchi, *Regulating Society* (New York: Free Press, 1983).

19.   For specifics about the Reverend James Jones and his terrible doings, see Ethan Feinsod, *Awake in a Nightmare* (New York: Norton, 1981).

20. For background on the crimes and practices of Manson and his associates, see Vincent Bugliosi, *Helter Skelter* (New York: Norton, 1974).

21. For translations favoring the lower case *m* see Delattre, *Commentary*, p. 1; and Justin McCann, *The Rule of Saint Benedict* (Westminister, MD: Newman Press, 1952), p. 7.

22. St. Benedict, *The Rule of St. Benedict*, trans. Anthony C. Meisel and M. L. del Mastro (Garden City, NY: Doubleday, Image Books, 1975), p. 43.

5

Monasticism At Its Crest

Do you wish me to . . . show you the miracles of the
saints among us? What could be more marvellous than a
person who formerly could hardly abstain three days
from lust, gluttony, revelling, drunkenness, debauchery,
and impurity, as well as a hundred other vices, whatever
they may be, and yet who now abstains from them for
years at a time, even for a whole lifetime? What could be
a greater miracle than so many young people, so many
youths and nobles, all those, in short, whom I see here,
remaining, so to speak, in an open prison, being bound by
the fear of God alone and persevering in hard penance,
something which is in my eyes beyond human power,
above human nature, and which goes very much against
the grain.
— Saint Bernard of Clairvaux's Second Sermon at the
dedication of the Church at Clairvaux

For over a thousand years after the Edict of Milan in
313, Catholicism was the dominant religion in Western Europe.
And, for most of these centuries, monasticism was the prime
means for devout believers to deeply relate to their religion.

The primacy of monastic life was due to several factors.
Monasticism was, above all, collective life. In contrast, diocesan
priests often lived in comparative isolation from other clergy
because they were supposed to live with their scattered
parishioners. Dispersion caused priests to be isolated from
intellectual support and institutional supervision, and sometimes
surrounded by distracting and corrosive influences. As a result,
the public status of secular clergy during this long era was often

low. On many occasions, this disrespect was essentially deserved. Throughout the medieval centuries, reforming popes made sporadic efforts to subject secular clergy to some mode of regulation and community life akin to Saint Benedict's Rule precisely due to the abuses that arose under the existing system.[1] Still, in general, the secular clergy were never regulated with the rigor typically associated with monastic life.

In contrast to the indeterminate controls affecting secular clergy, religious were supposed to live in communities isolated from outside influences, and where members were expected to monitor each other's observance. It was also easier for library materials to be copied and made available for monks. Furthermore, the relative isolation of monasteries from secular life meant that misconduct by members, when it occurred, would not be apparent to outsiders. Finally, the structure provided by Saint Benedict's Rule established important norms to direct and inform the conduct of religious.

Laypersons saw that the virtues of monasticism could provide civic life with a variety of forms of support. Contributions of resources to monasteries could be translated into major works of publicly visible art and architecture, as the monks used the resources for the "Glory of God." Monasteries enhanced the prestige of communities—just as modern urban areas hope to attract professional sports teams, or become the sites of major buildings. (Sometimes, monasteries even became the objects of pilgrimages, attracting numerous travellers.) Monasteries developed a trained class of copyists, writers, and administrators, who might assist both religious and lay activities. Monasteries provided shelter for some aged and infirm laypersons, and burial sites (on consecrated grounds) for especially selected laypersons. And, in some instances, a monastery served as a site of a cathedral (or bishop's principal church): in such cases, the administrative structure inherited from the rule facilitated efficient management. A monastery could also be a base for missionary and rationalizing forces in isolated and unruly areas.

But the paramount virtue of monastic life in the medieval era was the monk's special relationship with God. Because of the status attached to this relationship, adults voluntarily chose to join monasteries (or nunneries).   Parents were sympathetic to placing their children in monasteries to be reared as religious or, if the children were older, to encouraging them to choose to enroll. Catholics wanted monks to offer prayers on their behalf; and wealthy persons, and even poorer Catholics, contributed to the support of monasteries to permit and encourage such prayers to be offered. The contributions included titles to land, rights to collect taxes, precious metals, and other valuable assets. The matter of lay contributions in exchange for prayers and other forms of remembrance is important, and deserves deliberate attention.

Catholic Doctrine and Prayer

Traditional   Catholic   doctrine   holds   that   prayers, addressed to God or his saints, can bring divine intervention on behalf of living (or dead) human beings. The prayers may be addressed by a person seeking assistance, or by intermediaries on that person's behalf. The significance of this doctrine of prayer was heightened by the concept of purgatory: a state between Heaven and Hell, where souls of indeterminate virtue waited until they were released to Heaven because of their accrued suffering, or the intercessory prayers of their survivors. This concept of purgatory encouraged living Catholics to pray for deceased whom they viewed as worthy of sympathy. It also made other living Catholics hope that people would choose to pray for them after their deaths.

The doctrines pertaining to prayer are part of a body of Catholic theology that attributes to God an essentially reciprocal attitude. Prayer, charity, and forebearance entitle believers to certain benefits from God. Eventually, these doctrines helped to generate an elaborate body of *indulgences.* The indulgences signified the benefits *earned* by Catholics as the result of practicing particular virtues.   An important cause of the Protestant Reformation was the popular (and largely correct) perception that much of the income from the sale of indulgences by authorized religious was being used for worldly undertakings. Undoubtedly, such a doctrine of reciprocity—where the Church is, in effect, the middleman between believers and God—can be subject to abuse. But the doctrine has played an important part in the shaping of religious life. Its implications must be deliberately considered.

A high proportion of the events that concern individual human beings (and groups of persons) are determined by circumstances largely beyond their direct control: the effects of war, the moderation of drought, or the outcome of their own illness or that of someone they love. Catholic doctrine about prayer provided a means for concerned individuals to match their inherent concerns with their actual conduct. Even though they could not concretely affect some event, they could intervene through practicing prayer. Furthermore, once one admits the efficacy of prayer, it is logical to invite particularly holy persons to become specialists in prayer to offer their highly efficacious prayers on behalf of other concerned persons. And, finally, it is logical for believers not themselves prone to pray to contribute resources enabling prayerful people to focus their energies into prayer, especially prayer on behalf of contributing "sinners." In effect, a network of prayer specialists might evolve, supported by contributions by persons whose lives focus on other priorities. Indeed, the word *orator* is derived from the root *pray* or *plead.* It originally signified a person who addressed pleadings to some divinity on behalf of a whole group.

It is not hard to criticize some elements of the model just sketched. The nonpraying contributors may be persons whose lives are devoid of traditional virtue. The persons engaged in praying may be actually cheating the people who request their prayers, and who make their contributions at great sacrifice. But, after such cautions are uttered, certain basic human problems still persist: Human beings are recurrently trapped into caring about events and persons they cannot materially control. Still, we want to believe that energy, competence, and virtue can be transformed into certain benefits. As one friend put it to me, he heard someone belittle the concept of "God as a bookkeeper." My friend's reply was "God had better be a bookkeeper." He meant we are inevitably driven to assume that there is a rational relationship between sacrifice, forebearance, and one's deserts. And, if mankind has always procured the help of specialists—be they navigators, shamen, or doctors—why shouldn't there be specialists in prayer whose help can be solicited and earned? The plea that each of us, alone, must make and shape our particular universe is also a plea that we live disengaged from the many forces we cannot hope to materially control—without country, ethnic group, or perhaps even children. It is a plea for the pursuit of loneliness and alienation. Thus, the belief in the efficacy of prayer led to shared concerns between monks and laypersons, between missionaries and stay-at-homes, and (at least symbolically) between living and deceased persons who, according to Catholic doctrine, can pray for each other.

To put the matter concretely, during the seventeenth century, French Jesuit priests travelled into the Canadian wilderness to convert diverse American Indian tribes to Catholicism. Most of the missionaries suffered severe deprivations, many were tortured by hostile tribes, and some suffered terrible martyrdom. As one reads the reports of the missionaries, one is incredulous at the courage displayed by these European-born and academically trained missionaries.[2] They had chosen to live (and many to die) in an environment as strange to them as the face of the moon might be to us. During much of this missionary effort, in a convent of Ursuline sisters in France, different pairs of sisters maintained a twenty-four hour vigil before the Blessed Sacrament on behalf of the Jesuits' mission.[3] The Jesuits knew of the sisters' conduct, and the sisters periodically received thorough written reports of the fathers' trials. What effect did this exchange of knowledge about remarkable acts of mutual commitment have on the emotions and conduct of the affected parties?

When the Protestant Reformation occurred, one key point of dispute was the role of institutional intermediaries—such as the Catholic Church—in affecting a believer's expectations for salvation. The reformers typically took the position that salvation was a personal matter, it was not determined by the acts of intermediaries. But this answer did not settle the issue. The answer still might imply that other persons whom one had helped might intercede—via prayer—on one's behalf. And so the whole issue might again be reopened. Eventually, different denominations evolved diverse interpretations about what factors made eternal salvation more likely or certain.

Sometimes such doctrines made salvation seem almost the product of good luck—which hardly seemed reassuring, or justifiable. Thus, the dethronement of the Catholic church as an intermediary did not abolish controversy around this troubling issue.

The sum of this analysis is that many Catholics, from all social classes, wanted to be remembered—during their lives and after death—in the prayers of monks. To earn this remembrance, they donated resources to support the foundation of new monasteries and made additional endowments to existing monasteries. The donations provided monks with time and other resources to permit them to engage in prayer. And during these prayers, such as Divine Office, explicit petitions were addressed to God on behalf of donors, and particular donors were explicitly named by the chanting monks. Some noteworthy donors might be remembered in this manner for as long as a century or more.

Many themes regarding prayer are evinced in a deed executed in the year 909 by William of Aquitaine. He used the deed to endow the proposed monastery of Cluny in south-central France. The deed is worthy of lengthy quotation, since Cluny did become one of the major monastic sites in the European world:

> To those who consider things sanely it is evident that Divine Providence counsels the rich to use well those goods that they possess in transitory fashion, if they wish for eternal recompense. And Holy Writ shows this to be possible, for such counsel is manifest in the saying: "the ransom of a man's life is his riches." Wherefore I, William, by the grace of God count and duke, having pondered these things and wishing while there is yet time to make provision for my salvation, have found it right, yea necessary, to dispose for the good of my soul of some of the temporal possessions which have been bestowed upon me. For since I appear to have increased them much, I would not wish to deserve the reproach in the hour of death that I had used

them only for the needs of my body, but would rather, when my last moment shall take them all from me, give myself the joy of having used a part for my soul: the which may not be better done than by following the precept of our Lord: "I will make myself friends among the poor." That this benefaction may endure not only for a time, but may last for ever, I will provide at my expense for men living together under monastic vows, with this faith and hope that if I cannot myself despise all the things of this world, at least by sustaining those who despise the world, those whom I believe to be righteous in the eyes of God, I may myself receive the reward of the righteous.

To all those who live in the unity of faith and who implore the mercy of Christ, to all who shall succeed them and shall be living so long as the world endures, I make known that for the love of God and of our Savior Christ Jesus I give and deliver to the Apostles Peter and Paul the village of Cluny, on the river Grosne, with its curtilage and its house, with the Chapel that is dedicated in honour of St. Mary Mother of God and of St. Peter, Prince of the Apostles, with all the property that depends thereon, cottages, chapels, serfs both men and women, vines, fields, meadows, forests, water and watercourses, mills, crops and revenues, land tilled and untilled, with no reservations. All these things are situate in the county of Macon or near it, each enclosed within its bounds. I, William, with my wife Ingelberge, give these things to the aforesaid Apostles, first for the love of God, then for the soul of my lord the King Eudes, for the souls of my father and mother, for me and my wife, that is for the salvation of our souls and bodies, for the soul of Ava my sister who left me these properties by will, for the souls of our brothers and sisters, our nephews and of all our kindred, men and women, for our faithful servants, and for the maintenance and integrity of the

Catholic faith. Finally, since as Christians we are all bound together by the bonds of our faith and charity, may this gift be made also for the faithful of times past, present and to come.

I give on condition that a Regular Monastery be established at Cluny in honour of the apostles Peter and Paul; that monks shall form a congregation there living under the rule of St. Benedict; that they shall for ever possess, hold and order the property given in such wise that this honourable house shall be unceasingly full of vows and prayers, that men shall seek there with a lively desire and an inner fervour the sweetness of converse with Heaven, and that prayers and supplications shall be addressed thence without ceasing to God, both for me and for those persons commemorated above.

We ordain also that our foundation shall serve forever as a refuge for those who having renounced the world as poor men bring nothing with them but their good will, and we desire that our superfluity shall become their abundance.[4]

Cycles of Monastic Activity

Between the fourth and thirteenth century, which roughly encompassed the medieval era, patterns of monastic growth and dispersion affected most of Western Europe. Many monasteries were founded. Many of them were substantially endowed. And many monasteries became larger than those of Saint Benedict's time. Thus, by the eleventh century, about 800 monasteries (for males) were associated with the central monastery of Cluny.[5] The pattern of monastic growth proceeded by fits and starts, included elements of increase and decline. Thus, in England and Wales, between 1066 and 1200, the number of male monastic houses increased from 50 to 370, and the number of monks almost five fold.[6] Many factors contributed to these changes: the rise of notable monastic leaders; shifts in popular religious fervor; the development of efficacious forms of monastic organization; changes in economic affluence; demographic patterns; and shifts in the political environment (it is significant that an era of English monastic growth began at the time of the Norman Conquest). In about the year 1300, about 700 monasteries for men, and a larger number for women, were associated with the Cistercians, an order distinct from the Cluny monasteries.[7] Almost all the Cistercian monasteries were founded after 1100.

As the size and wealth of individual monasteries increased, role specialization developed among community members. Some community members were expected to manage property and relate to the external world on matters of marketing, purchasing, and politics. Other community members, typically priests, were trained in chanting and reading Latin texts, so they could participate in relatively elaborate presentations of the Divine Office. Employees and serfs became associated with some monasteries. In the late stages of medieval life in England, in some active monasteries, only 20 percent of persons associated with each monastery were full-fledged monks, regularly performing the Divine Office.

Almost all medieval monasteries were governed by Saint Benedict's Rule, or a variant of that Rule. The Rule originally conceived of monasteries as small, relatively poor, self-supporting, and largely self-governing institutions. It made only passing reference to the basic unit of Catholic church governance: the diocese, under the authority of a bishop. All the Rule did was to provide that the abbot was designated by the local bishop after the vote of the community, and that the abbot could be removed by the bishop in cases of gross malfeasance. But these were only limited forms of monitoring. Over centuries, the mechanics of the selection of abbots have been periodically revised as has the authority of bishops over orders residing in their dioceses. Still, during the medieval era, local bishops were a major organ of supervision over monasteries. Another complicating element of monastic government was the principle of *commendium.* It signified that an external civil authority—a local lord, or state official—had the inherited right to preemptorially designate the abbot of a monastery when a vacancy arose. Typically, this right had been granted to such civil authorities by the monastery or church in exchange for a significant endowment or economic or political favor. Often a commendatory abbot was simply a layman to whom the appointing person owed some patronage—since an abbot could choose to receive a substantial income from the operation of a well-established monastery (and laypersons were not inhibited by any obligations of poverty). In the short run, the operation of the commendatory abbot system provided monasteries or the whole church with immediate political or economic benefits. In the longer run, it proved highly corrosive to the vitality of monastic life.

One corrective measure against the possible decadence of an individual monastery was the temporary appointment, by a local bishop, of a reforming outside abbot whose responsibility it was to remedy the situation. The problems and opportunities confronting such reformers are suggested in the writings of Johann Busch (1399-1480).[8] Busch was a German religious who helped reform twenty-three nunneries in Saxony at the request of local bishops and wrote a book on his experiences. The range of problems confronted him was broad. Still, they are similar to patterns of decadence periodically affected the lives of both male and female religious during the era. The forms of nonobservance he discovered included; nuns eating meals in small groups away from the community; the extensive possession of private property; the lax performance, or nonperformance, of the Divine Office; avoidance of dietary restrictions; the affection for (provocative) semisecular dress by the nuns; the avoidance of regular confession; the routine visitation of supposedly cloistered convents by secular priests and laymen; sexual liasons; and inadequate supervision by the designated external monitor. Many of such violations were tacitly supported by relatives of the sisters who lived in the area. The relatives were sympathetic for the welfare of the sisters and would sometimes abet their misconduct. Other laypersons and prominent clergy, however, were distressed by the misconduct, and actively assisted Busch in his reformations.

In many instances, Busch found the practices of the designated nunneries satisfactory. Thus, he reported that "We found a prioress and nuns living in great poverty, very simple and humble, but of good will and ready for all good work; for they applied themselves promptly to obedience and to the obedience of their Rule, and very willingly brought to us all those things which they held in private possession [in violation of Rule]."[9]

Busch applied a basic set of tactics: asking sisters to surrender all private property; acting as a regular confessor to all members of the community; requiring community members to wear appropriate garments; supervising their performance of the Office; and training them in performance where necessary. Busch usually was assisted by a team of sisters who travelled with him and were sympathetic to the principle of strict observance. He sometimes worked with a community being reformed for up to a year to complete his task.

He often was confronted with serious resistance and had to apply himself with patience and ingenuity. In one case, it was rumored to a group of erring sisters that he might impose terrible penances on them if he acted as their confessor. He wrote:

> The frightened nuns were afraid to confess to me, because they heard that I was wont to inflict very severe penances, which was not true, as I afterwards told them. Then [the local priest designated to regularly oversee the convent] said to them: The bishop's mandate orders you to confess to him under pain of excommunication and if you refuse then you will be under an interdict. My good ladies, I counsel you to confess to him. I will place beside him my servant with a drawn sword and if he says one bad or harsh word to you it shall cleave his head. When they saw and heard that they could not escape they consented to confess to me, but they sent before them first one bold nun in order to beard me. Seated in the confessional, she began, "Sir, what do you here?" I answered, "I lead you all to the kingdom of heaven. . . ." Half the nuns confessed to me that day. To the third of them I said, "Sister, am I as harsh as you said I was?" and she replied, "You are a man of gold,

gentle and kind beyond all things." In the evening,
when we were supping I said to the [local priest]:
"What are your nuns saying about me? Am I as
severe as they thought?" He replied, "When it was
their turn to go to confession, the hair of their
heads stood on end, but when they came away
from you, they returned in great consolation." The
next day I finished the others before dinner, and
towards the end I asked one of them, "Am I as
hard and severe as you heard?" and she replied,
"Now you are honey-tongued. But when you have
got our consent and have tied a rope to our horns to
drag us along, then you will say to us: You must
and shall do all that I desire." I answered her,
"Beloved sister, fear not, for I shall always remain
kind and benign towards you."[10]

Despite the efforts of dedicated and sensitive persons such
as Busch, the oversight of local religious communities by bishops
or their designees during the medieval era was sporadic.
Bishops often had many more pressing responsibilities. The
oversight process was frequently a thankless task (some
resistent sisters once locked Busch in a cellar, and on other
occasions, groups of them attacked him and his associates with
sticks and stones). And, if the erring community owned
significant economic resources, such resources could sometimes
be used to buy off reform proponents.

Another form of monitoring evolved after the foundation
of the monastery of Cluny and its development under a
succession of able, long-lived, reform-oriented abbots. Due to its
prestige, abbots and other members of the Cluny community
were periodically recruited to help reform monasteries operating
under the rule. The logical assumption was that members of
the Cluny might be unusually qualified to instruct other
monasteries in how to improve their observance. Many of such
reform efforts were successful. Gradually, local bishops chose
to place the governance of (formerly) erring communities under
the more-direct control of the abbot of Cluny.[11] By the end of
the eleventh century, hundreds of monasteries had subjected
their local practices, and the appointment of their abbot, to the

governance of the abbot of Cluny. Such arrangements were carried out on a case-by-case basis, and many special variations arose. But the general principles held relatively constant.

The role of Cluny as a base for reform was facilitated because the abbot of Cluny, from early in its existence, was placed under the sole jurisdiction of the pope. He was exempt from the authority of his local bishop. Monasteries associated with Cluny received similar status. This undoubtedly assisted the flexibility and prestige of Cluny. The successive abbots of Cluny wielded great religious and secular influence. Several popes were associated with Clunic monasteries before their elevation. And the architecture, ornamentation and religious rites of Cluny became extraordinarily elaborate. In the year 1060, one visitor made the following remarks in a letter written to the abbot:

> When I recall the strict and full daily life of your abbey, I recognize that it is the holy Spirit that guides you. For you have such a crowded and continuous round of Offices, such a long time spent in choir service, that even the days of midsummer, when daylight is longest, there is scarcely a half-hour to be found when the brethren can talk together in the cloister.[12]

The prestige and wealth of Cluny and its affiliates gradually brought about activities that were seen as abuses. In about 1125, Saint Bernard of Clairvaux (1090-1153), a reformer from a non-Clunic monastery, publicly levelled a variety of written charges against Clunic practices:

> I have seen an abbot with sixty horses after him, and even more. Would you not think, as you see them pass, that they were not fathers of monasteries, but lords of castles—not shepherds of souls, but princes of provinces? Then there is the baggage, containing tableclothes, and cups, and basins, and candlesticks, and well-filled wallets—not with the coverlets, but the ornaments of beds. My lord abbot can never go further than

four leagues from his house without taking all his furniture with him, as if he were going to the wars, or to cross a desert where necessaries cannot be had. It is quite impossible to wash one's hands in, and drink from, the same vessel? Will not your candle burn anywhere but in a silver or gold candlestick of yours which you carry with you? Is sleep impossible except upon a multicolored mattress?[13]

Some monks concluded that too many Clunics had come into conflict with the letter and spirit of the rule. This conclusion was later supported by other authorities. Butler, a twentieth-century historian and Benedictine monk, said that "medieval [i.e., Clunic] Benedictinism was a transformation of St. Benedict's intention."[14] In particular, Butler was referring to the large proportions of time spent at office. The contemporary religious critics of Cluny believed it was important for monks to engage in significant amounts of manual labor. To attain such ends, the reformers, founded in 1098 a new monastery, Citeaux (in France), which was more faithfully observant of the Rule. The monks associated with Citeaux eventually were called Cistercians.[15] Saint Bernard became the most prominent Cistercian of his age. He had great energy, an acute mind, and was an able writer and orator. Partly due to his leadership, and the dry rot afflicting the Clunics, the Cistercians developed as their major successor—although many Clunic monasteries continued to exist independent of the Cistercians. Hundreds of new monasteries were founded throughout Europe under the leadership of small colonies sent out from Citeaux and its affiliated monasteries. These monasteries formed a system of independent federation, governed by the Charter of Charity, a constitution drafted with the advice of Saint Bernard. The affiliated monasteries annually sent representatives to a central international assembly, to review the operations of their institutions, and the constituent body.

The Cistercians deliberately chose not to decorate their monasteries and other buildings with jewels and precious metals. But their structures were not insignificant; they were imposing. The buildings were austere and dignified, and had a generally uniform style and layout. When we contemplate the notable beauty of the surviving Cistercian structures, or other works of monastic art, we should recognize that, generally, monks did not physically construct their own magnificent churches and other buildings, nor did they manufacture many of the great art works displayed in these buildings.[16] Usually, such works were made by lay craftsmen. In the area of the arts, monks' (and nuns') contributions were largely in the form of composing and performing choral works, copying and illuminating manuscripts, composing and translating certain forms of literature, and producing fine needlework. And, finally, they practiced the vital craft of patronage—commissioning and directing skilled artists to engage in the appropriate exercise of their art.

The Cistercians received substantial endowments as their prestige increased. Typical Cistercian monasteries were surrounded with large agricultural plots, which were used for farming and grazing. Through such productive commitments, the Cistercians hoped to remain focused on Saint Benedict's emphasis on manual work. But large estates compelled the monks to engage in farming and herding at sites remote from the oratory; as a result, they could not regularly assemble to perform the office. Gradually, lay brothers were enrolled who lived in residences or granges close to the farming sites. Meanwhile, the priest-monks living in the monastery proper performed the relatively elaborate office. The two classes of Cistercians that evolved were both monks—since, nominally, there was no need for monks to be priests. The two groups, however, assembled together for special occasions only, when all community members gathered to perform a special Office or other unique ritual. But, as a practical matter, the division of labor came to reflect a division of status. In nunneries, eventually, an equivalent division often prevailed—between *choir* nuns, who performed the office, and *lay* sisters who managed the maintenance of the nunnery. The same rationale as in the monasteries was involved; properly performing a complete Divine Office (in a foreign language) took careful training, and thus distinction between the two groups of the community was appropriate and necessary.

It might seem distressing that a division of status followed from a division of responsibilities. On the other hand, it conversely might seem incongruous for a learned and sophisticated monk to have only as much voice in the management of a monastery as one of its laborers or swineherds. Furthermore, important monastic policies needed to be settled by persons with knowledge and experience in complex affairs. The monks residing at the main residence, in daily contact with each other, were more informed about the major topics affecting order policy. The basic pattern of segregation was almost inevitable when monasteries became large and complex institutions. Then, a variety of tasks were generated, and task specialization became desirable.

Monastic affluence generated many problems. Some of the internal ones have already been mentioned. But it should also be recognized that, while the rule prohibited individual monks from owning property, accumulations of institutional wealth presented temptations for abuse that were often not resisted. Evasions of the Rule resulted, and local exemptions and variations were justified by abbots and other authorities. One frequent evasion was of the Rule's prohibition on monks eating the "meat of quadrupeds." It was one thing to maintain the provision in a poor, primitive Italian monastery, where meat was normally unavailable to many persons. But, the matter became far more complex in later, relatively prosperous, monastic communities, where fresh meat was properly available for persons in the infirmary, for older and disabled monks, for guests at the abbot's table, for special feast days, and so forth. Later commentators observed that a monastery's fidelity to (or breach of) the prohibition of meat often served as a reasonable index of general individual observance of the Rule.

The institutional church—certain popes, bishops, and abbots—was occasionally sympathetic to monastic reform during the medieval era. Reform became an issue at some church councils (formally assembled meetings of all bishops and other designated members of the church hierarchy). A decree was passed at the Fourth Lateran Council in 1215, for example, requiring all monasteries to submit to annual visitation.[17] During visitations, persons from outside the community would assess a monastery's fealty to the Rule. However, there was insufficient support for vigorous enforcement of such decrees. Thus, the reform efforts were largely ineffectual.

External problems arose because the relative wealth of some monasteries had repercussions in secular society. Monasteries and their wealth were not taxed, since churches and church property were exempt. This accelerated the accumulation of monastic wealth. Furthermore, many of the gifts (to monasteries) of land or the right to collect taxes were made on the condition that the gifts stay in the perpetual possession of the monastery. The monks could not sell, donate, or otherwise transfer such property. The givers, by establishing such constraints, hoped to insure their perpetual remembrance in prayer by successive cohorts of monks. Due to the constraints, it was technically possible for the capital of monasteries to grow infinitely over generations. They could become centers of wealth and influence. Simultaneously, as the enrollment of monks declined from time to time, the wealth sometimes drifted into the control of small groups of monks, who became relatively vulnerable to intrusions by important classes in secular society. Furthermore, particular monks, by reason of their designated offices, became the beneficiaries of specific endowments—somewhat like academic "chairs." It could be in the interest of such monks to keep monastic enrollment down, so that the capital would be divided among a limited group of users. Finally, the restraints on property alienation meant that capital could not easily be moved away from traditional monastic activities into other, more productive forms of investment, such as banking, shipping, or manufacturing.

Many monasteries did use some of their wealth for charitable activities. Nevertheless, their affluent situations, especially during periods when religious observance was lax, subjected them to envy and (sometimes deserved) criticism. Eventually, such exposure and vulnerability encouraged other powerful persons and social classes to seek and find excuses to expropriate monastic property.

Women in Medieval Religious Life

Any observations about the role of women religious during this era must reflect important complexities.[18] In general, women played a limited role in affecting public life in medieval Europe. Thus, women attempting significant public activities, such as organizing or managing a female religious community, were often directed or assisted by male associates. Furthermore, religious communities were closely related to the sacramental life of the church—such as Mass, Penance, and Holy Orders. These sacraments were, and are, administered by males. Thus, close cooperation with male clerics was essential for female religious communities.

In practice, many male monasteries, or particular monastic movements, simultaneously inspired the development of parallel systems of female nunneries. These parallel institutions were sympathetic to the themes of the male movement, and were assisted in various ways by priests from the brother monastery.

It would be simplistic to perceive of such patterns as merely instances of females accepting male direction. Typically, female monasteries were subjected to more severe enclosure (or seclusion) than male monasteries. This was partly because male monasteries sometimes conducted farming activities that engaged monks with their beyond-the-walls environment. Female seclusion also stemmed from the norms of the society, which assumed that unmarried and unenclosed women would be liable to abuse and exploitation. Such strict seclusion meant that the internal governance of a nunnery was almost solely under the control of the (female) community members. Depending on the size and affluence of the establishment, matters of governance could involve complex issues. Indeed, for those times convent life may have provided most female religious with larger areas of responsibility and authority than were available to females elsewhere in the society.

There was also the matter of the diverse work of nuns. Apart from the maintenance of their quarters and the preparation of food, they also chanted Divine Office, engaged in religious reading, and produced needlework, such as altar cloths and ritual garments. Or, to put it another way, nuns performed serious music, read significant literature, and manufactured notable works of art. Of course, as already mentioned, many religious communities engaged in only limited observance of their rule. Still, in principle, it would be wrong to assume reflexively that the religious life of women during the era was necessarily uniquely restrictive.

It should also be recognized that some medieval religious women assumed positions of unquestionable leadership in the development of nunneries or in other areas of religious practice. Thus, Saint Bridget of Sweden (1302-1373), who was connected with the royal family of Sweden, was impressed by the virtues of Cistercian life. She determined to form a religious order of women expressing an equivalent spirit.[19] In making her plans, Saint Bridget addressed herself to maintaining relationships between her proposed order and a group of cooperating priests. She adopted an approach which was later applied by several other organizers of female religious communities: she formed double monasteries—separate communities of male and female religious living in closely related residences, with the males being responsible for providing sacramental services for the nuns. The female members of such communities were typically more numerous than the males.

There is ample evidence that many such communities were created and maintained proper decorum. But, eventually, the occasional abuses and the potential scandal and temptations surrounding these institutions caused the gradual abandonment of the practice.

Some Monastic Themes

During the medieval centuries, several important and pervasive themes developed to complement the provisions of the Rule. These themes eventually were reflected in the diverse supplementary regulations and other guidelines for order members. All of these themes still exist in many contemporary orders.

One theme relates to chronology—simply, a periodic, perhaps daily, listing of the major events (and dates) occurring in the life of the community: illnesses, transfers of office, new professions, harvests, deaths, and the like. Other medieval institutions maintained such records also. Monasteries, however, were especially well-equipped to carry out semiliterary tasks, since they were partly inhabited by writers and copyists.

It is striking that the position of "chronologer" does not formally exist in most of our contemporary secular institutions. It is hard to identify the means through which institutional history is maintained in our era. The fact is that such information is typically generated as the by-product of routine records. But the difference between such records and a deliberate chronology is instructive. A chronology is flexible and open to include whatever strikes the community's members (or the chronologer) as noteworthy (e.g., the death of a member, a significant celebration). It can generate a richness that invites the persons writing it and those reading it to broadly reflect on the institution's history and direction. A common instance of such reflection can be found in the entries in monastic chronologies memorializing deceased community members. The following text is from an entry in about 1260 in the chronology of an English nunnery describing its deceased abbess:

> It is most fitting that we should always perpetuate the memory, in our special prayers and suffrages, of one who ever worked for the glory of God, and for the weal of both our souls and bodies. For she increased the number of the Lord's handmaids in this monastery from forty to eighty, to the exaltation of the worship of God. To her sisters, both in health and sickness, she administered the necessaries of life with piety, prudence, care and honesty. She also increased the sum allowed for garments by 12d. each. The example of her holy conversation and charity, in conjunction with her pious exhortations and regular discipline, caused each one to know how, in the words of the Apostle, to possess her vessel in sanctification and honour. She also, with maternal piety and careful forethought, built, for the use of both sick and

sound, a new and large farmery away from the main buildings and in conjunction with it a dormer and other necessary offices. Beneath the farmery she constructed a watercourse, through which a stream flowed with sufficient force to carry off all refuse that might corrupt the air. Moreover, she built there a place set apart for the refreshment of the soul, namely a chapel of the Blessed Virgin, which was erected outside the cloister behind the farmery. With the chapel she enclosed a large place, which was adorned on the north side with pleasant vines and trees. On the other side, by the river bank, she built offices for various uses, a space being left in the centre, where the nuns are able from time to time to enjoy the pure air. In these and in other numberless ways, the blessed mother Euphemia provided for the worship of God and the welfare of her sisters.[20]

From personal contacts, I know that many subunits of orders active in our contemporary world maintain thorough and informative chronologies.

The Chapter of Faults is another monastic practice that evoled during the era. The term chapter originally referred to a gathering of religious where some part—or chapter—of the rule was read. Eventually the term was expanded to include any formal monastic gathering.

Under the Rule, monks were encouraged to engage in self-correction and to be sympathetic to the criticisms of other community members. Later this precept was expanded to provide for periodic community meetings, where members were encouraged to publicly accuse themselves—and, if necessary, other community members—of rule violations and other wrongdoings. The Chapter of Faults, as this process was called, eventually became a frequent and routine part of most monastic life, and another instance of the stress placed on individual humility.

When Chapters of Faults were routinely conducted, it often was appropriate for the community to develop a uniform set of penalties, or penances, for typical acts of wrongdoing. The following example is taken from a written set of suggested uniform penalties, used by a community of Alexian brothers (in Germany) in about 1461:

> Below there follows what is considered a condign punishment for each kind of offence: that is, the penance will consist of taking dinner on the floor in the presence of the whole community, a fasting dinner of bread and water, and also [practice self-flagellation] or perform other works of reconciliation according to the discretion of the superior.
>
> Also, anyone who talks during times of silence and outside of time for meals or eats without permission, will do penance for one day.
>
> Likewise, anyone who speaks in insulting or haughty manner to another brother or sister, or who grumbles about the food or drink or clothing or anything else, or who leaves the house without permission, he will be subject to penance for three days.
>
> Also, no brother or sister is to hold a conversation with someone of different age or sex in a private room unless the door be kept open, to avoid any suspicion. Anyone guilty of the contrary conduct and when admonished does not amend his ways, he is to do penance for five days. Likewise, anyone who has sworn disgracefully by God or His saints, or one who has refused to accept the penance imposed upon him by the chapter, or one who has struck a brother or sister companion without however shedding blood, or one who has been known to have or convicted of having his own supply of money, or one who has quarrelled either with friends or with someone outside the house, in

all such cases occurring within the house—such a one is to be bound to perform penance for twenty days.[21]

Clothing and the management of members' hair also became important themes in monastic life. It is evident that, for most orders, particular forms of dress were retained over years and centuries for largely noneconomic reasons: to increase the members' sense of collective identity and their identification with the previous history of the community; and, to separate members from the immediate secular world and other groups of religious. The Cistercians, for example, were popularly characterized as the *white monks* inasmuch as their robes were white, made from the undyed wool of their sheep. Benedictine monks were designated *black monks*. Furthermore, in some orders of nuns, what were once "simple" peasant garments persisted, over centuries. They became, in effect, obsolete and costly clothes that were hard to manufacture, maintain, or wear. But these unique garments provided a system of identification and separation. One common element of periods of religious decadence was the tendency of religious to modernize or revise their required garments, or otherwise avoid clothing norms. This is nowise to imply that every modification in clothing represented institutional decay: in some tropic situations, order members often persisted in wearing woolen garments (at serious risk to their health) derived from their homelands, far beyond the point of logic. But, as we will recurrently see, the process of drawing a line between plausible modifications and corrosive revisions has often been complicated.

Gradually, religious orders wove the symbolism of clothing deeply into the process of profession. Persons being trained to enter an order were required to wear different types of clothing at different stages of training. And the steps towards entry were marked by publicly robing the initiate in the different garments.

The matter of hair, as noted, has always been significant in religious life. Shortly after the historic invention of monastic life, the tonsure became the normal hair style of monks: the top of the head was shaved bald, and the remaining hair was trimmed in a predetermined fashion. The tonsure was adopted from the hairstyle required of Roman slaves—since monks were slaves of Christ.[22] Female religious were required to have their hair cut closely, and totally covered with a veil.

Whether we are male or female, the hair on our head is one of our most important unique characteristics. It has a particular color, texture, and thickness. It can be manipulated into different forms through combing, dyeing, curling, cutting, or braiding, or covered by a wig. If an institution hopes to emphasize certain commonality among its members and focus their energies on predetermined and limited goals, it is a wise policy to constrict the hair options available to members.

The inevitable human experience of death also played an important part in monastic life. In the Middle Ages, the average human life span was far shorter than in our era. As a result, the typical citizen would come into touch with more deaths per year than a contemporary citizen; the likelihood was increased for monks because of their special concern with caring for and praying over their own ill and infirm members. It was likely most monastery members would die in the monastery, and under the care of community members. Gradually, religious communities evolved elaborate rites, chanting the Psalms, and so on, which were performed by community members at the bedside of apparently dying brothers (or sisters). Over a period of three to five years, the typical monk would have spent a significant amount of time participating in such rites. Communities, also, usually had their communal graveyards located on the grounds immediate to their residence, or even entombed members in their oratory. Many laypersons, as well as monks, attached a special importance to dying, or being buried, under monastic auspices. Thus, important lay donors were sometimes granted the right to spend their declining years enrolled as monks, or to be buried on monastic grounds.

The central formal aim of religious life was to enable community members to attain Heaven. Death was the terminaton of the period of earthly trials (to see if one was

worthy of Heaven). Hopefully, it was the fulfillment of the life
plan of every religious. Indeed, in most orders, persons who
were suffering an apparent mortal illness, but were still in
preenrollment training, could be graced with premature
complete enrollment to permit them to die with the blessings
available to full community members. Death was also the
supreme occasion for the particular dying religious to display
forebearance, charity, and faith. Thus, the frequent observation
by individual religious of others' dying conduct must have been
a powerful and affecting experience. Here is a description of the
death scene of a religious from a chronicler writing in the
fifteenth century:

> [the dying brother] studied to amend without delay
> whatsoever he remembered to have done against
> God's will, in thought or word or deed or by
> omission, recognizing clearly that no evil can
> remain unpunished, nor any good unrewarded,
> since God doth not pardon the sinner unless he be
> truly penitent. For he lived in vehement fear of
> God's awful judgment, now so close upon him; and
> he felt how intolerable it would be to feel even for a
> single hour the purgatorial flames, or that fire of
> hell that is not quenched, tormenting the sinful soul
> most bitterly even to the utmost farthing. . . . I
> have seen him oftentimes sitting silently on a seat
> in front of the choir with his eyes fixed on the
> graves of the brethren whose dust lies there,
> meditating long upon their bodies turned to ashes
> and the happiness and glory of their souls reigning
> in heaven, while he firmly hoped himself soon to
> follow them.

> Sometimes, as I sat by his side, he would say unto
> me: "The Lord hath called our best brethren first
> unto himself, even as a dove is wont to choose the
> best grains of wheat. . . . " within a brief while he
> began to draw near his end, and the subprior gave
> him the Holy Communion and anointed him
> according to the rites of the Church in the presence
> of the whole congregation of Windesheim and the

prior of Nordhorn. But when he besought the
brethren to pardon him and to forgive all wherein
he might have offended, he did this so humbly and
with such true self-knowledge and compunction of
heart, that almost all were moved to tears.
Thenceforward he sometimes lay, sometimes sat,
sometimes stood by the fire leaning upon the
shoulders of the brethren, but always struggling
most painfully for breath; then again he was laid
upon the bed and rested awhile. But he had
compassion on those who watched by his side, and
said to our lay-brother, the surgeon of the
infirmary, that he should lie down and rest awhile.

When the surgeon came back to him in the
morning, he said: "Beloved brother, I am still
here," as though he should say "I shall not long be
with you." So, as his natural heat departed from
his extremities to his vitals, his feet began to grow
cold, and the brethren would have warmed them
with fomentations and friction; but he said: "Know
ye not, brethren, that when a man is about to die
his feet first grow cold?" And then they ceased
from their endeavours. Yet at his last moments he
suffered no troubling imaginations nor wandering
fantasies sent by evil angels; but in full command
of his mind and reason, in very good peace and
quiet of heart, he rendered his happy soul to God,
in the presence of the brethren, on the Saturday
after St Andrew's day, during the *Gloria in excelsis*
of High Mass, a Mass of the Blessed Virgin, whom
he had most specially loved, which was sung with
solemnity before Advent.[23]

The Diversity of Monastic Modes

Not all successful monasteries were weakened by the
corrosive effects of affluence. Several monastic communities
and orders gradually developed that emphasized the
semihermetic traditions which antedated Saint Benedict's Rule.
The founders of these communities stressed the importance of
small, extremely isolated monasteries, where members spent

the greater part of each day in solitude and silent prayer. In effect, such communities focused on the examples of the Desert Fathers. Two such communities were founded in Italy, in Camaldoli and Vallombrosa, in the eleventh century.[24] They are still exenuant. The Carthusian order, founded in France in the twelfth century, expressed similar principles, which are still applied in some contemporary Carthusian monasteries. In practice, for all of these foundations, *rigor* meant: strict enforcement of silence; that most prayer was individual; significant periods of meditation; many meals eaten in private; limited amounts of manual labor (as much for diversion as for economic activity); members sleeping and studying in private rooms; and very little contact with the external world. Small groups of lay brothers served the institutions' needs for occasional external contacts.

In our era, these communities still exist in forms relatively similar to that which they first assumed (though they were sometimes suppressed by anticlerical movements during the intervening centuries). As several observers have remarked, these communities have never been reformed, since they never significantly changed their original purposes. One friend told me a story about these monks which may be apocryphal, but is at least provocative: If someone writes to one of these monasteries to ask about joining, his letter probably will not be answered, meaning (a) the monks are determined to focus their energies on religious life, and (b) if a potential recruit does not persist when his questions are unanswered, he probably lacks enough purpose to join and persist in following the appropriate Rule. The anecdote is a variant of Saint Benedict's injunction that potential recruits should be required to remain outside the monastery gate for several days before being permitted to enter.

Useful object lessons can be derived from these small, rigorous but persisting institutions. Withdrawal can help shield community members from distracting temptations. In all eras, a certain fraction of society will choose to adopt such an option. But, if the withdrawal is rigorously applied, the proportion of persons who will follow such a course is not large.

The Trappists were another religious community, based on Saint Benedict's Rule, which grew up after the medieval era, and which practiced a form of rigorous observance. Technically, they were designated as The Order of Cistercians of the Strict Observance. The designation *Trappist* is derived from the name of the La Trappe monastery, where the order originated under the leadership of Abbot Jean de Rance (1626-1700). Its founder, de Rance, incidentally, was originally merely a commendatory abbot who undertook to significantly reform the monastery under his nominal charge. The Trappists evolved away from the Cistercians, whom they saw as becoming decadent.[25] One of the Trappists' central principles was a determination to observe Saint Benedict's requirement that community members abstain from flesh meat. In addition, the rule of silence was closely observed, a demanding schedule of Office was maintained, and readings, agricultural labor, and meditation were the norm for all members. There are still Trappist monasteries in our era, in the United States and elsewhere in the world.

It is instructive to see, in summary form, some of the mutations that occurred over the centuries around Saint Benedict's Rule. First, there were simply individual monasteries which followed the rule. Next, many of these monasteries affiliated under the leadership of Cluny. Then the Cistercians formed an alternative monastic system. The Cluniac system eventually fell into complete decay (Cluny and many of its dependencies were extinguished by the eighteenth century, though a few disaffiliated monasteries survived). Although the Cistercians were divided by the formation of the Trappists, the basic Cistercian order survived and is still active in our era. The Trappists, too, are still functioning. Meanwhile, a number of monasteries (neither Cistercian nor Trappist) continue to apply Saint Benedict's Rule, and new ones are being formed. All—or almost all—of these monasteries eventually affiliated in a new confederation, called the Benedictines. (There are other monastic orders and communities omitted from this outline.) And the development of "monastic"—or cloistered or enclosed—orders of women is probably an even more complex story.

In the twelfth century, another form of religious life arose, partly at the instigation of Saint Bernard. This was the "military order,"[26] which developed partly as a means of assisting the Crusades. Two prominent communities of this type were the Order of the Temple (the Templars), founded in 1119, and the Order of the Hospital of Saint John in Jerusalem (the Hospitaleers), founded in 1130. The military orders were religious communities whose work was providing military and hospital services to assist the Crusades and pilgrims in the Holy Land. The two orders based their separate rules on variations of the Austin Rule, which is attributed to Saint Augustine. The orders essentially represented the first efforts to adapt religious life—celibacy, prayers, obedience, communal living, fidelity to religious principles, a rule, lifetime commitment, submission to the church—to an external mission. The adaptation was relatively successful. Both orders developed notable administrative, military, and political capabilities. The Hospitaleers, in addition to engaging in military conflicts, managed probably the most elaborate and well-maintained hospitals (for the assistance of pilgrims in the Holy Land) in their era. And the Templars, incidentally, operated a sophisticated system for financial transfers, to invest and transfer contributed funds from Western Europe to military organizations serving in the Holy Land. The general principles underlying their religious rules helped such varied efforts.

By the early fourteenth century, the Crusades had expired as a realistic movement. This raised questions about the legitimacy of the activities of the Templars and the Hospitaleers. For several centuries after the expiration of the Crusades, the Hospitaleers justified themselves through their hospital activities and their continuing heroic defense of Mediterranean islands (such as Malta) from Turkish incursions. The Templars did not make such a successful shift. The order's affluence, based on contributions collected and invested to assist the Crusades, provoked envy in secular leaders. The French king, Philip the Fair (1268-1314), led a movement to suppress the order and confiscate its assets. This caused a dramatic incident, which tells us much about the spirit prevailing in some orders. Philip accused the Templars of heresy. Through the application of torture, some Templars signed false confessions, which implicated other members. Still other Templars, despite their torture, refused to confess, and some of the members who did confess recanted their forced confessions. In the year 1314, fifty-four recalcitrant members of the order were taken to a field outside of Paris, and tied to stakes before a large crowd. They were told that if they confessed or recanted, they would be released. Otherwise, they would be burned at the stake. But confession would mean admitting Philip's (dishonest) accusations, and falsely implicating other Templars. The chronicler, who was present, reported that "all of them, with no exception, finally acknowledged none of the crimes imputed to them, but constantly persisted in the general denial," saying that "they were being put to death without cause and unjustly; which indeed many of the people were able to observe by no means without great admiration and great surprise."[27] All fifty-four died at the stake. Most of the Order's funds were eventually appropiated by various secular governments.

Maintaining Institutional Identity

By the late Middle Ages, there were innumerable examples of long-lived religious orders that had drifted afield from the original purposes of their founders. Members of religious communities had become conscious of the problems involved in maintaining the integrity of their institutions. Still, there was necessarily some need for institutions to evolve and adapt to unforeseen circumstances. Indeed, the very text of Saint Benedict's Rule (consider his resigned cautions about monks' use of wine) indicated the virtue of realism. Again, take the matter of eating flesh meat.

The Rule explicitly prohibited that practice—though it also frowned on the use of wine, but said that enforcing the prohibition was impracticable. But what might be a practicable dietary rule about meat for monks living in another country, at a time 1,000 years after Saint Benedict's death? One could surely find many reasons for opting for flexibility and reasonable adaptations. But reformers saw that some "adaptations," over brief periods of time, perhaps twenty-five to fifty years, led to scenes such as Saint Bernard described—where the Clunic abbot travelled with an entourage like a mighty lord. The problem of drawing the line was very complex.

Adaptations that seemed common sense or trivial sometimes led to effects that were entirely undesirable, and hard to reform. On the other hand, absolute refusal to adapt could well be unjustified. Throughout religious history, there was constant tension between "realists" and reformers who proposed that lines should be drawn over issues which may now seem absurd: whether religious should wear sandals (or go barefoot), compared to shoes and stockings; whether they should eat flesh meat; or whether they should live in regular residences as compared to haphazardly borrowed quarters. But, in many cases, the seemingly arbitrary lines drawn were devised by imaginative, charismatic reformers. These communicators perceived that focusing on such issues enabled them to simply and dramatically communicate broad goals to a body of potential supporters. Thus, such conflicts often basically turned on general principles relating to the observance of a Rule. The assumption was that followers who chose to accept particular symbolic demands would accede to the many other provisions the demands signified. So part of the communication genius of such leaders was their ability to identify and highlight such vital symbols.

Apart from the matter of reformation, there is the more general matter of institutional identity for diverse religious orders.[28] As centuries passed, different communities were formed, with different founders, to attain different ends. Often such developments were mutations, as some members left an existing community—on good or bad terms—to deal with some novel problem or opportunity. If the visions of these new groups were favored by circumstances, they might persist and grow. Eventually, such groups might form into new and distinct religious orders. Over centuries, procedures developed under which new orders received their rules, or charters, directly from the pope. But often, prolonged negotiations preceded the granting of a rule. The potential order usually had to prove itself through collecting a group of members, developing a significant sense of purpose, and evolving an identity different from other available existing orders. Thus, orders which have persisted for some period of time have an institutional identity, somewhat akin to the differences among the U.S. military services, or some major corporations (such as IBM, Xerox, or Standard Oil), or important universities. Their identities can be symbolically communicated, but such symbols often reflect real differences in practices, basic objectives, and the relations among order members. A variety of means have been applied to assist such order identification: particular ethnic identifications (i.e., relating to the country in which the order was first organized); different work or missions; special garments; identification with a specific, notable founder (e.g., Saint Benedict); particular forms of residences or other buildings; and special modes of meditation, prayer, or worship. Order members even usually affix the initials of their order after their personal signatures, to emphasize their own institutional identity (e.g., O.P., Order of Preachers, for members of the Dominican Order).

In persisting orders, recruits choose to join because they value the order's unique characteristics—recruits who dislike such characteristics are discouraged; recruits in training ("formation") are taught to honor and express such characteristics; routine activities of order members are congruent with such characteristics; necessary changes in the order are managed to maintain the integrity of the characteristics; and the characteristics, themselves, represent a thoughtful and realistic vision of human nature and Catholic doctrine.

Like other vital and persisting institutions, religious orders become extinct, shrink, enlarge, reform, merge, splinter, remain stable, die, or die and revive. Sometimes, the extinction of an order or community occurs entirely through the action of its (declining) members, and sometimes a declining and vulnerable order is suppressed due to external jealousy of its remaining assets. For instance, in the late monastic era, many monasteries (whose enrollment had shrunk) were suppressed by secular agencies who wanted to seize their property. Technically, such seizures did not necessarily stop people from choosing to become monks. But, without the previous assets, and with the likelihood that any additional assets collected would also be seized, the continuing life of the organization expired.

As one means of stability, orders have made considerable effort to identify their traditions with the contributions of a specific founder, or foundress: the person who "gave" them their Rule and otherwise initially shaped the institution. His conduct is presented as an example, his relics receive special reverence, and his writings and statements are carefully studied. Different founders represent different principles, and often are identified by diverse iconographic devices. The inevitable differences among founders in matters of style and conduct serve to heighten and clarify distinctions among orders. The relationship between the founder, the order's Rule and other principles, and the longevity of the order help generate stability during periods of institutional stress. Indeed, order members often participate in efforts, or "causes," to have their founders canonized by the church as saints, partly because such recognition legitimizes the traditions of the order.

The role of the church as a referee and supervisor is also important in order identity. The church has a long-range interest in fostering the vitality of its diverse orders. Many of these concerns are largely "spiritual": there are numerous instances of bishops or other members of the hierarchy making sacrifices to create or support units of cloistered orders within areas of their jurisdiction. Undoubtedly, they wanted prayer specialists praying on behalf of their concerns.

Particular church members will also have varied sympathies for specific orders, or for the formation of nonexisting orders. Existing orders often look to the church for various forms of help, and for the determination of intraorder and interorder conflicts. And the operation of orders is partly determined by the effects of canon law. Finally, under canon law, all newly formed orders must look to the church for the provision and/or acceptance of an appropriate rule. Over time, the particular decisions the church has made affecting order identity have necessarily been varied and complex.

Long-Term Monastic Decay

From about the fourteenth century onward, monastic life underwent a long-term process of decay: fewer members enrolled; the members enrolled made less profound commitments to monastic practices; and many monasteries were suppressed through government action, often related to the Protestant Reformation. The decline was partly caused by a general rise in urbanism and secularism, and by the Reformation. While the entire Catholic church was affected by these forces, monasticism was more affected than other forms of religious life. Putting it directly, the shifts that occurred were especially uncongenial to monasticism. It might also be said that monasticism had not yet "learned" to make an effective adaptation to the emerging modern world. As we will see later, a significant monastic revival eventually occurred in the church. Monasticism never reattained the level of vitality that it had during the medieval era, but it did rise significantly above its post-medieval nadir.

Notes

1. Herbert Workman, *The Evolution of the Monastic Ideal* (Boston, MA: Beacon Press, 1962), p. 235 et seq.

2. For details on the Jesuits in the wilderness of Canada, see James T. Moore, *Indian and Jesuit* (Chicago, IL: Loyola University Press, 1982).

3. Francis Parkman, *The Battle for North America* (Garden City, NY: Doubleday, 1948), ed. John Tebbel, p. 108.

4. Joan Evans, *Monastic Life at Cluny, 910-1157* (Hamden, CT: Acron Books, 1968), p. 4.

5. *New Catholic Encyclopedia* (Washington, DC: Catholic University, 1967), vol. 3, p. 966.

6. David Knowles, *Christian Monasticism* (New York: McGraw-Hill, 1969), p. 99.

7. *New Catholic*, vol. 9, p. 1038.

8. Eileen Powers, *Medieval English Nunneries* (New York: Bilbo and Tannen, 1964), p. 670.

9. Ibid, p. 681.

10. Ian C. Hannah, *Christian Monasticism* (New York: Macmillan, 1925), p. 133 et seq.

11. Knowles, *Christian Monasticism*, p. 48 et seq; and Workman, *Evolution*, p. 230 et seq.

12. Knowles, *Christian Monasticism*, p. 53.

13. Quoted in Hannah, *Monasticism*, p. 136.

14. Cuthbert Butler, *Benedictine Monasticism* (New York: Barnes and Noble, 1924), p. 299.

15. Louis J. Lekai, *The Cistercians: Ideals and Realities* (Kent, OH: Kent State University Press, 1977).

16. There are many noteworthy, well-illustrated books that provide displays of monastic art. Two examples are Christopher Brooks, *The Monastic World* (New York: Random House, 1974), and Knowles, *Christian Monasticism.* An evocative and literary book which focuses principally on a textual presentation is Sacheverell Sitwell, *Monks, Nuns and Monasteries* (New York: Holt and Rinehart, 1965).

17. *New Catholic*, vol. 8, p. 407.

18. For material on women in medieval religious life, see Lina Eckenstein, *Women Under Monasticism* (New York: Russell and Russell, 1963); Powers, *Medieval*; and Drid Williams, "The Brides of Christ," in *Perceiving Women*, ed. Shirley Ardner, (London: Malaby Press, 1975).

19. Hans Cnattingius, *Studies in the Order of St. Bridget of Sweden*, vol. 5, *The Crisis of the 1420s* (Stockholm: Alnquist and Weksell, 1963).

20. Powers, *Medieval*, p. 89.

21. Christopher J. Kaufmann, *Tamers of Death* (New York: Seaburg Press, 1976), p. 109.

22. *New Catholic*, vol. 14, p. 199.

23. Coulton, *Five Centuries of Religion* (Oxford: Cambridge University Press, 1950), vol. 4, p. 93.

24. Knowles, *Monasticism*, p. 61-65.

25. Leaki, *The Cistercians*, p. 181 et seq.

26. See Walter Nigg, *Warriors of God* (New York: Alfred A. Knopf, 1959); Jonathan Riley-Smith, *The Knights of St. John in Jerusalem and Cyprus, 1050-1310* (New York:

St. Martin's Press, 1967); and Desmond Seward, *The Monks of War* (Hamden, CT: Archon, 1972).

27. Quoted in Malcolm Barber, *The Trial of the Templars* (New York: Cambridge Press, 1978), p. 157.

28. For one discussion of the problems of institutional identity, see Orrin Klapp, *The Collective Search for Identity* (New York: Holt, Rinehart and Winston, 1969).

6
Into the Secular World

... Amongst the friars of "the Community" were not a
few who, whilst accepting the "milder" interpretations
and the modifications of the primitive simplicity, yet
endeavoured to restrict the more manifest relaxations of
the *Rule* and to live at least in the spirit of the primitive
fraternity so far as their personal life was concerned.
And amongst the "Spirituals" too there were those who
admitted that in the changing circumstances of the Order
there must be a certain adaptability to new needs,
provided that the essential poverty and simplicity of the
Rule were maintained as the foundation of the fabric.
These were the moderates of both sides. They could
hardly be said to form a party: they were as a leaven
preventing for a long time the utter disunion of the Order.
— Fr. Cuthbert, *The Capuchins*

In the late Middle Ages, a series of developments brought
about the formation of new types of religious communities.
These communities did not ignore the insights provided by the
history of monasticism. But they coupled that knowledge with
new recognitions and experimental modes—some of which
persisted, while others flared up and then expired. One
important development affecting the communities was the
increasing significance of the place of preaching in public life.

The Significance of Preaching

The people of the era, as in most other historical societies,
lived in an oral culture. Books (or, more properly, manuscripts)

were scarce and expensive, and few persons were literate. Many citizens necessarily spent large portions of their time in oral activities: talking, listening, singing, exchanging tales, or hearing various forms of public addresses. Such activities were a central means of amusement and popular instruction. And, as the level of urbanization increased, the sophistication of such interchanges heightened: participants were able to compare the performance of many different speakers (or "performers"), and thus elevate their standards of assessment.

A major area of oral expression was religious topics. In effect, they were a form of intellectual discourse. Or, if the listeners were not disposed to hear erudite theology, they were prepared to attend presentations that had an essentially religious character. Religious discourse was relatively popular, because almost all listeners had substantive information about the nature of Christianity, the clergy who presented such sermons were (supposedly) trained to make skilled presentations, and church buildings were natural sites for such presentations. Attending sermons and other forms of religious presentation served, for many citizens, as a type of pastime. In addition to the matter of rhetorical content and delivery, there was also the issue of the overall design of the rhetorical occasion: It was often possible or proper for an important religious address to be presented at a special convocation, which was framed by dramatic and carefully designed rites and ceremonies. But the organization of such occasions took practice and imagination.

The development of a pool of increasingly sophisticated listeners generated a challenge for the church. Many secular clergy lacked the formal training—in either theology or presentation—to be accomplished preachers. They did not know how to compose significant sermons or deliver them in an engaging style, nor to organize elaborate rites. Furthermore, secular clergy were handicapped by being expected to stay in one parish for a prolonged period of time. In contrast, a mobile orator, once he had "perfected" a particular speech, or series of speeches, could repeat essentially the same presentation at a variety of sites to different audiences—like a political candidate on the road, or a professor teaching some topic to successive groups of students.

On different occasions, monks accepted the roles of mobile preachers. The preaching of Saint Bernard of Clairvaux, for example, played an important part in exciting support for the Second Crusade (1144-1148). But there were difficulties in regularly assigning such roles to monks. First, their Rule typically required them to maintain seclusion from the world and to leave their monasteries only for extraordinary reasons. Second, the development of particular monks as talented preachers was largely an idiosyncratic process. Monks were not recruited to be preachers, and their regular training was not especially oriented in that direction. It is true that some monks did display notable scholastic talent. But scholastic talent did not necessarily carry over to skill in oratory. And so a gradual need arose in the church for the establishment of a system to regularly produce dedicated clerics, skilled in debate and oratory, and able to travel freely to fulfill their assigned roles. Such a system would give considerable attention to recruiting and training innately talented persons. Eventually, a variety of orders evolved which did satisfy this need for preachers. One order deliberately concerned with preaching were the Dominicans, whose history will be considered in more detail later. The constitution of that order (ca. 1210) clearly outlined how the order was to monitor the dedication and skill of members engaged in preaching:

> At general meetings of the whole Order, there shall be presented those who are thought by some brothers fitted to preach, and who have had license and command from their own prior, but not yet received the office of preaching from their higher superior or chapter. They shall all be carefully examined one by one by suitable brothers, appointed to deal with this, and the brothers with whom they have lived shall be carefully questioned on the grace of preaching which God has granted them, on their zeal, religious life, fervour of charity, purpose and intention; and when they have given their evidence, the brothers appointed will, with the consent and advice of the higher superior, approve whatever they judge the better course: that these brothers should continue still in study, or serve

apprenticeship in preaching with older brothers, or
are fitted and useful to exercise the office of
preaching on their own.[1]

A typical example of the style and impact of such skilled
preachers is provided by a relatively detailed contemporary
description of a series of Lenten services in an Italian city in
1617:

> There came to Piacenza to preach the Lent, Padre
> Giacinto da Casale, a Capuchin, a preacher of
> singular character, of wonderful goodness of life
> and of rare courage. . . . He began his course of
> sermons on Ash Wednesday, and the great
> concourse of people proved the expectancy and
> thirst for the saving water of the divine word. The
> great Duomo was dangerously packed; people came
> from far and from near, both men and women, to
> hear the preacher. The commotion and the
> fruitfulness began from the beginning; and every
> day was as a Good Friday, what with tears and
> striking of the breast and the voices of contrition.
> Frequently too, during the sermons were heard the
> voices of the demons in the unhappy obsessed,
> mingling with the words of the preacher, so that
> the church seemed veritably as a day of judgment.
> These rebellious spirits even set themselves to
> preach; and the father giving way they confirmed
> all he had said, crying aloud to the confusion of us
> poor sinners that now was their final ruin. And
> truly to my thinking he were more demon than
> man who would not be moved at seeing in the
> pulpit that face so uplifted with devotion, so
> emaciated as though he were one of the ancient
> anchorites who had come from his cell in the wood;
> or one who would not change his mind at seeing
> that countenance as pitiful in softening hearts as it
> was terrible in its detestation of sin, in
> reprehending vice and in threatening the dire
> chastisements of God; or finally one who could
> remain stolid listening to that voice, clear, sonorous

and penetrating, and to such burning arguments,
clothed with the zeal of God, and afire with the
ardour of the Holy Ghost. . . . Before he entered
the pulpit, a confused murmur of voices, because of
the multitude, filled the great church; at the first
word intoned by the father, the noise suddenly
subsided and there could be heard a silence as great
as the silence in a well-regulated cloister of
mortified religious. [The narrator then sums up the
results of the sermons] Such restitution of goods,
such confessions of those who had been unconfessed
for many years, such giving up of dishonest
practices and promises of amendment on the part
of the notaries and lawyers; so many youths, in
particular those of the nobility, asking to be
received into the father's order (the which could not
be because the number was too great for all to be
received); so many conversions of women of the
streets that the homes were too small to
accommodate them all and the father appealed for
funds to buy another house, and out of the funds
many were given dowries and found husbands; so
many feuds were settled and so many enemies
embraced each other, in the course of the sermons.
In the shops, the piazza and the houses, nothing
was talked of but the preacher and his sermons,
and amendment of life and the doing of penance for
past sins.[2]

An important effect of this concern with preaching was
the formal interest of religious orders in participating in higher
education: in having order members hold chairs at colleges and
universities; in having significant proportions of order members
earn degrees of higher education; and in assisting in the
founding and operation of colleges, universities, and "houses," or
subunits of colleges. The ultimate base for this interest was the
training of order members to preach, or to produce works of
scholarship supporting (or helping to refine) church policies.
These patterns were different from the forms of intellectual
training practiced in monasteries. In monasteries, the
intellectual training was incidental and relatively idiosyncratic.
In medieval colleges and universities, the training was

systematic, corporately managed, led to formal degrees, and was designed to train persons who would ultimately operate away from the institution, instead of staying to work as at the monastery. We should also recall the oratarical focus of medieval scholarship; speaking skills were as important as writing for academic success. Many faculty members of such colleges and universities were members of religious orders, and some students were junior members of orders.

There were evidently strong explicit and implicit pressures for religious orders (developed after the monastic era) to drift towards formal scholarly activities. For instance, the Franciscans, an order whose history will be more carefully considered later, were founded by Saint Francis, a brilliant but largely anti-intellectual leader. He viewed formal learning as an impediment to true religious devotion. Yet, as one Franciscan historian observed, "Within twenty years after the death of the Founder, the order had become one of the most learned institutions in the world."[3] The author then went on to list the many arrangements the order had provided to encourage and stimulate its members to heighten their formal learning: lectors were designated in each community to instruct all members, especially those who should go on to further learning; regional "schools" were established for order members from different communities so they could congregate for more elaborate training; and additional "schools" were organized at different universities, where the most promising order members went to complete their studies with the financial support of the regional units of the order (compared to the limited economic resources of each local community).

Stresses of Decline and Reform

A variety of events were setting the stage for the Protestant Reformation (during the sixteenth century). Many elements of monastic orders, and the church proper, showed evidence of decay: there was often lax observance of clerical obligations such as celibacy and poverty; many churchmen were excessively concerned with material display and the appurtenances of status; and, it has been argued, the church's monopoly as *the* organized religion of the West lowered the quality of its operations.

At the very time such disorder was developing, other forces in the church were attempting to reform many undesirable norms.[4] Some of these reform efforts simply represented the distress of sincere persons at the malfeasance they saw around them. In other instances, the reformers were simultaneously provoked by the conduct of groups of religious dissenters or heretics who disassociated themselves from the church. The church reformers contended that practices should be purified to prevent further dissension or to tempt the heretics back to the fold. Actually, many of the popular protests that surrounded the triggering of the Reformation were similar to other in-church reform efforts which occurred both before and after the Reformation. The difference between the Reformation and the in-church efforts was that the in-church efforts, on the whole, were channeled into constructive in-church reform (or they were stifled). In a sense, from the perspective of the church, the Reformation was a reform effort that got out of hand.

One remarkable characteristic of the institutional church has been its capability to direct reform efforts into channels which reinvigorate the church. The Reformation is a notable—but rare—instance of the failure of that capability. An important element of this channeling capability has been the diverse patterns of religious life. These patterns permit groups of especially devout believers to form into critical masses, and support and stimulate each other. At the same time, the groups are encouraged to submit themselves to the general governance of the institutional church—firstly, through soliciting the church's approval for their rule and, secondly, by accepting the general canon law, or overall rules, of the church.[5] It is quite possible for informal groups of Catholics to spontaneously assemble to heighten their sense of religious community. Such gatherings often occur. But if such a group seeks to formalize and enlarge itself, and persist—as a Catholic group—it will need to provide for the regular provision of the Sacraments to its members. And if its members do not regularly receive the Sacraments, it will not be a Catholic group. In this inevitable process of relating to the church, the group will subject itself to formal regulation.

Assume such a group represents the potential foundation of a religious order. Then, the members will be provoked to consider the application of the principles of religious life to their organization. For instance, they will be encouraged to establish boundaries, either symbolic or physical, to constrain the interaction between their community and the rest of the church. (In the case of religious orders, the symbolic boundaries consist of the formal process of member formation and profession; community members are persons who have submitted to this arduous process.) As a result of such boundaries, the impact of the church on (sometimes) "alien" orders is moderated, and the order is protected from direct contact with misfeasance that may exist elsewhere in the church.

The church gradually developed a variety of institutionalized forms of community life, in addition to typical religious orders. The nature of these nonorder communities varies widely. Furthermore, their particular status in the eye of the church is affected by the forms of the canon law that prevailed in different eras. Some of these groups had relatively transitory existences. Thus, the Beghards, a significant quasi-religious organization for males, was active in the Low Countries during the thirteenth and fourteenth centuries.[6] The group eventually expired, in part because of church repression (due to its heretical tendencies) and numerous institutional changes. Conversely, the Third Order of Saint Francis has continued in diverse forms from the thirteenth century into the present era. The degree of commitment that such groups required of their members was not uniform. In the instance of some groups, the demands made on members were only slightly less intense than the requirements of some religious orders; in other cases, the demands were much less—members were married, lived at home with their families, and viewed their affiliation as only one of several vocational, family and religious obligations. These groups often were essentially lay counterparts of particular religious orders. Such parallel groups were frequently termed *Third Orders*. The *First Order* of the community was its professed male members, the *Second Order*, the professed female members, and the Third Order, the nonprofessed male and/or female affiliates, who were usually counselled by members of the First Order. Due to these various

"nonreligious" groups, many aspects of religious life were
transmitted to lay church members in a somewhat moderated
form. This transmission spread the impact of different orders
and the general principles of religious life among church
members.

The unique strength of religious, or isolated, life led to a
peculiar anomaly. Members of male religious orders who were
priests (so-called regular clergy) were sometimes assigned to
parish work in place of diocesan clergy when no diocesan clergy
were available to fill a peculiar need. Or, alternatively, church
authorities or significant laypersons used their influence to have
order members assigned to parish work in place of diocesan
clergy precisely because of the evident virtues they had
displayed. And, in other circumstances, orders, or order
members, have undertaken deliberate maneuvers to obtain such
parish assignments, because of the prerequisites and economic
benefits such assignments might generate. The assignment of
order members to parish work has generated problems and
opportunities for orders. Parish work has confronted some
order members with some of the same temptations and
diversions their order's initial segregation was designed to avoid.
It has (sometimes) generated jealousy and hostility between
diocesan clergy and regular clergy.[7] And it has provided order
members with opportunities to do good works and recruit
additional members into their orders. But, whatever the pros
and cons of such patterns, it is indisputable that order members
have become a church resource for maintaining parish activities.
During the twentieth century, perhaps 20 to 40 percent of all
"parish priests" are regular clergy.

Another development in church structures warrants
mention. Monasteries were typically externally monitored by
local bishops. As more elaborate forms of orders evolved, the
church came to rely on other means of external supervision.
Local units of orders increasingly became regulated by the
parent order, and not the local diocese. Then, the overall
international order was supervised by the whole
church—theoretically, based in Rome. This shift provided
orders with more independent systems of self-governance, since
the members collectively governed the local units. Bishops were

not, however, totally removed from authority. They retained jurisdiction over recent, or purely local orders and had some forms of authority over local units of national and international orders. But there was undoubtedly a long term trend towards greater order independence from local external monitoring, greater subordination of local units to their overall order, and greater subordination of orders to the overall church.

In addition to the potential distinction between diocesan clergy and members of religious orders, there is also the matter of distinctions among persons who choose particular orders. Over time, the diverse modes of religious life gradually increased. Some older forms persisted, and other forms developed and (sometimes) persisted. What evolved in different religious orders were a number of alternative modes of conduct, which appealed to different types of persons, and which were associated with different forms of institutional work. Due to this evolution, throughout church history, clerics (or female religious) enrolled in various orders have been qualified to perform diverse special services for the church because of the skills and insights refined by their particular ways of life. Gradually, different orders evolved different identities, or charismas, and these identities further affected their recruitment, training, and development.

In effect, Catholic policies regarding religious life have shaped the church into an extraordinarily heterogeneous system. In contrast, it seems in many Protestant sects that whenever a doctrinal or personality conflict arose, a separate new sect had to be formed. There were not effective means to maintain religious diversity and fidelity in a common system.

Two Examples

Two important religious orders were founded in the early thirteenth century: the Dominicans and the Franciscans. The circumstances surrounding their foundations nicely demonstrate the mixed themes of internal reform, the church's tolerance for diversity, and the commitment (of many reformers) to the overall welfare of the church.

The Dominicans were founded under the leadership of Saint Dominic (1170-1221) to assist the church in countering the spread of dissent and heresy by developing a body of trained preachers to publicly confront and counter the arguments of prominent heretics. Saint Dominic was particularly moved to form such an order as a result of his experiences in combating the heresies of the Albigenses in southern France. Those experiences led him to conclude that only highly trained clerics who led humble and exemplary lives could counter such opposition. All too often, the local priests, through their dissolute practices, were part of the cause for the dissent. And repression alone could not work without concurrent reform in the church itself. Thus, the Dominicans aimed at fostering both internal reform and competent confrontation of heresy.

The immediate circumstances surrounding the formal approval of the Dominican's rule are significant. The Fourth Lateran Council (1215) concluded, with some cause, that the proliferation of religious orders and rules was harmful to the vitality and cohesion of the church. A decree was issued that no more orders or rules were to be created. Persons desiring to participate in religious life had to fit their concerns into the structure of existing orders. At the same time, it was evident that Dominic was an able person, and his proposed order was already performing significant and novel services. Eventually, Saint Dominic asked the permission of Pope Innocent III (pontificate, 1198-1216) for his order to adopt a version of the Augustine Rule, which was already being observed by some existing religious communities.[8] Thus, in one sense, no new order was created—another group of persons simply decided to adopt and live under an existing rule. All persons concerned, however, knew very well the real objectives of the simple manipulation.

The circumstances surrounding the founding of the Franciscans will be considered later in some detail. But the relevant point here is that Saint Francis (1182-1226) and two successive popes (Innocent III, and Honorius III, pontificate, 1216-1227) engaged in prolonged negotiations over the rule to be applied to the Franciscan order which was being formed. The order was to be dramatically different from the orders that previously existed. But, despite this difference, Saint Francis continuously emphasized the order's responsibility for obedience to church authority. Concurrently, the popes strove to develop a rule which was responsive to the creative demands articulated by Saint Francis. The rule that eventually issued did not permanently resolve the problems of coherence in the Franciscan community. Tension often surrounded the continuing development of that community. But the Franciscan order (and other orders that evolved from it) accomplished many notable deeds. It is true that some elements of the order finally entered into direct conflict with the church. Still, the main themes of Franciscan/church relations have, on the whole, been supportive. Undoubtedly, one reason for such relative harmony was the tradition of constructive engagement first established by the two popes and Saint Francis.

It is relevant to recognize that reform and decline in the church have not displayed uniform patterns. Sometimes church decay has been evident at the papal level, while some local entities have concurrently displayed great piety; sometimes, parts of orders have been observant, while other portions have simultaneously been decadent; sometimes, important prods for reform have come from the papacy and other central agencies; and sometimes whole orders have become sources of reform and inspiration. The most important generalization about reform and decay that can be justified by the long-term history of the church is that both elements have developed from a variety of sources.

Dominic and Francis

As much as two men can, Saints Dominic and Francis characterized the religious spirit of the late Middle Ages. They each founded important orders, the Dominicans (or the Friars Preachers), and the Franciscans (or the Friars Minor). Both orders have persisted as significant institutions into contemporary times. The orders differ considerably from each other, and also from their predecessors. The differences are partly due to important differences in style, or charisma, between the two founders.

Dominic was a Spaniard. He entered into clerical life in a relatively typical fashion. As a person of notable ability, he was eventually sent on various missions with his bishop. As a result, he became concerned with the spread of heresy, especially the Albigensian heresy in Southern France. He became part of a group of clerics seeking to combat such heresy through preaching, and eventually assumed leadership of the group. The group especially stressed the joint importance of competent preaching plus the exemplary lives of the preachers. (It should be noted that these activities sometimes coincided with the ruthless military crusade, under church sponsorship, conducted against the Albigenses.) Saint Dominic led his group in France for about ten years (1206-1217), and finally it became the basis of the order he helped form. (By 1347, the order had about 21,000 members.)[9] He also founded a community of women to assist the order's efforts through prayer, and to provide shelter for females who wished to withdraw from heretical activities.

One informative story about Saint Dominic can be derived from the documents presented to the church on behalf of his "cause" for canonization (the formal process of adjudicating a deceased person worthy of sainthood). The story is also a remarkable example of charisma in operation. It was recited by a Dominican who had been personally recruited by Saint Dominic:

> The witness said that, when he was a student at Bologna, Master Dominic came to Bologna and preached to the scholars and other good men, and the witness confessed his sins to him, and it seemed to him that he was attracted to him. Late one evening, when the witness was sitting down to dinner in his hostel with his fellows, Brother Dominic sent two brothers to him, who said: "Brother Dominic orders you to come to him at once." "When I have had my dinner I will come to him," he replied. "No," they said, "come at once." So he got up, left his companions, and came to Dominic; he found him with a number of brothers at the church of St. Nicholas. Brother Dominic said

to the brothers: "Teach him how to seek pardon."
When pardon had been granted, he took Stephen's
hands in his; and before he could draw back
Dominic had clothed him in the habit of the Friars
Preachers, saying: "I will give you arms, with
which you are to fight the devil all the days of your
life." And the witness was mightily astonished,
then and later, by what instinct Brother Dominic
thus summoned and clothed him in the habit of the
Friars Preachers, since they had had no previous
talk of his conversion to the religious life. He
believes that he did it by divine inspiration or
revelation.[10]

Saint Dominic and his immediate successors deliberately
directed themselves towards the development of a written
constitution to provide for the overall governance of the order.
The constitution would differ from the order's Rule; the Rule
would govern local and personal conduct, while the Constituion
would govern systemwide relations. The first constitution was
developed under his guidance. Its later revisions exuded a
congruent spirit.[11] The constitution provided for the formation
of regional units, or provinces, of the overall Order. Each
province encompassed a significant number of houses. The
constitution delegated significant voting authority to all
professed brothers (who were also priests). All officers of the
order, plus elected delegates, met periodically at a general
chapter to revise and review existing policies and rules. Despite
the many democratic themes of the constitution (as far as the
professed priests were concerned), the constitution provided for
more deliberate and formal centralized administration than the
structures that had previously bound together various monastic
orders. Previously, Benedictine monasteries were relatively
independent, or were aligned with some central entity by
written, but somewhat diffuse, controls. Many elements of the
Dominican constitution were adopted by later formed religious
orders. In effect, that constitution was prototypical.

Saint Dominic was a dedicated, farsighted, but relatively
"ordinary" unusual person. His aspirations evolved, but there
was a logical relationship between his activities, his words, his

plans, and the order he founded. Saint Francis was another matter.

Saint Francis was born in Assisi, Italy, and reared in a relatively well-off merchant family. He was recognized, in his city, as a high-spirited young man, and volunteered and participated in two unsuccessful local military campaigns. Gradually, he developed an increasing interest in devout activities and engaged himself in the reconstruction of abandoned and ruined churches. When Francis was about twenty-four, his father became concerned about his withdrawal from public and material affairs. He brought him before the local bishop to be reprimanded for his conduct. His father wanted him to pursue a role appropriate to his family's status. Francis chose this occasion of public rebuke to finally disassociate himself from traditional family and community life—which he saw as inconsistent with a profound Christian mission. Before the group, he stripped himself nude (of his colorful secular garments) as a symbol of his discarding his previous status, and of his commitment to his new role. For the rest of his life, he was continuously engaged in defining exactly what that role was to be.[12]

For a while after his public commitment, Saint Francis continued to engage in church reconstruction. Concurrently, other males joined him in his activities. Gradually, a body of principles evolved about the governance of this group. Its members made a strong commitment to the practice of poverty. And, by "practice," they meant that they would only wear a simple, worn beggar's robe and would own no property. (While individual monks were obligated to observe poverty, groups of monks could collectively own the buildings, land, implements, and other property of their monasteries.) Franciscans would live solely by begging, and were thus sometimes termed a mendicant order. Reliance on begging sometimes meant that an area would become "beggared-out," and had no more resources to donate. The beggars then had to move on. Each day, one or two members of the group might be designated as beggars to go out to collect food for the group. Group members were expected to live in caves, abandoned buildings, temporarily "loaned" rooms, or other expedients. The Dominicans made an equivalent commitment to live by begging. But that order's simultaneous commitment to supporting scholarship was inconsistent with diverting members to destabilizing activities such as begging, which required members to move frequently in pursuit of food. Thus, the Dominican mendicancy requirement was quickly modified. Some groups of Franciscans persisted in mendicancy over centuries, however.

Saint Francis's opinions about the governance of his followers were complex. He put great stress on their obedience to church authorities. He also recognized the frustration that administrative responsibility engendered within himself; indeed, in 1221, five years before his death, he resigned from formal leadership of his order and designated a vicar general as successor. For the rest of his life he served as simply another (very influential) friar. He also stressed egalitarian relationships among members. He never became a priest himself and required that lay brothers have the same voice in order policies as members who were ordained and typically well-educated. (But, by 1242, the rule was changed to greatly diminish the influence of lay brothers compared to the priests.)[13]

Francis was reluctant to oblige members to apply formal procedures, or establish a regular hierarchy in the order. The Rule he drafted for the governance of the order was almost entirely a collection of excerpts from Scriptures. They were unexceptional, but relatively imprecise. After his death the Rule underwent many revisions.

The order that Francis almost accidentally was founding became extraordinarily successful. Three thousand friars and novices attended one of the first general chapters in 1221.[14] Much of the order's early—and even continuing—success was due to the tradition of immediate and personal spontaneity and devotion established by the life of Saint Francis. From its early work, dedicated to the reconstruction of churches, many members gradually became engaged in preaching, scholarship, teaching, and charitable and missionary activities. Some idea of the force of Saint Francis's presence can be gained from a description, written by a contemporary priest who was not a Franciscan, of one his sermons:

On the Feast of the Assumption, when I was
studying in Bologna, I saw St. Francis preaching in
the piazza in front of the Palazzo Publico, where
almost all the citizens had gathered. The opening
words of his sermon were: angels, men, devils; and
he treated of these three rational and spiritual
beings so well and so perceptively that many
educated men in his audience were filled with no
small admiration at the sermon of this uneducated
man. He did not deliver his sermon in the usual
way, but in a rousing fashion. All he said was
aimed at quenching hostility and procuring peaceful
agreement. His habit was dirty, his appearance
contemptible and his face ill-favoured, but God gave
the man's words such effect that many noble clans,
whose violence and long-standing feuds had raged
with much blood-letting, were induced to agree to
peace. So great were the reverence and devotion of
the people for him that men and women pressed on
him in throngs in their eagerness either to touch
the hem of his garment or to carry off a scrap of
his clothing.[15]

It is pertinent to recognize that Saint Francis coupled his
vital attractions with a certain degree of humor. Undoubtedly,
such humor—which theme has often been downplayed in
religious life—constitutes another source of the appeal of the
saint and his order. One story nicely illustrating this matter
was recorded by a contemporary of the saint after his death:

I dwelt for a few months in a certain hermitage
with St. Francis and other brethren, to care for
their beds and their kitchen; and this was our
manner of life by command of the Founder. We
spent the forenoon hours in prayer and silence,
until the sound of a board [struck with a mallet,
like a gong] called us to dinner. Now the Holy
Master was wont to leave his cell about [7:00
a.m.]; and if he saw no fire in the kitchen he would
go down into the garden and pluck a handful of
herbs which he brought home, saying, "Cook these,

and it will be well with the Brethren." And whereas at times I was wont to set before him eggs and milk food which the faithful had sent us, with some sort of gravy stew, then he would eat cheerfully with the rest and say, "Thou hast done too much, Brother; I will that thou prepare naught for the morrow, nor do aught in my kitchen." So I, following his precepts absolutely, in all points, cared for nothing so much as to obey that most holy man; when therefore he came, and saw the table laid with divers crusts of bread, he would begin to eat gaily thereof, but presently he would chide me that I brought no more, asking me why I had cooked naught. Whereto I answered, "For that thou, Father, badest me cook none." But he would say, "Dear son, discretion is a noble virtue, nor shouldest thou always fulfil all that thy Superior biddeth thee, especially when he is troubled by any passion."[16]

The circumstances of Saint Francis's death help us to further appreciate the complexity of the traditions he represents. As he aged, he increasingly withdrew from missionary and preaching activities. In somewhat debilitated health, he went with a few companions to meditate in a remote mountain hut. During his withdrawal, his companions observed that his body was afflicted with the stigmata—his hands developed wounds akin to those afflicted on Christ at his crucifixion. The saint viewed this affliction as a recompense which he could make in gratitude for the sufferings of Christ on his behalf. He continued his solitary meditations, and died in the company of a few companions. His religious and secular contemporaries regarded him as a saint.

Saint Francis provided his companions and successors with an engaging and dedicated personal example. As the founder of a persisting institution, however, his model generated problems as well as opportunities. The aim of absolute institutional poverty was a key issue. There was ample evidence that the accumulation of capital, even through the collective acts of individual religious communities, could lead to severe distortions of order priorities. On the other hand, it was hard to see how any persisting religious order could exist without some forms of possession. If order members were to preach, they needed to reside at some fixed place for some period of time, to be trained. They needed books and a place to study. And, in some geographic areas, the sole reliance on begging for food might not be practical. In other words, an order might need to control—if not own—building, books, and money to buy food. (Eventually, the church encouraged some segments of the Franciscan order to solve this problem by having property dedicated to order use where title was held by nonorder members.) Furthermore, beyond the minimums of holding property, there were other issues. Thus, the Rule drafted by Saint Francis explicitly forbade members from owning or riding on horses (though riding might be permitted in the case of severe affliction). But in an era when riding horseback was the expeditious means of travel, was it realistic to require members to visit each other solely via travel on foot? Again, when Saint Francis died, his successor raised funds and built a great church commemorating the order's founder. Was this consistent with the saint's vision? These questions led to concrete, practical matters of conduct. John of Parma (who served from 1247-1257), when vicar general of the order, conducted a tour of the order's numerous residences, scattered throughout Europe. In obedience to Franciscan principles, he carried it out entirely on foot. It took several years. It is easy to identify the inefficiencies such principles generate; it is also possible to see the powerful appeal such a style of leadership might possess.

The plea for practically absolute poverty represented a proposal for a decentralized, spontaneous, and unstable religious order. Members of such an order could not maintain efficient coordination based on foot travel. Lacking in stored resources, members would have to aggressively cultivate relationships with local sources of day-to-day charity. Probably a significant number of members would enroll for short periods, then leave, since the formation process would necessarily be brief, and tensions on members would be relatively severe (if someone became ill, there was no preexisting system maintained by the order to provide food, care and shelter). Francis recognized these problems. But he emphasized that his proposed mode of life was equivalent to that practiced by Jesus and his disciples. Some biblical evidence could be cited to support his point. Furthermore, the Franciscan's fidelity to the principle of poverty had a strong sympathetic impact on many secular and clerical observers. One twentieth century writer summarized the following thirteenth century English story to make this point:

> A knight of Northampton, Richard Gobion, provided a house for the Minors, but when his young son joined the Order he told them to leave. St. Francis insisted that his Order should own no property and wished their lack of rights to be no fiction but a reality. The ownership of all houses was to remain vested in the donor, either individual, family, guild or municipality, or failing such, in the Papacy. If a donor rescinded his gift the friars were to acquiesce and relinquish their lodging without protest. The Northampton friars filed out, while the knight waited angrily outside the door to watch them go. Last went an infirm old man carrying a Psalter [a manuscript of collected psalms]. The knight was suddenly moved by their humble obedience to their principles, repented and begged them to remain.[17]

Many people admired Saint Francis, but felt his proposal needed to be modified before being applied as a religious rule. But the process of modification was extremely complex. It involved changing the practices developed by a notable saint. There was also a recognition that the inherent tensions between religious life and material goals was a vexsome problem. Furthermore, the literal principles propounded by Saint Francis, whether practical or not, have appealed to some groups of people throughout all ages of history. As a result, formal and informal organizations (some religious, some solely secular) have periodically developed to apply the principles of Saint Francis to diverse immediate social problems. It is probably not coincidental that in our time, it was a Franciscan priest who was responsible for opening a shelter for exploited young people in New York City's Times Square area—a cesspool of vice and bleak despair.

Over several centuries, innumerable controversies arose among the Franciscans about the principle of poverty (and how it was to be applied), and the other doctrinal and policy matters that concept affected. Several distinct groups developed in the order. The groups were largely defined by their interpretations of Saint Francis's principles. A brief listing of many of these groups—which sometimes evolved into separate orders—is informative: [18]

1. The Friars Minor. The order originally founded by Saint Francis. The name means "brothers of lower status" to emphasize the concept of humility.

2. The Conventuals. Groups that eventually chose to live in (and, in effect, own) permanent residences or "convents." (That term signified a residence for either male or female religious.)

3. The Zealanti (or zealots). Favored closely, almost literally, applying the rule, especially the prohibitions against property. They were later called the Spirituals.

4. The Observants. Favored the relatively strict interpretation of the rule.

5. The Discalced. Another group supporting strict interpretation. Their name was derived from *dis-calced,* or "without shoes," meaning they went barefoot or wore sandals.

6. The Recollects. A strict interpretation group which evolved from groups of Observants that had declined in fidelity to the rule.

7. The Capuchins. Another strict-interpretation group formed by dissatisfied members of the Observants. Their name was derived from the unique hood or cowl of their robes, which they contended was similar to that worn by the saint. (The special aspect of the Capuchins later caused a species of hooded monkeys to be called capuchins.)

Eventually, the criticisms leveled at the church and other Franciscan groups by the Spirituals became extremely severe—and vice versa. Finally, Pope John XXII (pontificate, 1316-1334) initiated proceedings to have the Spirituals declared heretics. As an outcome of this action, about 150 Spirituals, largely from the south of Italy, were burnt at the stake. At present, three relatively distinct Franciscan orders exist.

The Franciscans have been affected with many sharp controversies.[19] However, the order (and its spinoffs) has also had a productive history. In the year 1700, for example, the various segments of the order had a total membership of 65,000 brothers.[20] It has conducted numerous missionary activities, participated in and founded important institutions of learning and scholarship, and otherwise played a significant role in church and Western history. In a way, events have vindicated the conflicting theories of different persons concerned with the order; the spontaneity favored by Saint Francis was a fertile source of tension and disorder, and simultaneously a vital mobilizing force; conversely, the structuring systems proposed by the institutional church (and some Franciscans) have suppressed some aspects of Franciscan vigor, and helped transform the order(s) into a long continuing institution.

Due in part to the counsel of Saint Francis, a parallel female religious community was founded by Saint Clare of Assisi (1194-1253). The community, eventually called The Poor Clares, was affected by the principles and controversies surrounding Saint Francis. Saint Clare determined that her nuns, who lived in seclusion, meditated, and performed the Office, should, like the Franciscans, not own any property, either personally or as an institution. Presumably, they would live cloistered lives in borrowed property and receive daily food offerings from lay residents of their area (which might be collected by nonprofessed sisters). This proposal contrasted with the typical arrangements for female religious, who usually lived in endowed communities. The church was reluctant to formally authorize The Poor Clares as a female religious community without an endowment. The church's assumption was that, in practice, it would become responsible for the maintenance of the congregation if the proposed *ad hoc* systems of sustenance failed. This liability would be especially severe in the case of female religious—unmarried women of diverse ages who had not been trained for gainful employment. Finally, after persisting discussions around the issue of absolute poverty, the church authorized the establishment of the order along the lines proposed by Saint Clare. The order, like the Franciscans, gradually underwent various mutations and is still active at this time. Today, the Primitive Observants of the Poor Clares have the largest proportion of the total membership of 17,000.[21]

An instructive instance of the interrelationships between male and female orders is found in some devotional texts written for the Clares by Saint Bonaventure (1217-1274), who also served as vicar general for the Franciscans. The materials coincidentally demonstrate some of the themes of personal devotion to Christ typical of Franciscans:

> Draw near, dear handmaiden, with loving feet to Jesus wounded, to Jesus crowned with thorns, to Jesus fastened to the gibbet of the cross; and be not content, as the blessed apostle Thomas was, merely to see in his hands the print of the nails or to thrust your hand into his side; but rather go right in, through the opening in his side, to the very heart of Jesus where, transformed by most burning love for Christ, held by the nails of divine love, pierced by the lance of profound charity, and wounded by the sword of deep compassion, you will know no other wish or desire or hope of consolation except to die with Christ upon the cross, so that you can say with St. Paul: "I am crucified with Christ. . . . I live; yet not I, but Christ liveth in me".[22]

Orders and the Inquisition

Christianity first developed in the religiously heterogeneous environments of Palestine and the late Roman Empire. In these environments a considerable degree of tolerance existed among diverse patterns of belief—or Roman authority necessarily compelled such toleration. When Christianity became the preponderent European religion, it assumed the posture of exclusivity probably inherent in any evangelical religion when it attains dominance. In other words, if a religion is capable of exciting missionary enthusiasm, it will tend to punish and restrict disaffectors when it has attained authority.

The Church gradually evolved a body of doctrine regarding heresy: the teaching or acceptance of distorted Christian doctrines. Heresy was more obnoxious than simply being a nonbeliever, such as a Jew or Muslim. Alliances formed among some Catholic temporal rulers and the church to suppress various heresies. The alliances developed for many reasons: the sincere beliefs of the parties about the evil of heresy; the fears of one or both parties that their own religious or temporal authority might be threatened by public dissent from established doctrines; the pressure (for action) by one or the other of the parties; or the desire of one or both parties to use the suppression of heresy to increase their economic or political status (heretics might be political enemies, or their property could be confiscated).

The Inquisition was established by Pope Gregory IX about 1233. It was a major church tool for the suppression of heresy.[23] The pope assigned to the Dominican order the principal responsibility for operating the system, though the Franciscans also were actively involved later. The units of the Inquisition typically cooperated either explicitly or implicitly with local or national secular governments. The church, acting through the Inquisition, was responsible for the detection, investigation, and adjudication of possible heresy cases. Punishments were managed, in different situations, by either the church or the government. Where direct popular resistance arose to the operation of the Inquisition, and this sometimes occurred, the church expected the appropriate government unit to use force to support the Inquisition. When such support was not provided, the Inquisition could not operate.

The conduct of the Inquisition generated bureaucratic and intellectual problems for the church. Dedicated, trained, and disciplined managers were desirable. In many instances, the inquisitorial process was taken quite seriously: There was genuine concern with evaluating the pros and cons, and arriving at a conclusion of guilt or innocence supported by evidence and precedents. As a result, it was appropriate that inquisitors be skilled in dialectic. Some of the complexities involved are portrayed in the *Practice of the Inquisition into Heretical Perversity* (ca. 1307-1323), a manual written by the Dominican inquisitor, Bernard Gui (1261-1331). Gui wrote in his preface to this widely circulated text:

The Inquisitor must be constant, persevering amid dangers and adversities even to death. He should be willing to suffer for the sake of justice, neither rashly precipitating danger nor shamefully retreating in fear, for such cowardice weakens moral stability. While remaining adamant to the entreaties and blandishments of sinners, nevertheless he must not so harden his heart as to repel appeals to grant delays or to mitigate penances according as circumstances of place and time may suggest, for such procedure savors rather of cruelty. By the same token he should refrain from too lenient an attitude which degenerates into dissoluteness. . .[24]

The *Practice* also included a hypothetical examination of a suspected heretic, which covered several pages.

The proceedings of the Inquisition, and many of its punishments, are abhorrent to our era. Indeed, some of the forms even went beyond the typical legal procedures of medieval Europe. The accused could not confront the witnesses against him. He could not have effective counsel during his interrogation by a skilled examiner. Torture could be—and was—used against the accused and witnesses to gather evidence. Informers were entitled to rewards from the property of convicted persons, and the entire (remaining) property of such persons was turned over to the church or state (a considerable incentive for the generation of convictions). Severe offenders were sometimes punished by public burning at the stake, usually conducted by government authorities. Lesser offenders were fined, imprisoned, or otherwise chastised. The quality and effect of the Inquisition varied widely according to the religious and social climate of different areas, the values of the religious and temporal persons engaged in the activity, and the applicable church policies. Gui, already quoted, for example, heard over 900 cases during a long career. He sentenced 246 persons to life imprisonment (commuting 139 of those cases), and abandoned 40 heretics to the secular arm—which meant burning at the stake.[25]

The operations of the Inquisition were relatively inhibited in England and northern Europe, active in southern France and Italy, and most vigorous in Spain. In particular, the Spanish Inquisition became relatively subordinate to the state. It was as much an arm of government repression of dissent (and the confiscation of private property by the government) as an institution of the Roman church. What presumably happened is that the long trial of the reconquest of Spain from the Moors developed a certain strain in the Spanish character (and Spanish leaders). They were especially attracted to agencies for generating stability and uniformity through militant suppression. The Inquisition was active in Spain from 1480 to about 1800, a longer period than in any other European nation. During those years, it is estimated that 20,000 persons were burned at the stake in Spain for heresy.[26]

These distressing statistics can be better appreciated if we concurrently consider the great concern with witchcraft generated in Europe among all Christians (and many governments) during the sixteenth and seventeenth centuries. Estimates of the number of Europeans burned alive for this offense during those years range from 200,000 to over one million.[27] Many of the "witches" condemned by the Catholics were identified by the Inquisition, though numerous secular and Protestant agencies were also involved in this persecution. Many Catholics were also among the persons critical of the accusations pertaining to witchcraft. For example, a Spanish inquisitor (in 1610) markedly lessened accusations in that country by criticizing the forms of evidence accepted and refusing to allow the confiscation of the property of convicted witches.[28]

Notes

1. Roslind B. Brooks, "The Ancient Constitution of the Order of the Friars Preachers," *The Coming of the Friars*, ed. Roslind B. Brooks (New York: Barnes and Noble, 1975), p. 197.

2. Fr. Cuthbert, *The Capuchins* (Port Washington, NY: Kenikat Press, 1971), p. 357.

3. John Moorman, *A History of the Franciscan Order, From Its Origins to 1517* (New York: Oxford University Press, 1968), p. 123.

4. See, Edward McNall Burns, *The Counter-Reformation* (New York: D. Van Nostrand, 1964), pp. 22-50; for discussion about the Catholic Reformation——which is not the same thing as the Counter-Reformation, see Pierre Janelle, *The Catholic Reformation* (Milwaukee: Bruce Publishing, 1949).

5. For an informative discussion of the role of canon law in shaping religious life in the early 1960s (shortly before the effects of Vatican II occurred), see Review for Religious, *Questions on Religious Life* (St. Mary's Kansas: Saint Mary College, 1964), compiled from materials published in *Review for Religious.*

6. Ernest W. McDonnell, *The Beguines and Beghards* (New York: Octagon, 1969).

7. For discussion about the tensions between Franciscans and the secular clergy, see Moorman, *A History*, p. 120 et seq.

8. Brooks, *The Coming*, p. 108.

9. *New Catholic Encyclopedia* (Washington, DC: Catholic University, 1967), vol. 4, p. 977.

10. Brooks, *The Coming*, p. 181.

11. John-Baptist Reeves, *The Dominicans* (New York: Macmillan, 1930), pp. 46-73; and Brooks, *The Coming*, p. 98 et seq.

12. The literature about St. Francis, and what he "really" signified, is voluminous. From shortly after his death on into the twentieth century, scholars and groups have tried to interpret a body of somewhat ambiguous conduct and limited evidence. One useful source is John R. H. Moorman, *St. Francis Assisi: Writings and Early Biographies* (Chicago: Franciscan Herald Press, 1977).

13. Brooks, *The Coming*, p. 97.

14. Moorman, *A History*, p. 105.

15. Brooks, *The Coming*, p. 136.

16. G. G. Coulton, *From St. Francis to Dante* (Philadelphia: University of Pennsylvania Press, 1972), pp. 72-73.

17. Moorman, *A History*, p. 113.

18. Brooks, *The Coming*, p. 110.

19. For some consideration of these divergencies, see *New Catholic* entries related to Franciscans, vol. 6, pp. 36-72; Cuthbert, *The Capuchins*; and Moorman, *A History*.

20. *New Catholic*, vol. 6, p. 43.

21. Ibid. vol. 11, p. 566.

22. Moorman, *A History*, p. 260.

23. For some writings on the Inquisition, see, e.g., John A. O'Brien, *The Inquisition* (New York: Collier and Macmillan, 1973); J. Guiraud, *The Medieval Inquisition* (New York: AMS Press, 1968); Henry Charles Lea, *The Inquisition of the Middle Ages* (London: Eyre and Spottiswoode, 1963); and G. G. Coulton, *The Inquisition and Liberty* (London: William Heinemann, 1938).

24. O'Brien, *The Inquisition*, p. 11.

25. Ibid. p. 21.

26. Ibid. p. 104

27. Norman Cohn, *Europe's Inner Demons* (New York: Basic Books, 1975).

28. O'Brien, *The Inquisition*, p. 127.

7
Helping to Revive the Church

Ah, my brothers . . . what do these lights shining and
sparkling in the midst of the night mean, if not that He
whose memory we are now honoring has through His
birth dissipated the shadows and the ignorance of the
world; having done this the first time so many centuries
ago, He is about to grant us today, for the first time in
these centuries, the same grace and mercy. There are
purposes and reasons, which can only be adored, for
which He has not done this sooner; but it is a grace and a
favor toward us, which cannot be sufficiently estimated or
acknowledged, that His providence has arranged this
blessing for our country while we are still living.
—Christmas sermon delivered by Canadian Huron Indian
convert to tribe members in 1638, written down and
translated by Jesuit missionaries, and contemporaneously
reported and published in France in the *Relations*

Martin Luther (1483-1546) was a Catholic priest and a
member of the Augustinian order—a monastic order observing
the Austin Rule. He had received the extended academic
training that qualified him to act as a public preacher. His
order was afflicted by many of the tensions about rule
observance that affected many orders in the late Middle Ages;
thus, its members were divided between groups designated
observants and *conventuals.* Luther was affiliated with the
observants. In effect, his training, commitments and
responsibilities were akin to those of many other religious of his
era. Even his dissatisfactions with many church practices were
widely shared by other Catholics. It is finally noteworthy that

188 Traditional Catholic Religious Orders

the turbulent movement he helped ignite had profound effects on the nature of religious life even down to our time.

Before Luther and the forces he mobilized became public issues, there had been continuing pressures in the church for greater reform. These efforts have been characterized as the *Catholic* Reformation.[1] The name signifies that there was a reformation effort in the church itself, which paralleled—and indeed, antedated—the Protestant Reformation. This effort evinced itself in diverse successful—and unsuccessful—attempts to reform individual religious communities, or whole orders, and to initiate an appropriate "council," or international meeting of the church hierarchy, to reorganize church governance. (The hope was that such a council could establish procedures to correct the many existing evident deficiencies in church policies.) Despite the sporadic success of reform efforts in particular orders, no council was called during the early years of the Protestant Reformation. One reason for such lack of a council was the desire of some church groups to stifle pleas for reform.

Eventually, despite continuous efforts to suppress dissent, the reactionary forces in the church lost control of the situation. The Reformation then grew into a large-scale anti-church movement. This led to an enormous medley of consequences—wars, religious massacres, the defection of millions of people from the church, the establishment of new and competing religions, and the popularization of significant and original conceptions of human nature and religion. Ironically, one of the many important and unexpected consequences of the Reformation was a considerable revitalization of the church. This revitalization was assisted by religious orders, particularly newly developed orders. Simultaneously, the new systems of church governance that evolved in response to the Reformation affected the structure and form of religious life.

It is significant to note that the newly established Protestant churches, and most of their successors, deliberately chose to form religious systems that did not provide for institutions akin to Catholic religious orders—even though the new churches did follow some other elements of the Catholic tradition. This disjunction with tradition had many implications for Protestant secular and religious life, which cannot be adequately explored here. As one instance of these implications, consider the observation by Thomas Macauley that religious orders served as a form of institutionalized enthusiasm with the result that devout, energetic, imaginative (and potentially eccentric) believers could carve out a niche for themselves as founders or active members of orders; at the same time, these persons could remain relatively committed to the general principles of the overall Church. Macauley contended that such persons in Protestant environments might either abandon, or be driven from, their existing church and perhaps form new and divisive sects.

The Reformation triggered in-church reform since it provided powerful evidence of the deficiencies of the status quo. Thus, previously unthinkable proposals for internal reform became more thinkable. Furthermore, the common psychological phenomenon of polarization both intensified religious controversy and gave special energy to the persons enlisted in the controversy. As a result, some persons who might have been passive, moderate Catholics in earlier eras were provoked by the circumstances of the moment to heightened levels of dedication and sacrifice. While Catholicism was the universal religion, its value was taken for granted. But when there was a real chance it could be extinguished by militant opponents, it assumed greater worth in the eyes of many believers. Furthermore, Catholicism had gradually embedded itself into the fabric of European government, and public and private life. The power of these ties in some countries and areas became more evident as the efforts of the Reformation persisted and spread.

It should be emphasized that many of the Catholic reformers did not think, "The church is threatened, let us do something, or let us form an order to moderate this danger." To the contrary, their writings and day-to-day work often evince a concern with the concrete religious and social problems around them, and a general desire to serve God and advance the church. But their individual acts occurred as part of an overall climate, and on behalf of an institution that had deliberately decided to reform in response to external threats. In sum, the

Reformation was a partial trigger for many dynamic and novel religious developments in the church that occurred in the centuries succeeding Luther's posting of his ninety-five theses in 1517.

A major event that deliberately affected the structure of religious life was the Council of Trent (1545-1563). The council was called by Pope Paul III (1534-1549) in response to the Reformation. It attempted to effect a reconciliation among the disputing forces and to concurrently help reform the church. The council's efforts at reconciliation with the Protestants failed, partly because some church leaders did not want to pay the price needed to attain reconciliation. The council then lapsed for a number of years, since some church factions were hostile to its themes of internal reform. Eventually, the council was reassembled and drafted a body of principles and decrees for the operation of a reformed church.[2] Those principles have effected the operation of the Church into the modern era (though they were significantly impacted by the pronouncements of the Vatican II Council, 1962-1965).

The new principles recognized that the survival of the church was in question. Drastic reforms were necessary. The reforms adopted provided for tighter controls from the top, systems for monitoring to avoid diverse forms of abuse (and "experimentation"), a clear demarcation of differences between Catholic and Protestant denominations, and the adoption of policies that heightened the rigor of religious life. The reforms accepted the existing climate of polarization. They have generally been characterized as the Counter-Reformation. In effect, the church symbolically and administratively girded its loins for a long and arduous conflict. The name of the council came to characterize the spirit of its policies, and historians have coined the term *post-Tridentine church*. In our era, that term has usually had negative connotations. It signifies many forms of closedness, restraint on spontaneity, apparent anti-intellectualism, centralization, and bureaucracy. Evaluating the council from the perspective of its day—1563, however, it is noteworthy that principles adopted in the sixteenth century have had continuing vitality down into the twentieth century. Furthermore, in an institutional sense, the principles worked.

The closing of the council did, in effect, mark the high water-mark of the Protestant Reformation. There were few noteworthy disaffectations from the church after the council. In addition, many disaffected Catholics returned to the church after the council, due partly to the missionary activities towards Protestants the council fostered. One important concern of orders which affected the council was the matter of religious formation.

Religious Formation

The term *formation* has been applied to describe the process through which a person is socialized to participate in religious life. The term has come into use relatively recently.[3] Its spirit, however, is consistent with traditional religious perspective.

The process of formation is a unique characteristic of Catholic religious life. Reflections on that process—about recruitment, training, and selection into religious life—antedate the existence of Saint Benedict's Rule. Over many centuries, the formation process has been subject to a number of experiments and variations. The knowledge derived from this costly experience is relevant to the operation of the church. It also can be of general benefit to persons concerned with design of diverse voluntary institutions—ranging from community organizations, schools and colleges, to businesses hiring employees. Thus, the ways in which the process evolved and was refined is of considerable importance.

The council recognized that many deficiencies existed in the modes of formation practices in existing communities. These deficiencies rebounded to the general injury of the church. To correct the problems, several principles were pronounced, then legislated into canon law.

All religious professions before the age of sixteen were declared unrecognizable by canon law: The church would not enforce such commitments.[4] The adoption of an age of consent represented a significant institutional decision.

Orders were required to establish central novice houses, or novitiates.[5] In these sites the training of novices would be conducted by a designated, and carefully selected, novice master. The period of novicehood had to last at least a year. (Monastic orders and cloistered sisters were generally exempt from this requirement for the complete segregation of novices. These institutions were traditionally decentralized, and their rules assumed that novices would be trained in the houses where they might spend the rest of their lives.) Novitiates were established to revise the previous situation, where local, decentralized training of individual (or small numbers of) novices in scattered communities was left to coincidence. The defects of this haphazard process were often evident. Thus, a historian of our era summarized the status of a hospital in Paris operated by Augustinian nuns in 1630 as follows: "The nuns had no novitiate. Each newcomer was assigned to an older sister who was quite as much concerned to attach the newcomer to herself as to instruct her in what little she knew of nursing. The result was that the nuns were divided into factions and were relaxed and inefficient."[6] Furthermore, when each community had only a few novices (instead of novices being pooled from several communities), there was insufficient incentive for a community to establish systematic forms of training. Conversely, in a novitiate, the novice master could be someone deliberately selected for his (or her) qualifications. And the creation of a pool of novices meant a more organized curriculum could be developed and tested.

The organization of novitiates also meant that individual novices could be centrally assessed, and their talents compared to those of their peers. A potential system for personnel management was created. Particularly able novices could be identified at early stages by skilled novice masters, offered pertinent training and encouragement, and assigned responsibilities appropriate to their talents. Inept novices might be more deliberately identified by a centralized process, applying formalized criteria; they then might be asked to leave, or provided with constrained assignments. Constrained assignments were often available due to the common order practice of giving members identifiably different statuses. Such differences were often founded on the order's rule. Thus, among some orders of nuns, there were choir sisters and sisters. Choir sisters were particularly responsible for performance of the Office and had the requisite qualifications (e.g., a knowledge of Latin, an appropriate voice). Typically, assigned statuses were accepted by the members as permanent roles.

The centralization of formation that the council decreed did not only apply to order members. A somewhat equivalent process was also provided for secular, or parish, priests. But the relatively high level of structure already existing in religious life made it possible for orders to comply with such formation requirements with greater facility and rigor.

Gradually, the formation process articulated by the council was further elaborated, partly resulting from church decisions and partly because of the policies of individual orders. The process tended to become increasingly prolonged, and the nature of the training more complex. By the twentieth century, in one very rigorous order, the Jesuits, a period of fifteen years would elapse between a candidate's entering the noviate (after graduating high school) and his ordination as a Jesuit priests—the final step in the formation process. One observer, in the first half of this century, estimated that about 60 percent of the Jesuit candidates completed the whole process.[7] The "dropped" candidates either left the order completely or accepted less than full priestly status. (Some members of the order never intended to become priests and were formed through a different, and less demanding, process.) The shift toward prolonged formation was the result of diverse factors. New (and old) orders were increasingly prone to give members assignments remote from their community base. The persons receiving such assignments required more prolonged formation; prolonged formation would provide them with deeply embedded attitudes and values that would persist without frequent reinforcement. An extended formation would also eliminate persons who would not hold up under severe stress. With a selective screening process, which identified able people, it was logical to provide those chosen people with more elaborate formation.

Prolonged formation was also assisted by social and economic change. Training is usually expensive. It removes both trainees and trainers from immediately productive work, such as farming. But, as the general level of affluence rises—as it did over the centuries—more resources became available to underwrite formation costs. The gradual prolongation of the human life span, due to a variety of changes, was an additional cause of attenuation of formation. The longer the average life span, the wiser it is to provide youths with prolonged formation. Training became increasingly prolonged as such formation appeared to "work." Well-formed members were given assignments that subjected them to extraordinary stress—traveling to remote countries, spending their lives in arduous assignments, and confronting strong pressures and temptations. In general, the fealty of such persons has been notable. Thus, the greater the aspirations of many orders, the greater the emphasis they gave to formation.

There were necessarily wide variations among orders in the form and substance of their formation process; the structure of formation was affected by the *work* of particular orders. Still, a general procedure, or model, can be sketched. Formation was typically a multi-stage process. Applicants were first *postulants*—persons requesting admission. They served alongside members of an operating religious community and performed modest chores, to obtain some idea of the nature of religious life. They wore garments which evinced their nonmember status. Postulancy was not required by canon law, but many orders applied this practice. If a potential member wished to persist after postulancy (and the order favored this persistence), he was elevated to novicehood. He was assigned to a novitiate, provided with different, distinctive garments, and given more formal training.

Novices were restricted from having contact with relatives, lay friends, and even professed order members. The training element of formation aimed to help initiates focus on religious matters. There would be frequent Bible readings and discussion, training and readings regarding mental prayer, and classes in theology, church (and order) history, and the rule of the order. Novices might be trained to participate in choir or the performance of the office, and this might obligate them to learn Latin. The novice master would direct great attention to the formation of an appropriate demeanor in novices. This would be discussed in small group meetings and in one-to-one discussions. The whole process was relatively stressful. Novices were frequently called to ask themselves, Is this what I want to do with the rest of my life? Is God calling me? The meditative elements of the formation process further heightened such introspection.

Some idea of the content of formation can be obtained from the following extract from the autobiography of a contemporary former sister. The extract portrays a process that has probably been repeated over many previous centuries:

> While we were novices, classes on psalms began with Mother Superior's painstaking translation from Latin to English as we looked into the ribbonless, stiff, old breviaries we'd been given. Mother told us that each of the 150 psalms occurred every week in the Church's official prayer, the Divine Office. We should apply ourselves to translating and to understanding the psalms, so that we would be able to pray them well when we had the privilege of joining in the office.
>
> "Sisters, let's consider the psalm we have just translated." It was Psalm 139. "The first level of meaning tells of David's cry to God for help against his enemies. The second level of meaning is the Church's prayer to Christ for redemption. Let's look closely at the third level of meaning to see how you can pray these words for yourselves.
>
> "Deliver me, O Lord, from evil men; preserve me from violent men, from those who devise evil in their hearts, and stir up wars every day."
>
> "Who are these violent men? I suppose you think no wicked men are bothering you?"
>
> We laughed hesitantly.

"They are the ungodlike tendencies of your hearts: feelings of rebellion when you're told to stop doing what you're at and go do something else; feelings of self-assertion when you want to be the important one instead of the one who mops floors. These are the violent men. Your soul wants to be at peace with God, content with Him alone. But your evil inclinations stir up daily war in your soul."

The smiles faded awkwardly from our faces.

'They make their tongues sharp as those of serpents; the venom of asps is under their lips.' Through your sinful inclinations Satan whispers that union with God isn't worth the sacrifices. It takes faith, supernatural strength, to repel his suggestions. In the next verses you pray for that strength: 'Save me, O Lord, from the hands of the wicked. . . . O God, my Lord, my strength and my salvation; you are my helmet in the day of battle.'

'Grant not, O Lord, the desires of the wicked; further not their plans; may the mischief which they threaten overwhelm them. May he rain burning coals upon them; may he cast them into the depths never to rise.'

"Sisters, here you ask God to purge your evil inclinations . . . With burning coals!" Mother's eyes burned intensely, as if they themselves were purging gray coals. "If God takes you at your word, He will send you keen sufferings. It takes courage to pray these verses. You could pray just to have the courage to mean these verses.

"Sisters, religious life is a life against nature. Every moment for all our lives we struggle to act supernaturally instead of giving way to our natural inclinations. . . ."[8]

The introspection pervading novicehood was focused by confessors, or spiritual advisors, who were appointed for each novice, plus the supervision of the novice master. It is understandable that order members were disposed to encourage novices to complete their formation and enroll in an order. Still, once enrolled, members (in most countries) had the power to assert their civil law rights and leave without the consent of the order. Furthermore, under canon law members also could make application to leave with the consent of the church. Such requests were infrequent. But both the civil and canon law rights of professed members signified that it was impractical for orders to retain members by coercion. In addition, it was not in the interest of orders to enroll and retain inherently unsympathetic members—they could create great stress for all other members. And, once a member had become professed, it was practically impossible to expel or terminate that member. Thus, orders had strong incentives to use formation as a means of identifying and turning away or redirecting applicants who might enroll and later, after a costly training process, embarrass and distress the order in manifold ways.

It should be recognized that, throughout history, many persons have undoubtedly chosen to enter religious life for partly nonreligious motives—to earn a living, or to undertake a career (such as teaching); in other words, many enrollees had mixed motives. This could be particularly true for persons reared in environments where ecomomic security and career alternatives were limited. A major aim of the formation process was to insure that such possibly undermotivated persons were prepared to be truly committed to religious life. In other words, the process implicitly recognized the mixed motives affecting many novices. Nevertheless, the assumption was that a powerful formation system could either transform or screen out such persons.

Some portion of the time of novices was dedicated to tangible activities such as housekeeping and service responsibilities. Novices were expected to apply themselves to these responsibilities with dedication and enthusiasm. But internal reconstruction was the central aim of formation.

The process could be perceived as subjecting trainees to unnatural stress. A typical novitiate anecdote reveals the potential pettiness of the process:

> One Sunday afternoon I was walking meditatively in the convent yard, close to the laundry on the south side. I noticed that the windows in the laundry offered me a full-length profile of myself. Instead of meditating on heavenly things, I suddenly began admiring the graceful folds in our habit. "Sure is good to be a Dominican," I reflected, and proceeded to rearrange the folds at my left side, then at my right. "Vanity of vanities, and all is vanity!" Somebody's voice jerked me out of my feminine reverie. I twirled around. There stood Sister Frieda, the novitiate sewing instructor. I suddenly felt hot and cold at the same time. I wanted to say something to excuse myself, but no words came.[9]

Still, it is important to recognize that the aim of the formation was exalted: to generate an important human transformation. The following story, from Saint Joan de Chantal's testimony on behalf of the canonization of Saint Francis de Sales, suggests the sorts of self-denial that were its ultimate goal:

> He often gave away his outer clothes, his linen and his shoes; once, as his valet assured me, he even handed out the shoes he was actually wearing. The servant was a eyewitness of this act of charity, and he was also the person responsible for buying the clothes that were given to the poor. And I think that if the Blessed had had charge of his own money he could not have stopped himself from giving it all away. The year after he died two Jesuit Fathers told me that they had met the village schoolmaster of Faucigny who showed them a vest which the Blessed had given him one winter when he was too poor to buy warm clothes. He asked him if he had nothing warmer to wear than what he had on, and when the other said no, the

Blessed went into his little inner room, took off his woollen vest, put on the rest of his clothes again and handed him the garment in a discreet way. This vest is now held in great veneration.[10]

It is also relevant that many religious, in leading their professed lives, had responsibilities that required considerable secular skills—teaching, translating, work in the applied sciences. On the whole, however, the learning of secular skills was treated as subordinate to the process of emotional formation. If a member required schooling to attain those skills, schooling was generally postponed to relatively late in the formation process. The first priority of formation was to identify and shape particular emotional traits; the transmission of cognitive knowledge would come later—if the persons seemed truly committed order members.

In most orders, each stage of progress towards profession was marked by rites of increasing importance. The rites were, in form, rather like the rites of passage often described by anthropologists;[11] they might include music, both choral and instrumental; the public signing of documents; the presence of church and order dignitaries; the abandonment of old garments and the taking on of new ones; the delivery of a sermon on the significance of the ceremony; welcoming gestures or remarks by order members; the pronouncement of oral promises or vows (a vow is a promise to God); and the adoption of a new name by the candidate. On some occasions, family members might be invited to attend. One sister, writing in 1956, described her order's profession rites as follows:

It is difficult to say which is the supreme moment, and to decide where the highlight of the Profession service really is—in the solemn declaration which one makes of one's life-long determination to live for the love of Almighty God alone, and by means of his Grace and to abide steadfast; or when one signs the Community register, using one's secular name for the last time; or when one receives the lighted candle, the symbol of the light of Christ, which after the Mass is over, will be put out and not lighted again until one's death; or the solemn

reception of the cross, the token of consecration to
Christ, the veil, the token of humility and purity
and of service, and the ring, the token of fidelity; or
the sevenfold blessing which the Bishop gives to
oneself alone.

Perhaps it is none of these things, nor even in the
Profession service as such itself, but in the act of
Communion, when one abides one's poor oblation in
His all-perfect Offering.

I know at every Profession that I have witnessed, I
always think (and most other Sisters feel the same)
what a truly "aweful" thing it is to be a Superior.
For at the end of a Profession, the Bishop
commends the newly-Professed Sister to the
Superior in these words: "To your loving care I
commend this our Sister. See that you watch for
her soul as one that must give account thereof in
the day of Judgment."[12]

(The bishop's charge to the superior is directly derived from
Saint Benedict's Rule.)

It is easy to identify certain traits that might be
maximized through formation—either the process would cause
participants to learn them, or persons lacking such traits would
tend to be screened out. Obedience would obviously be
important. Also tact, interpersonal judgment, industriousness,
loyalty, introversion, a disposition to accept the consequences of
one's conduct, charity, and foresight. Conversely, one can
imagine traits that would be suppressed by the process:
spontaneity, lassitude, direct assertiveness, selfishness,
individualism, acquisitiveness, and dispositions towards personal
(nonsexual) intimacy. One would assume also that traditional
religious orders, comprising persons who exhibit the former list
of maximized traits, would, as institutions, tend to display a
similar style of operational activities.

It is instructive to contrast some elements of the
formation process with the techniques now prevailing in

American formal education at the high school and college level. In particular, formation is aimed at a relatively clear goal: a particular vocation the candidate is considering. Novices are encouraged to deliberately decide whether they want to complete the process, and "graduate" into their order. The persons managing the process are already involved in that vocation: they are essentially order members who incidentally have been assigned responsibilities relating to formation. The cohort of novices undergoing formation may well have future relationships with each other as order members. Conversely, in American education, students are usually trained for relatively generalized and diffuse roles. The assumption, in both high school and college, is that it is proper and good for all students to graduate—it is rarely officially admitted that some students should drop out. The persons conducting the teaching of students are almost always professional educators, rather than to people who work in the fields the graduates will enter. Many educators will never see their "products" again. And American students may never see each other after graduation.

These contrasts give some idea of how and why the process could be so much more powerful (as a mode of formation) than the process typically provided by modern education. Formation managers have a greater incentive than teachers and professors to shape their charges. They have a better idea of what is ultimately required for novices to carry out their desired vocation than educators have about their pupils' after-graduation work. Novices have a relatively clear idea of what they want to learn: how to be good members of the X order, as compared to being "simply" effective adults. And it is much more legitimate for a novice to decide he does not want to profess than it is for a student to drop out of college or high school; due to this legitimacy, the energies of persons being formed are not sapped by the confusions and ambivalence of uncommitted peers. The fact that novices will (or may) have lifelong relationships with each other, and with their trainers, also makes relationships developed during formation more profound and justifies giving greater attention to them.

In sum, professed traditional religious usually have acquired more coherent images of themselves than contemporary students of equivalent ages. This generalization can be fleshed out by an anecdote told me by a colleague writing a history of an order of Catholic teaching sisters in America. In interviewing some of the older sisters, he was amazed at the equanimity they displayed in reciting their early teaching experiences, where—at the age of perhaps twenty, with no more than a high school degree—they were assigned after profession to teach elementary classes of fifty to sixty children. The sisters recalled that, all things considered, the classes went relatively smoothly, though the work was arduous. Both my historian friend and I attributed the sisters' classroom efficacy partly to their powerful formation process. It enabled them to carry out potentially stressful roles with great confidence and determination. Furthermore, while their training had focused on the exercise of authority over them, it had simultaneously provided them with clear examples of how to exercise efficacious authority over others; such examples can be very helpful to people engaged in teaching.

Another friend told me of one of his experiences in attending, during the 1930s, a Catholic-parish elementary school in New York City staffed by an order of sisters. One particular sister had a habit of occasionally leaving the class, putting students "on their honor" not to talk during her absence. When the sister returned she would usually ask any students who had talked during her absence to stand up to confess. There were always a few violators, and most of them did stand up; then they received moderate, but unpleasant, punishments. My friend, in recollecting the experience, remarked that the sister probably intended to teach her students to (a) be obedient; (b) tell the truth in the face of temptation; (c) accept deserved punishment with dignity; and (d) to return to full participation in the community after being punished. My friend felt that his teacher had given him a valuable lesson.

Philosophical Premises of Formation

There are evident philosophical premises underlying formation which deserve explicit attention, although such attention is rarely articulated in Church documents. Formation places great stress on obedience and determination. Yet, as we will see, members after profession were often given assignments that required them to display considerable adaptability. It seems incongruous that persons completing such a constraining socialization would be prepared to operate in novel situations with the necessary degree of adaptability or creativity. Indeed, it may be said that the church, as a human institution designed to operate under stress, gives greater priority to strength of will, compared to flexibility and creativity. One can identify some causes for this disposition.

The Protestant Reformation was the most severe blow ever received by the institutional church. To the extent that the church can be blamed for the Reformation, its basic fault was in failing to carry out its own expressed principles. If the Church had done essentially what its doctrines said it should do, there might not have been a Reformation. Thus, the Reformation taught the church the repercussions that could flow from lack of fidelity to evident doctrine. It also demonstrated the enormous temptations to stray from doctrine which surrounds clerics, religious, and the church hierarchy. Thus, the Tridentine spirit rated the virtue of creativity of secondary importance. It held that constancy to doctrine was central to institutional efficacy and growth.

But the post-Tridentine church was a militant institution. Part of that militancy was defensive: it desired to reattain what it had, and reacquire the status lost in many Protestantized areas of Europe. Coincidentally, the spirit of militancy coincided with the European age of discovery, exploration, and colonization. As a result, this domestic militancy also favored the extension of Catholicism into the newly discovered areas. Some of these themes are expressed in a letter written in 1646, by Saint Vincent de Paul to a member of the Catholic hierarchy:

> I must confess I have, I think, a great affection and devotion for the propagation of the Church in infidel lands, which arises from the fear I entertain that God may gradually bring her to naught in Europe and that little or nothing may remain of her here in a hundred years' time, on account of the corruption of our morals, the new opinions which are

spreading more and more, and the general state of public affairs. In the last hundred years, the Church has lost, through two new heresies, the greater part of the Empire and the Kingdoms of Sweden, Denmark, Norway, Scotland, England, Ireland, Bohemia, and Hungary, so that only Italy, France, Spain, and Poland now remain to her, and there are many heresies both in France and Poland. Now, these losses of the Church during the last hundred years give us reason to fear that, in another hundred years, the Church in Europe may be totally lost and, bearing this fear in mind, blessed are those who can cooperate in the extension of the Church in other lands.[13]

Ironically, the patterns of both European (or domestic) and non-European militancy required orders and order members to display extraordinary adaptability and creativity. When institutions engage in successful expansion, they must adopt modes of operation different from the means applied in static situations; they must, for example, learn new languages, analyze foreign cultures, devise extraordinary procedures. As we will see, the expansion efforts were relatively successful; thus, we have a paradox: an institution stressing obedience and relative dogmatism, but simultaneously displaying considerable adaptability.

This dichotomy invites further analysis. Dogmatic institutions that act in militant (and aggressive) fashions will be gradually forced to learn from circumstances and adapt. Thus, we have persons such as Saint Vincent de Paul and Saint Ignatius Loyola (1491-1556), both of whom meticulously refined particularly novel approaches to organizational problems in religious life. Loyola circulated draft versions of the proposed Jesuit constitution to Order members for ten years before submitting the final versions for approval. And de Paul observed, "Those who rush defeat the demands of God."[14] And yet, these saints coupled patience with a persistence in engagement. In the end, they helped develop institutions or plans that were both novel and viable.

Such constructive effects require that dogmatism be integrated with a determination to affect events. Without such a determination, an institution and its leaders may simply drift into stagnation or isolation. The alternative institutional combinations we are considering can be easily characterized.

High dogmatism/low assertive institutions might be monasteries. Low dogmatism/low assertive institutions could be like communes. High assertiveness/low dogmatism institutions might be undoctrinaire, militantly reformist, semi-utopian institutions (perhaps like some aggressive anarchist party). High dogmatism/high assertiveness might be found in rigorous and often efficacious institutions, such as some religious orders. Each alternative in institutional form has certain elements of instability. Thus, the quiescence of monasteries gives them low visibility and recruiting capability. Their dogmatism, however, has a certain staying power. High dogmatism/high assertiveness institutions have considerable potency. But they make great demands on members. It is, simply, hard for an institution to stay at the necessary intensity for long periods of time: to keep recruiting the proper people, and providing them with appropriate formation.

These considerations have important implications for the development of creative policies in major institutions—like the church. There is an assumption that creativity is encouraged in relatively flexible environments. And one can see some truth in that. But creative achievements—when they are implemented—may ultimately be more substantial in relatively stable environments. Such environments provide resources for implementing new ideas, as well as pools of critics and refiners to improve the quality of the original proposals. We all know, however, that stable institutions can also act to suppress novel ideas—both for good and bad reasons. The institutional challenge is to develop relatively stable environments where creative ideas can receive at least balanced consideration. For some forms of activities, and in some periods of history, the church appears to have met this challenge.

A highly creative era in the history of religious life occurred between about 1500 and 1725. One way of describing the religious activities of this period is to calculate the comparative rates of the formation of new orders. This comparison might serve to measure changing rates of "religious activism." But the meaning of such a measure would be ambiguous. During early church history, most religious were either males or females living in communities that applied one or another interpretation of Saint Benedict's Rule. Their monasteries (or convents) were all "counted" as affiliated with one or another of a few specific orders (e.g., the Cisterians, the Benedictines). In later periods, after about 1500, groupings of religious tended more to form separate orders, with distinct missions. Furthermore, the rate of new order formation could be affected simply by changes in the absolute number of church members in different eras. Still, comparatively high rates of order formation do mean that diverse religious institutions are being founded, often with original missions. The data disclose that twice as many religious orders were formed during the seventeenth century than during any other century from the beginning of Catholicism through the eighteenth century.[15] And many original activities were carried out by these orders. There are two evident ways of briefly describing and analyzing such developments: we can identify the principal persons associated with these measures and describe their activities, or we can select particular thematic activities and identify the persons and orders carrying out these themes. Each approach has evident virtues and limitations. My treatment will focus on the prominent persons concerned, and identify important thematic elements whenever appropriate.

Pairs of Saints

Male and female order founders—or order reformers—often acted in concert, and coordinated their mutual efforts. A first precedent for this were the efforts of Saint Benedict and his sister, Saint Scholastica. Saint Scholastica, according to Pope Gregory, founded a convent applying the principles articulated by St. Benedict in his rule.

Many religious leaders of the era demonstrated a similar propensity towards coordination. Undoubtedly, such cooperation enabled each party to benefit from the other's help, and to provide each other with unique insights. One pair of reformers was Saint Teresa of Avila (1515-1582)[16] and Saint John of the Cross (1542-1591).[17] They were both members of the Carmelite order. The Carmelites evolved from a colony of male Christian hermits who lived about Mt. Carmel, near Jerusalem. In about 1247, after the decline of the Crusades, members of the community became refugees in Western Europe. In Europe, they governed themselves according to the Albertine Rule, which expressed principles for the management of a rigorous, semihermetic community.[18] Eventually, a female Carmelite order evolved as a counterpart of the male communities.

Saint Teresa was a member of a Spanish Carmelite community. Gradually, she became distressed at the relatively low level of religious rigor practiced in her community. She ultimately became the leader of a movement to reform her community, and later her order. Her efforts were partly triggered by her strong personal mystical devotion to Christian themes, which she expressed in significant writings, and partly assisted by her noteworthy common sense and *energy*.[19] Saint John was also Spanish, and a member of the counterpart male Carmelite order. He was likewise a notable mystic and reformer.[20] Both Saints, individually, and acting in consort, faced great resistance in stimulating reform, rigor, and withdrawal in their respective congregations. Saint John was even imprisoned by the Spanish Inquisition for a time. Teresa's considerable practical insights are revealed in the texts of hundreds of her letters generated by her activities. One typical letter was written to a priest assisting in her reform efforts. It described some of her activities directed towards reforming a particular community:

> The sisters here moved into their new house on the Feast of the Immaculate Conception. The move was accompanied by great rejoicings. There was a procession with the Most Holy Sacrament, which was brought from the other house. The nuns were very happy: they looked just like little lizards coming out into the sunshine in summer. They had certainly suffered a great deal in the other house; and, though nothing whatever is finished here

beyond eleven cells, they have ample living room
for many years even if nothing more is done.

Oh, my Father! How badly I was needed here,
both for the transference of the nuns—they would
never have got in so soon without me—and for
other reasons. God, of course, could have freed
them, but I cannot myself see what other means
there was of getting them away from that
atmosphere. The nuns have realized now how
foolishly they had been behaving; and, the more I
learn of the way the nun who was here governed
the house, the more decided I am that it would be a
very rash thing to give her any office again. The
poor Licentiate [the priest monitoring the convent]
seems to me a real servant of God, and I think he
is the person least to blame. He listens very
seriously to all I tell him about what must be done
here, and his humility and regret at having been
the partial cause of the trouble have left me greatly
edified. . . .

In some ways I allowed them too much freedom,
and we ought not to have put so much trust—or
any trust at all—in people who are so young,
however holy they were, for, when people have no
experience, they will work great havoc, even with
the best intentions. We must take things in hand,
my Father, from now onward. I hope in Our Lord
that everything will be all right now, for the
Prioress we have brought here is a very God-
fearing and sensible person, and so skillful in ruling
the nuns that they have all grown very fond of
her.[21]

Saints Teresa and John were identified with the Discalced
(or shoeless) Carmelites, who signified their commitment to the
"primitive" rule by refusing to wear shoes (they either went
barefoot or wore sandals). The history of the various divisions
of the Carmelites provides a striking—but not entirely
novel—instance of the divisions and subdivisions which occurred

over the centuries in some orders. Figure 1 is a diagrammatic history of these variations. Note that only three Carmelite orders now survive: the original Carmelites (ultimately called the Calced Carmelites); the Discalced, founded by Saints Teresa and John of the Cross (both with male and female branches); and an order of French nuns, related to the Discalced Friars.[22]

SOME MOVEMENTS OF RENEWAL IN THE CARMELITE FAMILY FROM THE XVth TO THE XVIIIth CENTURIES

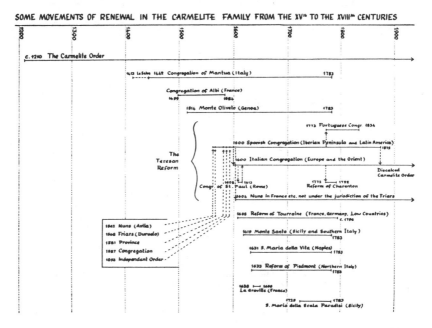

Figure 1. Some Movements of Renewal in the Carmelite Family from the XVth to the XVIIIth Centuries

Some of the spirit of purity and reformism which has affected the Discalced Carmelites is suggested in a brief poem written by a twentieth—century Discalced sister in praise of the primitive tradition:

> Oh! oh! happy Carmel,
> Beware; for the fox
> Painstaking and cunning,
> Is trying to destroy your peace.
>
> Have your eyes about you.
> Be on the watch,

And call to keep guard with you
Theresa and Albert.[23]

Figure 2 portrays the legislative history of the Carmelite order and its components. The original Albertine Rule and the mitigated Rule of Innocent IV apply to all branches of the Carmelites. But, over seven centuries, innumerable revisions and variations due to circumstances have moderated and elaborated the Rules.[24]

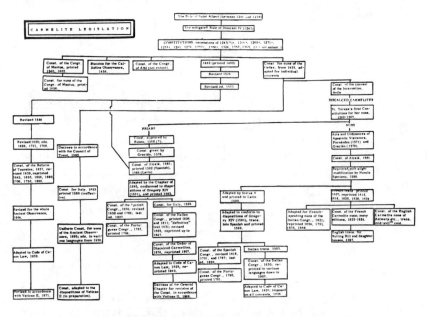

Figure 2. Carmelite Legislation

Another pair of order founders were Saint Francis de Sales (1567-1642)[25] and Saint Joan de Chantal (1572-1641).[26] Saint Francis was the Catholic bishop of Geneva, Switzerland, and a noteworthy preacher, writer, and pastoral leader. In 1604, he became the confessor of Saint Joan, who at that time was a widowed mother and a devout woman. Saint Joan's religious disposition was heightened by the example of Saint Francis. After his death, she offered the following testimony on behalf of his canonization.

I once asked him if he ever went any length of time without actually and explicitly turning his mind to God, and he said "Sometimes for as long as a quarter of an hour." [Saint Joan, in her recital, also quoted] the story of a priest who admired St. Francis' meekness and kindness. The priest said, "At one time, when I was severely ill, my most comforting thought had been how clearly God's infinite goodness was reflected in the Bishop; for if a man can be so good, how good you must be, O my loving Creator, how sweet and gracious!"[27]

Following the counsel of Saint Francis, Saint Joan decided to form an order of women dedicated to prayer and works of mercy towards the poor and sick. Such an activity would be highly consonant with Saint Francis's principle that evangelization came first from the practice of charity. The plans for the proposed order were very original. They violated the then prevailing norm of claustration (which the church applied at that time to all orders of women). Eventually, the Order of the Visitation of Holy Mary was formed under Saint Joan's leadership. But in 1613, shortly after its commencement, it was compelled (by the local bishop overseeing its foundation) to accept a Rule that required its members to remain cloistered. The order persisted. By Saint Joan's death, it had eighty houses, and it still persists in our day.[28] But it has remained a cloistered order.

Yet another pair of order founders were Saint Vincent de Paul (1581-1660),[29] and Saint Louise de Marillac (1591-1660).[30] Saint Vincent led a long, colorful, and productive life. He was a French priest who was captured by Barbary pirates in the Mediterranean, was sold as a slave in North Africa, converted his master to Christianity and escaped with him to France, became the chaplin for prisoners assigned as oarsmen in the French galley fleet, went to Paris and organized innumerable charitable and Church reformation activities, formed the Ladies of Charity (a national Catholic laywomen's organization to carry out charitable activities), and eventually worked with Saint Louise to establish the Daughters of Charity, the first noncloistered order of women—which he consistently denied was to ever be an order.

212 Traditional Catholic Religious Orders

Saint Vincent also founded the Congregation of the Missions, a male order. Its initial principal work was conducting evangelistic activities in the French countryside, where the shortage (and low quality) of parish priests deprived rural areas of church support. His priests travelled among villages, administered the sacraments, and conducted well-organized programs of religious instruction and preaching. During summers, when peasants were occupied in farming activities, the order members studied and prayed at a central residence. As the order enlarged, the scope of its activities became extremely varied. By Saint Vincent's death, it had 500 members.[31]

A central theme of Saint Vincent's approaches was the personal element of charitable help. Many occasions arose when he vigorously solicited money and other resources for different causes. But, whenever possible, he coupled such pleas with requests for direct, personal aid from benefactors. Thus, some members of the Ladies of Charity were women of noble status. The issue arose whether they should be exempted from the organization's rule which required members to provide direct service to poor persons—prepare meals, carry them to homes, and serve them to sick people. Saint Vincent wrote the following to the woman serving as director:

> If you now relieve each one of the duty of having the food cooked, you will never be able to impose this rule in future. And if some of them undertake to pay to have it cooked elsewhere, after a while you will find them demurring at the cost. And if you yourself pay money to have it cooked, how much is it going to cost you? Then, too, after a while we will have the Ladies of Charity saying that the soup should be carried to the poor by the women they get to make it, and in this way the Charity will fail.[32]

Saints Vincent and Louise worked to form the Daughters to provide a pool of young women, from low-income backgrounds, to work alongside of the upper-class Ladies. Vincent suspected that if the Daughters ever became a formal religious order, they would be compelled to accept claustration (as happened to Saint Joan de Chantal). Thus, he constantly told the Daughters they were not a religious order, only a quasi-religious body. But the pressure of practical circumstances, and the entreaties of the church, eventually led the Daughters to form an organization that was essentially an order—but an order that was expected to work in the world, outside of the cloister. By the time of the deaths of Saints Vincent and Louise, there were forty houses of the Daughters in France. In 1963, the community had 2,900 houses throughout the world.[33] In addition, a number of other orders of sisters later were formed, explicitly calling themselves "of Charity" (e.g., Sisters of Charity of Halifax), and applying the Rule first developed for the Daughters.

Varieties of Religious Missions

The activities of Saint Vincent and the Daughters of Charity remind us of the important role religious communities have played in diverse charitable activities throughout the world. This role began with the first monastic communities. Monasteries were expected to show hospitality to travellers and distribute food to beggars and poor persons. Later, orders such as the Hospitalers provided shelter, protection, and hospital services to Holy Land pilgrims remote from their homelands.

The early charitable activities of religious orders were broadened, partly in response to innumerable social and economic changes in Western Europe. Those changes included intensifying urbanization and the increasing efficiency of transportation and central government. Due to such changes, social problems were concentrated in particular areas, and it also became easy to shift help or resources to remote afflicted persons or communities. Over a long period of time, an elaborate network of religious orders arose that dedicated themselves to providing such assistance, transmitting aid from more affluent Catholics to more needy ones. Some sense of the activities of these orders is provided by the following words of encouragement Saint Vincent de Paul addressed to his female lay associates in 1653:

It is now twenty years since God gave you, ladies, the grace to undertake and maintain many works: the feeding and instruction of the poor at the H ô tel-Dieu, the board and education of foundlings, the care of providing for the bodily and spiritual needs of the *galeiens*, the aid you sent to remote and war-torn provinces, besides all you have contributed to the missions throughout the country. These, ladies, are the works of your society. Imagine women doing all that! . . . The Brother who distributes your alms said to me, "Monsieur Vincent, the wheat sent to the faraway provinces saved many lives; many families had not a grain to sow; no one would lend them any; the land lay fallow and the countryside was deserted because of the death or departure of the people who lived there." In one year alone as much as 22,000 *livres* has been expended on seed corn, giving these poor country people work during summer and food for the winter. You see, ladies, by the good accomplished what a great misfortune it would be if you were to give up the work you *began.*[34]

The orders that gradually evolved provided much of the aid to the needy, afflicted, and young, which is supplied in our day by social workers, psychologists, counsellors, welfare workers, teachers, nurses, hospital administrators, youth workers, and community organizers. The final outcome of these helping patterns is suggested by the description of a religious vocations exhibit sponsored by the Catholic church in London in 1965. The exhibit included presentations of 57 male and 140 female religious communities active in Great Britain. A vast number of community missions, or works, were articulated at the exhibit.[35] These included:

1. The evangelization of Africa
2. Contemplatives intent on prayer and sacred study
3. Keeping alive the faith of Italians by means of spiritual and social assistance

4. To serve Mary and spread devotion to her Seven Sorrows
5. The Christine education of girls of all types in schools and apostolic work connected with it
6. The practice of Christian charity towards the sick
7. To provide a religious life for girls wishing to care for and educate children from birth to seven years of age
8. To promote the glory of God and the sanctification of our members through the care of the sick in hospitals and homes for convalescents
9. Conducting approved schools for delinquent boys
10. Sharing the social conditions and manual work of the poor
11. To act as a living link between the church and the Jewish people

There were certain drawbacks and virtues to the assumption of such responsibilities by religious communities.[36]

The order members often were partly motivated by their desire to convert those they helped to active Catholicism. The degree of pressure exerted to attain this end varied widely. Still, even among the most minimalist religious who provided help, the goal of evangelization was still greater than if the helping activity was purely secular. (Some persons may conclude that coupling efforts at proselytization with helping activities may corrode the quality of the helping provided.) The level of help supplied to the poor by these orders was usually less than that available in our era—although the lower level was partly due to the generally lower level of economic resources in earlier periods of history. The help was often structured in a relatively nonprofessional framework: it was not shaped by principles of "scientific" psychology, nor evaluated by formal academic criteria. And the helpers themselves often had only modest academic training.

As to virtues, the persons helping were usually strongly motivated to produce beneficial effects: The formation process tended to graduate dedicated, self-disciplined order members. Furthermore, the religious framework of the helpers signified that they did not view it as essential that their efforts generate tangible, beneficial effects in the here-and-now. This made the helpers less vulnerable to burnout, which is typically generated by the gap between tangible goals and aspirations (but religious goals were partly intangible). The religious values underlying the help also provided a base of ideological harmony between givers—who might be either religious or laypersons—and most receivers. They were all part of the same community of believers, and all possessed a certain basic equality before God. The fact that they had different economic statuses was comparatively irrelevant according to religious criteria: Saint Benedict's Rule, for instance, even talked about how we should be grateful to sick persons, who provide us with occasions to practice charity.

Another important way of characterizing the nature of religious help is to recognize its stress on the themes of charity and mercy. Indeed, two important orders of women were called the Sisters of Charity, and the Sisters of Mercy (and many local or regional orders—which later became international—adopted that appellation). Both *charity* and *mercy* stress the obligations of the giver, a person whose status is implicitly superior to that of the receiver. Charity and mercy are voluntary acts, based on an essentially supernatural obligation. We can contrast this focus on the voluntary donations to the more modern emphasis on the rights of receivers to "fairness," and other forms of redistributive justice. Mercy and charity presume a nonadversarial relationship between givers and receivers. They cast the process of providing help as a non-zero sum activity: the donors benefited through earning grace and recognition from God, and donees received various forms of material help--plus the religious message transmitted by the donors. In modern fairness situations, the circumstances become more zero sum: the persons asserting their rights to economic justice say, "You have something that is mine. I want it from you, and you should surrender this thing to me." At best, the person who is taxed (or otherwise pressured) to help the poor can say that his semicoerced tax or contribution has fostered "justice."

Psychologically speaking, however, it seems far less gratifying to pay a compulsory tax than to voluntarily contribute to support the charities maintained by evidently dedicated religious and initiated by conspicuously virtuous saints.

It is at least arguable that the philosophy underlying the help provided by orders—with its strong stress on personal responsibility, gratitude, and obedience—provided very beneficial motivation for many receivers (the persons helped). The morale of the receivers may have been helped by the knowledge that the religious helping them were motivated by their desire to serve others, as compared to earning their livings. Finally, it is an open question whether there really are sciences of social work, teaching, or nursing. Undoubtedly, there are bodies of knowledge that can be useful to persons carrying out such work. But it is inaccurate to characterize most of such knowledge as science. The characterization may even engender serious and counterproductive misconceptions. Thus, the traditional hostility of some religious communities to "scientificizing" their work may oftentimes have been well advised.

Some sense of the help provided by religious is transmitted by the *Practical Rules* developed by Saint John Eudes (1601-1680). Among his many other activities on behalf of the Church, he founded the Order of the Good Shepherd, a religious community of women, to provide care, instruction, and counsel for delinquent girls and young women. His advice to order members (in the *Practical Rules*) on how to manage their charges is much in keeping with the spirit of the traditional formation process:

> Speak little and punish rarely. Win the children by manners contrary to which they have been accustomed in the past. It is best to treat the rudest of these poor children with the finest consideration and the greatest delicacy. Spare them anything that would excite them to impatience or dishearten them.

Proud persons have a great repugnance to asking pardon. It is often better not to oblige them to do it. The slightest show of contempt drives such persons to revolt. Public reprimands are generally unprofitable. These children are more easily touched by being shown that their faults render their good qualities useless.

Authority is a certain air, a certain ascendancy which commands respect; it is neither age nor stature nor tone of voice, but a character of the mind, equal, firm, always self-possessed, guided by reason, never acting by caprice of passion. Do not expose yourself to being disobeyed or treated with disrespect. Observe your children, learn from each of them. Each class, as well as each individual, has a peculiar character which should be observed and studied.[37]

The degree of proselytization of receivers practiced during such helping activities varied widely. But, even when the level of explicit preaching was low, certain inevitable messages were communicated. The order members wore distinctive costumes. They often made routine references to God and prayer as sources of help and consolation. Facilities were naturally made available for persons helped to attend Mass, or receive sacraments. The persons helped were invited to offer prayers of thanksgiving to the donors. (Failure to invite such prayers would imply that poor people were incapable of offering efficacious prayer, an assumption in conflict with doctrine.) And, most importantly, if order members did display exemplary commitment and efficiency, those helped would be prone to respect and admire their religious values.

As the number and variety of orders increased, the discrepancy between the number of male and female orders became more apparent. Thus, a tabulation of all Catholic orders—most of which were formed after the sixteenth century—discloses that 79 percent of those orders were for females.[38] This notable imbalance invites some discussion.

One cause of the imbalance is that there have simply been many more female than male order members. In part this is because being a religious is the only formal role open for females in the church. Males, however, can also serve as diocesan priests. And, partly, there has probably always been an imbalance of females (compared to males) formally affiliated with the Church. Perhaps this imbalance has been due, to a degree, to the limited number of effective roles for unmarried females in the secular world. There is also an evident disposition for women's orders to be more local than those for men. As a result, the typical female order is somewhat smaller than the typical male order. Thus, we have orders such as the Dominican Sisters of Edmonds, Washington, or the Franciscan Sisters of Mill Hill (Maryland). (In 1965, each of these orders comprised about 200 members.)[39] Still, we must recognize that even apparently locally focused order's names often are simultaneously associated with remote communities, created in locations thousands of miles away. These communities have spread from their home base through varied serendipitous circumstances. For instance, the Franciscan Sisters of Mill Hill also maintain two missions in Natal, Africa. There are also some male orders with equivalent geographic limitations, but there are simply more such female orders. Perhaps this pattern has developed partly because women have been less geographically mobile then men. Thus, they are attracted to their own, indigenous orders, as compared to moving out to establish new orders, or forming local religious communities as subunits of geographically dispersed orders. It may also be that there is some psychological disposition of females to prefer association with independent, proximate, and more intimate communities, as compared to being associated in larger, hierarchal, more formal institutions.

The development of significant external work for religious orders affected the patterns of recruitment into religious life. Undoubtedly, the typical hospital sister or teaching brother differed somewhat in temperament from religious living in enclosed orders, who spent most of their time in prayer, meditation, and performing the office. As it were, the total membership of all religious orders in 1650 comprised a different mix of persons than in 1100. It is even possible that the change in the nature of religious activities increased the size of the potential recruit pool: The proportion of potentially meditative persons in a society is less than that of semi-extroverts. Or, alternatively, perhaps the Middle Ages worked so as to produce young adults who were more like monks, while modernized Europe produced more active types of potential order recruits.

Other Founders

The Jesuits—the Society of Jesus—was probably the most significant order founded in the era. They were an order for men, and their founder was Saint Ignatius Loyola (1491-1556).[40] He was a Spanish nobleman and military officer. At the age of thirty he was hospitalized for about a year, for treatment of a painful battle injury. During this period he read religious literature and speculated about dedicating his life to religious service. After he recovered from his injury, he spent many months in meditation and gradually assembled a small number of like-spirited, devout companions. The group determined that they might serve the church better by further (and higher) education. They successively attended several institutions and eventually completed their studies in Paris (Ignatius commenced his Paris studies at about the age of forty). While engaged in their studies, and afterwards, the group sought to identify an appropriate work for themselves and to develop into a formal religious community. Several experiments were attempted: the development of a parallel women's community; travelling to the Holy Land to convert the Muslims; and conducting hospitals and equivalent activities. Eventually, the group identified a diversity of unique priorities: taking a direct oath of fealty to the pope (in addition to the three traditional vows), and concentrating their work on upper-level education (high school and college) and missionary activities. Saint Ignatius played the central role in designing the proposed order, although he assiduously sought the counsel of his associates. At the death of Saint Ignatius, the Order had 930 members; by 1565, it had 3,500; and in 1629, it had 15,500.[41]

To permit the order to pursue its determined priorities, its structure included novel elements of design. The order relied on an extraordinarily long period of formation. Before profession members received elaborate socialization plus formal academic training (and were carefully evaluated before full admission). The provisions of the order's constitution reserved preponderent authority to senior and better-trained members. These persons—perhaps 5 to 10 percent of the order's members—had perhaps 70 to 80 percent of the authority. The superior general of the order is elected for life, and holds a high level of central authority. Since the founding of the order, the average term of the superior general has been eleven years—which suggests a relatively high level of administrative stability.[42]

The matter of community life was also treated in an original fashion. Until the formation of the Jesuits, order members had essentially lived in groups, or communities. Such groupings were seen as desirable in themselves and furthermore fostered the performance of Divine Office. As nonmonastic orders began to develop, adaptations were essayed, and the requirements of saying the Office were moderated. Still, the themes of group life and the performance of some form of the office was maintained. Jesuit rules, however, did not require group life, the wearing of distinctive garments, or the performance of the office (although all of these things were usually permissible, and often done). But there was still a uniform obligation of daily, substantial, structured mental prayer. The prayers were a series of meditational exercises developed and composed by Saint Ignatius. The exercises displayed his considerable spiritual and psychological insight and were adaptable to the need of persons living and working in environments unsympathetic to spiritual life. In effect, the exercises signified both continuity and change: certain patterns stayed the same, since each Jesuit still engaged in significant, structured daily prayer, as other order members had for centuries; certain patterns changed, since these prayers were designed to be routinely recited in privacy and silence. The form of these exercises had an important influence on the practice of mental prayer in Catholic life, both by priests and even persons in secular life.

It was evident the structure that evolved for the order was partly influenced by Saint Ignatius's military background. Members were expected to accept many constraints and extraordinary discipline. They were simultaneously subject to rigorous academic training, and oftentimes finally given assignments that required them to display considerable independence, creativity, and flexibility. For example, for many years (1620-1666) a group of Jesuits served as scientific advisors to the emperor of China (partly with the eventual aim of persuading the emperor to adopt Catholicism as the official state religion). They translated European works into Chinese, wrote original works in Chinese, developed a revised calendar, and provided advice about metallurgy. Undoubtedly, one reason for the order's adaptability was its rigorous and attenuated formation process, and its careful screening procedures.

The secondary schools and colleges conducted by the Jesuits were deliberately designed to instruct pupils who would assume influential roles in adult society. The schools did not engage in vigorous proselytization and were open to non-Catholics. Some sense of the efficacy of such schools is suggested by the experience of Voltaire (1694-1778), who was educated in a Jesuit school from the age of ten until seventeen. Later in life he was an active anticlerical. Still, he continued to hold great affection for his Jesuit teachers. Nineteen years after leaving school, he sent a copy of a book he had written back to one of his masters, with the following remarks:

> If you still remember a man who will remember you all of his life with the most tender gratitude and highest possible esteem, receive this work with some indulgence, and regard me as a son who, after many years, comes to present his father the fruits of his labor in an art which he learned from him.[43]

The deliberately noncommunal element of the Jesuits made order members easily available for remote assignments, and their expressed fealty to the pope provoked them to adopt an international perspective. Their training also provided them with a broad knowledge of languages. Thus they were often assigned diverse diplomatic responsibilities, on behalf of the papacy, or of governments aligned with Catholic interests. Gradually, the success of the Jesuits provoked a form of intra-Church polarization. Some secular "Catholic" governments, or factions in such governments, became hostile to policies favored by the Jesuits on domestic and international issues. Furthermore, different orders found diverse reasons to oppose Jesuit policies—as the Jesuits opposed theirs. The term *Jesuitical* sometimes came to connote a distorted form of casuistry. A feeling for the hostility engendered toward the Jesuits, their conduct, and responsibilities can be had in the words of an English Protestant archbishop, uttered in 1694: "No religion that I know in all the world has ever had such lewd and scandalous casuists. Their main business seems to be, not to keep men from sinning, but to teach them how near they might lawfully come, without sinning."[44]

Undoubtedly, such criticisms could be applied to some of the tactics of the Jesuits—as well as the tactics of other orders engaged in practical affairs, and to many nonreligious secular agencies. Whether the Jesuits engaged in more casuistry than other orders or agencies accepting equivalent responsibilities is a difficult question. But it is probably true that the Jesuits were assigned (or accepted) more gray-area responsibilities on behalf of the church than other orders and carried out many such assignments with dedication.

Another significant order formed during the era was the Brothers of Christian Schools, founded by Saint John Baptist de la Salle (1651-1719).[45] La Salle, an ordained priest, became concerned with the problems of organizing and conducting charity schools for boys and adolescent males. Gradually, he gathered around himself a group of like-minded men and worked at developing a religious order dedicated to this activity. La Salle determined that these schools should not aim to transmit a classical education—in this particular, he wanted to distinguish them from the schools conducted by orders like the Jesuits. His secondary instruction would focus on practical affairs, such as prose writing in the vernacular, and bookkeeping. He stressed that material should be transmitted in conjunction with a strong emphasis on religion and character-related themes. At La Salle's death, the order had 270 members; in 1960, 16,300 members.[46] The spirit of La Salle's educational philosophy is suggested by some quotations from the *Directions for the Conduct of Schools*, which he drafted for his order:

The teachers should take care that the pupils bring with them every day their breakfast and lunch, and, without obliging them to do so, a little basket will be placed in an appointed place in the classroom, into which the children, when they are so piously inclined, may put what bread they have left over to be distributed among those of them who are poor. The teacher will see that they do not give away any of their bread unless they have enough left for themselves. Those who have bread to give will raise their hands, showing at the same time the piece of bread which they have to give, and a pupil who has been appointed to receive these alms will go to get them. At the end of the meal, the teachers will distribute the bread to the poorest and will exhort them to pray to God for their benefactors. . . .

From time to time, the teachers will give rewards to those of their pupils who are the most exact in fulfilling their duties, in order to incite them to do so with pleasure and to stimulate the others by the hope of the reward.

There are three kinds of rewards which will be given in the schools : First, rewards for piety. Second, rewards for ability. Third, rewards of assiduity.

The rewards for piety will always be more beautiful than the others, and the rewards for assiduity better than those for ability. . . .

Experience, founded on the unvarying teachings of the saints and the examples which they have set us, affords sufficient proof that, to perfect those who are committed to our care, we must act toward them in a manner at the same time both gentle and firm. Many, however, are obliged to admit, or at least they show by the manner in which they behave toward those in their care, that they do not easily see how these two things can be joined together in practice. If complete authority and too much power, for example, are assumed in dealing with children, it appears difficult that this manner of controlling them (although it may proceed from great zeal, it is not according to knowledge, as Saint Paul says, since human weakness is so easily forgotten) should not become too harsh and unbearable.

On the other hand, if too much consideration is had for human weakness, and, under pretext of having compassion for them, children are allowed to do as they will, the result will be wayward, idle, and unruly pupils.

What, then, must be done in order that firmness may not degenerate into harshness, and gentleness into languor and weakness?[47]

The *Directions* are 130 pages in length. To modern education theorists, they would seem to focus excessively on matters of pupil control, compared to psychological development and formal instruction. For example, the *Directions* include detailed instructions for the application of corporal punishment using a rod. The precise dimensions of the rod are prescribed, plus the occasions justifying its use. But after such ominious discussion, brothers are told that punishments of more than three blows should be rare, and more than five blows could not be given without the permission of the brother superior (or principal).

The contrast between the *Directions* and more contemporary educational approaches is partly due to the larger size of the classes (60 to 100 pupils per class) managed by individual brothers. Furthermore, their subject matter, while a significant variation for their era, was far less diversified than in our era. But we should also recognize a difference in educational priorities. Beginning teachers in our era regularly remark that their most demanding problem is the maintenance of pupil discipline; the beginners often opine that they were poorly trained in this particular.[48] It may be the Christian Brothers had a more realistic view of the needs of teachers than modern theorists.

La Salle was concerned with maintaining a distinction between the purposes of the order's schools and those maintained by more classically oriented orders. He concluded an order comprised solely of brothers, as opposed to priests, would be best suited to maintain that distinction. Brothers did not have the extended formal education (including training in Latin) typical of priests. Thus, they would have neither the training nor inclination to inject a classical perspective into their schools. La Salle tried to insure that governance of the order was placed in the hands of brothers—and not priests. And, to our day, Christian Brothers schools have maintained a focus on practical scholarship, and the education of middle- and lower-middle-class youths. For example, the most prominent Christian Brothers high school in the Chicago area has graduated a disproportionately high number of students who became local elected officials.

Overseas Missions

During its early years, the church had largely grown through missionary activities. And the era succeeding the Reformation was the first stage of a long period of European exploration and conquest of much of the overseas world. Once again Catholic missionaries (as well as Protestant ones) were engaged in spreading the faith to the world.[49]

In this process, Catholic missions were inevitably entangled with issues of international exploration, trade, and imperialism. The church had a commitment to bring Catholicism to all peoples. It was practically impossible for such transmission to occur without the cooperation of national governments—who controlled the means of overseas transportation and supply and provided the military forces needed to protect remote colonies from hostile powers and unfriendly natives. Furthermore, many citizens and officials in Europe were actively sympathetic with the missionary aims of the church. Such activities were part of the tradition of their religion. Many explorers and settlers were also Catholics and wanted priests and sisters to travel with them to provide prayerful support for their activities, and also to supply some of the social and charitable services that were developing in their homelands.

It is also notorious that missionary activities sometimes provided other forms of useful assistance for many colonial enterprises. They justified such enterprises (as missionary efforts) to uncertain persons in the homeland. They lifted the morale of explorers and colonials. And they supplied a mechanism for converting hostile natives into allies of the colonial administration.

The early intra-European missionary efforts were largely carried out by itinerant monks. The missions of the colonial era, however, were essentially staffed by members of more recent, uncloistered orders—the Jesuits, the Franciscans, and the Dominicans, among others. Some missionary efforts were also assisted by diverse female orders. Thus a convent for Ursuline nuns was established in Quebec in 1639 to provide education and medical attention for Amerindian converts. The various uncloistered orders provided an adaptative base for the organization of missions. They developed schools for the training of missionaries, and systems for recruiting and screening potential missioners. (The remote Jesuit missions in Paraguay, called the *Reductions*, were staffed with volunteers. Between 1650 and 1750, only one of every fifteen order members who volunteered for this arduous service was accepted and assigned. Those that were accepted knew that they would probably spend the rest of their lives on this mission.)[50] Scholars were assigned to develop dictionaries. Other educated missionaries wrote reports that were transmitted to congregational headquarters in Europe, and often printed and disseminated among Catholic laypersons to enlist support. Techniques developed in Europe for operating schools, hospitals, and other charitable activities were adapted to foreign environments. Gradually, indigenous order members were recruited and trained overseas, and became part of the orders' international hierarchies. The traditional religious stress on self-denial and discipline was enormously important in motivating missionaries to accept, with comparative equanimity, deprivation, isolation, and sometimes, martyrdom. The basic doctrinal themes of charity, community, and leading by example provided order members with powerful techniques of persuasion.

Some idea of the importance of such dedication is provided by details about the arrival of the first contingent of twelve Spanish Franciscan missionaries in Mexico City in 1524, four years after the arrival of the army led by Cortez. The so-called twelve apostles, true to their Rule, walked 250 miles barefoot from the coast to the city. Cortez led a procession of troops and native leaders out from the city to greet the friars. The chronicler who witnessed the event reported that "when Cuauhtemoc [the Aztec ruler] and the other chiefs saw Cortez kneel to kiss the friars' hands, and when they saw that the friars were thin, with torn habits and without hats, on foot and without horses, and on the other hand Cortez, whom they took to be some kind of idol, kneeling before them, they and all the indians followed his example."[51]

The precise tactics of missionaries and their practical effects were as diverse as the reasons for such activities. Missionaries provided explorers and conquistadors with arguments to justify the harsh suppression of native regimes. They eloquently protested the exploitation of natives as unChristian. They strove to extinguish traditional native styles of life in favor of techniques introduced by the Europeans. They attempted—sometimes with significant success—to protect native groups from exploitation (and even corrupting contact) by white persons. They encouraged systems of religious conversion based on force and coercion—and tried to win the hearts and minds of natives through charity, the display of wisdom, and temperance. They sometimes applied policies which foreclosed indigenous Catholics from assuming roles as clerics and order members—and gradually evolved policies which made full participation in church organization available to all Catholics. They directly conspired to overthrow native regimes, to replace them with colonial authority, and acted as loyal counselors to important native leaders, to win the voluntary acceptance of Catholicism by existing native governments. They encouraged the destruction of native cultural artifacts, and directed the systematic study and analysis of native languages and traditions. In some instances, long and elaborate missionary efforts, such as those of the Jesuits in Japan, ended up producing little or no lasting effects. In other instances, such as in South America, missionary (and colonial) efforts were responsible for aligning whole continents with Catholic values.

The topic of overseas missions is obviously extraordinarily complex. Still, it can be constructive to contrast such efforts with the earlier (and notably successful) Catholic conversion activities carried out in Europe, largely before the tenth century. It would be incorrect to describe the overseas missions as failures. But, it would be fair to describe them as less successful than the previous European activities. Several causes can be assigned for this lesser success:

First, even allowing for improvements in transportation between the fifth and sixteenth centuries, colonial missions were typically more remote from their bases than the earlier European missions. This made it harder for the home countries to supply support, and the prestige of the home country was less evident to the persons and cultures being proselytized.

Second, the barriers of climate and disease were more severe than the earlier situation in Europe. In some African missions, 100 percent of the first contingent of missionaries died within the first five years after the establishment of the missions as a result of the primitive knowledge about sanitation and disease (and the lack of developed resistance to local diseases).

Third, missionaries usually arrived at overseas mission sites as allies of the exploring or colonial power, since that power provided their transportation. During the earlier missions in Europe, missionaries often provided their own locomotion and were less affected by compromising foreign alliances.

Fourth, the conflict between the missionary goal of conversion, and the imperial goals of trade, conquest, and colonization, handicapped the efforts at conversion. In Europe, missionary efforts had often been undertaken to securely independent countries. Tensions between Protestant and Catholic missionaries (and Protestant and Catholic imperial powers) handicapped the efficacy of Catholic missionaries.

Fifth, tensions sometimes arose between different orders, as well as different nationalities. In Japan, in 1597, twenty-six Catholics largely aligned with Spanish Dominican missionaries were executed by the government, while Portuguese Jesuits and their communicants were tacitly tolerated.[52] The preexisting tensions between the Jesuits and the Dominicans with regard to missionary activities in Japan were among the innumerable causes contributing to the mixed pattern of persecution and moderate toleration.

Finally, the cultural gap between the overseas missionaries (and their homelands) and some of foreign societies visited was greater than the earlier gap between the Christianized nations of Western Europe and non-Christian European societies.

At later stages in the era of colonialization, changes in the European zeitgeist began to affect the vitality and objectives of religious orders—which were still largely European-based institutions. These changes led to a significant decline in Catholic and religious vitality, even in basically Catholic European societies. It is to the nature of this decline, its ramifications, and the religious response, that we now turn our attention.

Notes

1. For background on the Catholic Reformation, see Pierre Janelle, *The Catholic Reformation* (Milwaukee, WI: Bruce Publishing, 1949).

2. For a discussion of the trend and its implications, see Edward McNall Burns, *The Counter-Reformation*; A. G. Dickens, *The Counter-Reformation*(London: Thames and Hudson, 1968). and Jean Delumeau, *Catholicism Between Luther and Voltaire.* (Philadelphia: Westminister Press, 1977).

3. The Sister Formation Conference is based in Washington, D.C., and was founded in 1957. As an organization, it has been sympathetic to the liberalizing themes arising in Catholicism since the Vatican II Council. *New Catholic Encyclopedia* (Washington, DC: Catholic University, 1967), vol. 13, p. 261.

4. *New Catholic*, vol. 12, p. 328.

5. Ibid., vol. 10, p. 546.

6. Thomas Maynard, *Apostle of Charity* (London: George, Allen and Unwin, 1940), p. 134.

7. F. E. Peters, *Ours* (New York: Richard Marek, 1981), p. 28.

8. Nancy Henderson, *Out of the Curtained World* (Garden City, NY: Doubleday, 1972), p. 32.

9. Ibid., p. 33.

10. St. Joan de Chantal, *St. Francis de Sales: A Testimony*, trans. Elizabeth Stopp (Hyattsville, MD: Institute of Salesian Studies, 1967), p. 69.

11. For a classic work on this topic, see Arnold van Gennep, *The Rites of Passage* (London: Routledge & Paul, 1960).

For a more recent relevant work, see George A. Weckman, "The Rites of Entry into Closed Religious Communities." (Ph.D. diss., University of Chicago, 1969).

12. Rosemary Howard-Bennet, *I Choose the Cloister* (London: Hodder and Stoughton, 1956), pp. 56-57.

13. Mary Purcell, *The World of Monsieur Vincent* (New York: Charles Scribner and Sons, 1963), p. 205.

14. Maynard, *Apostle*, p. 11.

15. Calculations derived from Oliver Kaspner, *Catholic Religious Orders* (Collegeville, MD: St. John's Abbey Press, 1957).

16. For one biography, see E. A. Peers, *Mother of Carmel: A Portrait of St. Teresa of Jesus* (London: Student Christian Movement, 1946).

17. For one biography, see Chrisogono de Jesus, *The Life of St. John of the Cross*, trans. Kathleen Pound (New York: Harper Brothers, 1958).

18. For history of the Albertine rule, see Bede Edwards, *The Rule of St. Albert* (Alyseford, England: Carmelite Priory, 1973).

19. For St. Teresa's mystical writings, see *Life*, trans. David Lewis (Westminister, MD: Newman Book Shop, 1947); *The Interior Castle*, trans. E. Allison Peers (Garden City, NY: Doubleday, 1972); and *The Way of Perfection*, trans. E. Allison Peers (Garden City, NY: Doubleday/Anchor, 1961).

20. For St. John's mystical writings, see St. John of the Cross, *The Collected Works* (Garden City, NY: Doubleday, 1964).

21. St. Teresa of Avalia, *Letters*, trans. E. Allison Peers (London: Burns, Oates and Washbourne, 1951), vol. 2, p. 691.

22. Edwards, *The Rule*, p. 64.

23. Ibid., p. 37.

24. Ibid., p. 64.

25. For one biography about St. Francis, see Maurice Henry-Couannier *St. Francis de Sales and His Friends*, trans. Veronica Morrow (Staten Island, NY: Alba House, 1964).

26. For one biography on St. Joan, see Elizabeth Stopp, *Madame de Chantal* (Westminister, MD: Newman Book Shop, 1963).

27. St. Joan, *Testimony*, p. 97.

28. *New Catholic*, vol. 3, p. 451.

29. For writings on St. Vincent, see Maynard, *Apostle*; and Purcell, *The World*.

30. For one biography on St. Louise, see J. Calvert, *Louise de Marillac* (London: Geoffrey Chapman, 1959).

31. *New Catholic*, vol. 14, p. 686.

32. Purcell, *The World*, p. 121.

33. *New Catholic*, vol. 3, p. 471.

34. Purcell, *The World*, p. 124.

35. Geoffrey Moorehouse, *Against All Reason* (London: Widenfeld and Nicholson, 1969), pp. 91-92.

36. For general discussion about the pros and cons of voluntary versus tax-related charity, see Edward A. Wynne, *Social Security: A Reciprocity System Under Stress* (Boulder, CO: Westview Press, 1980).

37. St. John Eudes, *Selected Works*, ed. by W. E. Myatt and P. J. Skinner (New York: P.J. Kenedy, 1948), vol. 3, p. 210.

38. Kaspner, *Catholic.*

39. *New Catholic*, vol. 6, p. 55; vol. 4, p. 987.

40. For a recent life on Loyola, with bibliographic materials, see John C. Olin, *Autobiography of St. Ignatius Loyola* (New York: Harper and Row, 1974).

41. *New Catholic*, vol. 7, p. 900.

42. Ibid., p. 890.

43. Theodore Besterman, *Voltaire* (London: Longmans, 1969), p. 33.

44. John Tyllotson, Archbishop of Canterbury, *Sermons*, in H. L. Menken, *A New Dictionary of Quotations* (New York: Dodd, Mead, 1964), p. 608.

45. For one biography of St. John, see Edward A. Fitzpatrick, *La Salle, Patron of Education* (Milwaukee, WI: Bruce Publishing, 1951).

46. *New Catholic*, vol. 3, p. 632.

47. Jean-Baptiste La Salle, *Directions for the Conduct of Schools* (New York: McGraw-Hill, 1935), pp. 55-60.

48. See, for example, Kevin Ryan, *Don't Smile Until Christmas* (Chicago: University of Chicago Press, 1970).

49. Joseph Schmidlin, *Catholic Mission Theory* (Techny, IL: Mission Press, 1931) .

50. S. J. McNaspy, *Lost Cities of Paraguay* (Chicago: Loyola University Press, 1982), p. 29.

51. Bernal Diaz del Castillo, *History of the Conquest of New Spain,* trans. Maurice Keating (London: J. Wright, 1800), p. 387.

52. Michael Cooper, *Rodrigues, the Interpreter* (New York: Weatherhill, 1974), pp. 121-62.

8
Confronting Modernity

In 1976, a written survey was conducted among the 50 members of an American Trappist monastery. The study concluded that "Love and consideration for one's fellow man, adherence to the monastic vows, spirituality, and integrity emerge clearly as the principle qualities upon which respect [for other members] is based . . . "
— L. Richard Della Fave and George A. Hillery, Jr., "Status Inequality in a Religious Community"

A former sister reported the following anecdote about her formation process: "During the afternoon classes, Mother Superior's glances, whispered suggestions, and her gestures with their silent voices prodded us into convent class deportment. We were not to speak without permission. We ought not to have our hands, arms or elbows on the table. We should prop up the book we use with another book behind it."
— Nancy Henderson, *The Curtained World*

As Western society moved towards developing "modern" attitudes, many conflicts arose between those attitudes and elements of typical Catholic doctrine and practice. The tensions engendered by these conflicts critically affected order life. A number of these conflicts developed due to the increasing hostility of some social groups towards what they called "religious superstition." The topic of superstition and Catholicism is important enough to warrant deliberate examinaton.

The Secret History of Superstition

During all human history—including our own era—there has been a substantial difference between the themes that later history treats as significant, and those activities that comprise typical life. Normally, large proportions of human energy are directed towards activities that future observers will classify as fads, superstitions, and popular misconceptions. Historial studies often give such matters short shrift. Those trivial—or unwarranted—activities have not established precedents that have prevailed into our time. Conversely, in looking at the past, we typically focus on the themes that have articulated patterns that still affect the tone of our own lives.

One deficiency in this sorting of the past is our failure to appreciate the full weight of typical life. As a result, we neglect to consider the relationship between the *full* past and the real nature of contemporary life. A good instance of this neglect is the matter of superstition. For most of Western history, superstition has been an important force affecting popular life. Yet historical materials have generally ignored this prevalence, except when it is coupled with some concrete, dramatic phenomenon, such as the burning of witches. Because of this disinterest, we often assume that incorrect, magically-oriented concern about the nature of ordinary events is a trait peculiar to primitive peoples, or (in Western society) essentially medieval patterns of thought. One effect of this unsympathetic and superficial treatment is our failure to appreciate the role of superstition in affecting popular life during most (all?) of human history.

Church doctrine held that God might occasionally directly intervene in human affairs to produce particular effects. Miracles could happen. This belief, in itself, might be characterized as a form of superstition—depending on one's particular theology and cosmogony. But, as one Catholic scholar put it, "We should not assume that God regularly suspends the operation of natural laws." Divine intervention, miracles, or supernatural apparitions were typically regarded by the church as extraordinary events. Or, where such visitations might occur with some frequency—as during meditations—systems of control were provided, such as spiritual advisors. The purposes of the systems were to constrain and focus this powerful process.

The fact that the church regarded divine intervention as abnormal satisfied certain institutional needs: a group of persons frequently affected by personal divine visits would be affected with a high degree of instability, as different group members put different interpretations on such powerful and necessarily ambiguous incidents.

Despite this conservative disposition on the part of the institutional church, many Catholics, especially in earlier eras, tended to personalize and concretize some of the concepts pervading church doctrine. This meant that many everyday events were perceived as routinely shaped by divine intervention. Often, such intervention was presumably effected by numerous human acts of propitiation. Some theologians felt this process of personalization distorted parts of church doctrine. But the church often failed or refused to draw definitive lines between many forms of correct and incorrect belief. As a result, many evidently dedicated Catholics evolved substantial bodies of personal beliefs and had experiences that we would, today, be likely to call superstitious or psychotic. An interesting example of this is the autobiography, or journal, of the French abbot Guibert de Nogent (1053-1124). Guibert was a literate, and evidently effective, Benedictine monk and abbot. Yet one-third of his journal is occupied by descriptions of his semiroutine contacts with devils and other destructive supernatural forces. Some of the incidents involve the actual sighting of devils by Guibert or another person. Other incidents involve Guibert's attribution of some event to the deliberate intervention of good or bad forces. For instance, in his journal Guibert tells of one of his early personal demonic confrontations. He had been considering the importance of leading a right life, and possibly becoming a monk:

> One night, during this period, I was lying in bed, seeming to be safer with a lamp close that gave a bright light, when suddenly and close by (from above, I thought), there arose shouting of many

voices in the dead of night, and a voice without
words, but full of woe. Thereupon, dizzy with the
shock, I was rapt from my senses and fell with
sleep, in which I thought I saw a dead man, who,
someone cried out, had been killed at the baths.
Crying out with terror at the phantasy, I leapt
from my bed and, looking round as I slept, I saw
the lamp extinguished; and in the midst of a cloud
of gathering darkness my eyes fell on a devil in his
own shape standing near. At that horrible sight I
would have gone mad, had not my master [since
Guibert was serving as an apprentice], who was
usually on guard to control my terrors, adroitly
soothed my perturbed and wandering wits. It was
not unknown to me even in the tender years of
childhood that the desire for a right mind then
burning in my heart enraged the devil in no small
measure to stir up wretchedness in me . . .[1]

After preliminary incidents of this sort, it is easy to understand
why Guibert might be disposed to search for, detect, and believe
in the devil's intervention in numerous later life events.

The church's policy regarding such patterns of belief (or
superstition) was necessarily mottled.[2] Putting it simply, in
many instances it summarily suspended judgment regarding
many allegedly supernatural episodes; other incidents it
formally declared to be undeserving of belief or worthy of
suppression. Furthermore, prominent Catholics themselves
sometimes differed on how to interpret or assess stories of
particular visitations or miracles, adopted implausible
interpretations of ambiguous events, or simply shared the
incredulity of many lay believers. But probably the most basic
element of church policy regarding these matters was that the
church paid little or no attention to them. Essentially, the
incidents were ignored because the church lacked the resources
or energy to intervene in most such situations. In most Catholic
countries through most of history, high proportions of nominal
church members were only remotely connected with the church:
there were not enough priests to permit adequate intervention;
many priests themselves were poorly trained; and many

nominal believers had low levels of knowledge of doctrine or religious practices. Under such circumstances, a luxuriant growth of religiously-unsanctioned folk beliefs existed alongside a complex body of formally sanctioned transcendent beliefs. Predictable patterns of cross-fertilization transpired between these two bodies of belief.

The patterns of interaction between "superstition" and Catholic doctrine are, I would argue, broadly similar to the many intellectual currents in our own era. Often our contemporary analogues do not involve religious matters—the issues are usually secular. Nonetheless, in our era, as in all societies, there are generally accepted political and social principles that are used to justify a variety of disparate collective and individual acts and statements. The integrity of relationships among these principles and our patterns of everyday conduct is sometimes intellectually problematic. In other words, our conduct is often inconsistent with general principles we proclaim and the principles themselves conflict with each other. The nub of the matter is that the world is extremely complicated. It is impossible for human societies to devise systems of thought and action that are regularly coherent and provable. And so we intellectually patch things up and accuse earlier societies—which applied equivalent practices—of superstition. As for our own conduct, we devise more hortative terms.

The cross-fertilization between popular Catholic beliefs and superstitious conduct helped determine the nature of religious life: Guibert's reports of frequent human confrontations with the devil were one effect of this fertilization. Sermons, prayers, and meditations were designed to deal with such topics. Religious were trained to analyze and interpret potential metaphysical incidents. Ritual occasions were developed to articulate and confront such problems.

Some order members and communities of members deliberately exploited public superstitious beliefs through the manipulation of artificial and real religious relics and other activities. And systems for the suppression of bad and false beliefs were established and maintained.

The Impact of the Enlightenment

As the evolution of Western society proceeded, a body of opinion was formed which was inconsistent with the supernatural beliefs prevailing in medieval times. The new opinions have been generally characterized as the Enlightenment.[3] The conflict between the Enlightenment and medieval perspectives was partly due to the development of formal, experimental physical science. The new knowledge gradually demonstrated the deficiencies of many existing folk and philosophic beliefs. The conflict also evolved from the development of new and different superstitious beliefs. These new beliefs were not necessarily more right or wrong than their predecessors. They simply better matched the ripening zeitgeist. The new supernatural beliefs touched on topics such as the belief in human progress, the assumption of the natural goodness of man, and the premise that all phenomena were susceptible to scientific analysis. Like all vital supernatural beliefs, these new beliefs were unprovable. They had to be accepted on faith. During the Enlightenment, however, the new beliefs possessed an inherent widespread appeal. The force of the Enlightenment was particularly powerful vis-a-vis the church, since many members of the church hierarchy were embarrassed at the prevalence of folk beliefs among Catholics, especially in rural areas. As it were, the protagonists of the new beliefs—the philosophers—became the intellectual reference group for many significant Catholics. An increasing disjunction arose between what was believed by better-educated Catholics and less sophisticated believers.

The diffusion of the Enlightenment had a profound impact on European religious orders between 1700 and 1800. The church had earlier taken a position of essential hostility towards the development of physical science. That hostility was expressed in acts such as the suppression of the theories of Galileo (1564-1642). And the traditional supernatural values maintained in the Church were profoundly embedded in religious life—in the performance of the Office, the practice of the meditation, the veneration of the relics and traditions of order founders, and in innumerable other rites and norms. As the Enlightenment advanced—at first, in France, but then gradually elsewhere in Europe—church practices and doctrines fell under increasing criticism. Many of the critics themselves were church members, and even order members, who were carried along by powerful intellectual currents. Partly as a result of such shifts, the number of persons enrolling in orders gradually and steadily declined. The decline affected all orders, but especially the contemplative orders, whose activities were most embedded in traditional mystic perspectives.

The effect of this shift in intellectual currents was aggravated by changes in political circumstances. Through all of church history, significant relationships usually have existed between the church and local and national government institutions. These relationships were even embedded in church doctrine, which explicitly assumed that some form of division of labor between church and state should be negotiated and applied; then both institutions might better serve their divergent responsibilities. The particular balance of power in different circumstances largely determined the division which evolved. For much of European history, the church had important advantages in dealing with secular governments. Such governments were often quite decentralized. As a result, they were handicapped in confronting an international church whose hierarchy often possessed important administrative training. But, as European political evolution proceeded, the balance gradually shifted. In general, national governments increased in strength. The Protestant Reformation also diminished Catholic influence, because it extinguished the church's former monopoly as the sole Christian religion. And the spread of the Enlightenment further undercut traditional Catholic authority, since one aspiration important to the movement was the development of relatively benign, rational, and more nationally powerful governments.

As these shifts proceeded, some governments, even in the "Catholic" countries, applied their growing power to increase their resources and influence, and lessen the authority of the church. These measures were, themselves, accretions of earlier forms of government intervention into religious affairs. Thus, the practice of governments appointing commendatory abbots—who milked the revenues from monastic properties—had prevailed for many centuries in France. But additional forms of diminishing church independence and properties evolved. In France these shifts, characterized as Gallicanism, included measures making the designation of bishops and other appointed church officials largely dependent on the determination of the French king. In Austria, in the latter eighteenth century, the new policies were called Josephism, after Emperor Joseph II. He severely restricted enrollment into monastic life, required monks to assume the responsibilities of secular priests, and sequestered many sources of religious revenue for government purposes. Another significant by-product of increasing Church/state conflict was the suppression of the Jesuits.

Because of that order's conspicuous commitment to the international church—as evinced by its members' unique oath of loyalty to the pope—it was a powerful instrument for protecting overall Church interests. Such protection became more necessary as many members of the church hierarchy became increasingly beholden to national governments. Gradually, some national governments took steps to diminish the freedom of Jesuits within their jurisdictions. Government edicts were issued expelling the Jesuits from France in 1764 and from Spain in 1767. Eventually, in 1773, Pope Clement XVI (ponitificate, 1769-1774) dissolved the society, in a temporizing effort to respond to the many national pressures constraining the church. The dissolution meant that individual Jesuits were then expected to affiliate with other existing orders or become diocesan priests. The order, true to its principles, accepted this decision without any public display of dissent. In a number of overseas missionary situations, suppression actually meant the extinction of large-scale, effective missionary activities.

The suppression had other practical implications beyond depriving the papacy of powerful support. It symbolized the relatively limited vision and vigor of a succession of popes during the eighteenth century; the deficiency undoubtedly handicapped the church's response to many of the novel challenges confronting it. The suppression also communicated an important message to many other, non-suppressed orders: militantly supporting overall church interests, in the face of more limited national priorities, might invite severe retaliation against such orders. When retaliation was attempted, the Roman church could not or would not offer vital support.

The French Revolution

The decline of religious life in particular, and the vigor of the church in general, by the late eighteenth century, represented a relatively dramatic historical shift. The Catholic Reformation and the CounterReformation had disclosed the church's remarkable powers of recovery in the face of late medieval decadence and the Protestant Reformation. And the development of new orders, such as the Jesuits and the Daughters of Charity, had provided further signs of institutional adaptability. But, despite such achievements, the spread of the Enlightenment and the development of nationalism had taken a heavy toll. Perhaps the final, and most powerful, blow struck in this assault on traditional religious life was the French Revolution.

During the early stages of the Revolution, such as the meetings of the Estates General (in 1789), the Revolution's programs received explicit support from many members of the French church. These clergy were affected by the spirit of the times, and held only moderate loyalty to the church as an international institution. As the Revolution progressed, more direct church/state conflicts developed. The successive revolutionary governments carried out (or acceded to) the seizure of church property; church lands were taken over by peasants, or sold by the government to speculators. Some churches were closed or used for nonreligious purposes, others were temporarily adopted as "temples" for the practice of secular religions based on the worship of the Goddess of Reason. At different stages in the Revolution, secular priests and religious were pressured to adopt positions sympathetic to the Revolution—and sometimes its antireligious policies. The level of resistance to these pressures was mixed. Some priests and religious consistently refused to change their practices, and accepted martyrdom. Others went into foreign exile, or continued their commitment to the Church by continuing to publicly act as priests (where local lay loyalty to the church loyalty was strong), or served as underground priests. Many engaged in various forms of temporization, including acting as paid (and compromised) religious agents of the new state. The many forms of suppression by the Revolutionary government were motivated by a number of complementary factors: the desire of the government, or persons having an influence on the government, to get possession of church property; hostility towards the Church, partly on general priciples, and partly due to its identification with the Old Regime; the comparative weakness and vulnerability of the church; and resentment towards an institution connected with foreign governments that opposed the Revolution. The antireligious policies of the Revolution became part of the intellectual baggage carried through Europe by the armies of Napoleon. Thus, they were put into effect in many parts of the Continent.

At the very time the Enlightenment and Revolution were enjoying their greatest success, their most critical weaknesses were begining to appear. The relatively thorough suppression of the church in France was not followed by a purely secular society. Instead, there were many government efforts to establish an emotional center for legitimacy: a secularized religion, or a Napoleonic monarchy. These measures included some of the forms of traditional Catholicism, but lacked much of its public appeal. The elaborate and venal entanglement of the French Revolutionary state in religious life (through its efforts to establish a national pro-Revolutionary church) lent greater vitality to the earlier tradition of relative church independence. The cynical exhaustion of Revolutionary impulses, and the lengthy, costly and bloody Napoleonic Wars all served to undermine the appeal of the forces of irreligion in France. Eventually, Napoleon, for reasons of state, determined to consent to the reestablishment of the traditional Catholic religion in France. The precise (and implicit) terms of the bargain, the Concordat of 1801, were the subject of continuing church/state controversy. As a result, the place of Catholicism in French life remained unsettled until well into the twentieth century. But the nub of the matter is that the philosophies and programs of the Enlightenment, when put into practice, fell distressingly short of their alleged goals.

Whatever the deficiencies of the eighteenth century church, they appeared far less distressing after the alternative policies had been exhaustively assayed. The superstition attributed to the church contrasted not unfavorably with the superstition of the Terror and the Revolution. The benefits of science looked less attractive after they had been translated into the weapons and techniques of popular mass war. The virtues of nationalism seemed less appealing when nationalism provided the basis for recruiting and motivating national armies, far larger than any traditional monarch could mobilize by hiring professional soldiers. The charming doctrine of the goodness of natural man suffered a loss of vitality when the effects of that doctrine became apparent in practice.

The Reaction

During and after the Napoleonic Wars, a widespread reaction took place throughout most of Europe against many of the principles which set the stage for the French Revolution. The reaction is historically perceived in terms of the political leaders who articulated its programs (e.g., Metternich, the Duke of Wellington). But this perception is deficient unless we recognize that the leaders were able to mobilize followers because the doctrines of the Revolution had lost their appeal among many persons and classes. In the political sphere, the reaction was characterized by various forms of political conservatism. In the intellectual and aesthetic sphere, the reaction came in the form of romanticism. To our modern temper, these countermovements may seem irrelevant or limited. But, if we conduct a more serious analysis, we can see that the countermovements were rational responses to a flawed and arguably failed activity. Put simply, the more people saw of modernity, the less attractive it looked. Since all important popular decisions must be made on symbolic and affective levels, the irrationality of reflexively revering the past may be better than revering some undesirable and unpredictable future.

Some of the evidently destructive effects that the Revolution and the Enlightenment had on church policies had secondary benefits for the church. The confiscation of many church properties—including the Vatican States, literally, a nation governed by the popes—made church administrators less concerned with controlling and administering tangible assets, and the people living on them. Conversely, in order to cover the costs of church operations, it became necessary to rely more on income collected from church members. In sum, church leaders had less cause to be aligned with the interests of large landowners and military allies (who helped maintain their title to the Vatican States), compared to a broad group of potential contributors. Another effect of church/state polarization was the evolution of a church that did not reflexively identify with governments in power. Of course, this lack of identification sometimes descended to overt church/state conflict, and even suppression by the government. But often there was simply a recurrent tension. And, since there were usually classes of citizens hostile to particular government policies, a natural sympathy frequently arose between these classes and the outcast church. The religious toleration theoretically favored by the Enlightenment also had an impact. Thus, during the nineteenth century, many restraints on Roman Catholics, that had persisted in Great Britain since the Reformation, were removed in response to widespread gradual changes in English political values. As a result, a number òf orders created (or recreated) communities in the British Isles during that century.

We must keep in mind that the spirit of the Revolution—like that of the eighteenth-century church—left the lives of many ordinary citizens comparatively unaffected. As a result, many persons and families, through the whole period of the Revolution and the Napoleonic Wars, continued to practice—without great fanfare—their traditional modes of Catholic faith. Thus, by the Bourbon Restoration in 1815, two vital themes were already underway in Europe which affected religious life: persisting Catholics were at work reviving their religious institutions, and potential or dormant Catholics were being mobilized (in the spirit of romanticism) to revitalize extinguished or decayed religious orders.[4] Due to these developments, the nineteenth century became a period of noteworthy religious growth. More religious orders were founded in that century than in any other century, and 55 percent of all orders ever founded were founded in the nineteenth century.[5]

In addition to the creation of new orders, a growth occurred via the revival of extinguished or decadent orders. In France, Jean Lacordaere (1802-1861) persistenty and successfully worked to bring about the reestablishment of the Dominican orders in the face of government resistance and innumerable organizational problems (for example, the traditional Rule of the order was not appropriate for the operation of small convents, and so, sensitive adaption had to be made that still maintained the spirit of the Rule).[6] Again, the order of the Trappists had been driven out of France during the Revolution, and the surviving emigres had to be assembled and encouraged to reestablish their community in France.[7]

Also during the nineteenth century, a renewed militancy—or recovery of nerve—developed in the central church. Successive popes, for a variety of reasons, determined that the church should take a relatively strong position resisting many of the currents affecting Europe. This determination was evinced in various ways. In 1814, Pope Pius VII (pontificate, 1800-1822) revoked the decision to suppress the Jesuit order. The Bull of revocation aimed to restore to the church " . . . ceaselessly tossed by billows, those strong and experienced rowers who would conquer the might of the waves."[8] Between 1814 and 1900, the order's membership climbed from 600 to 10,000.[9]

Several popes strongly defended the independence of the church against the intrusive claims of diverse secular and anti-Catholic regimes, principally in Europe. These claims of independence eventually won the respect of diverse non-Catholic interests, who saw the integrity of the international church as one counterpoise against the growing claims of the nation-state, and the overweening attractions of nationalism. Pope Pius IX (pontificate, 1846-1877) brought about the acceptance of the doctrine of papal infallibility by the First Vatican Council (1870).

There is no uniform standard that causes one to judge all of these papal acts *correct.* But the pattern involved did provide Catholics and order members with an image of a relatively vigorous church. That church, in general, took positions consonant with the main traditions of religious life.

Undoubtedly, this image positively assisted the growth and revival of orders.

Another part of the revival in religious life occurred through the development of new orders to meet diverse novel challenges. One of these new challenges was the spread of urbanization. This shift meant that the traditional proximate, informal supports found in many small rural communities were less available to citizens dwelling in crowded, heterogeneous cities. Furthermore, the problems afflicting urban dwellers were simply more apparent than those affecting rural residents. In response to these circumstances, a number of new male and female orders developed that focused on the charitable, medical, and educational needs of the new populations. In effect, during the nineteenth century, in lieu of increased government services, many urban areas moved towards enlarging the services provided by religious orders.

New orders also evolved to heighten and communicate important (and sometimes original) devotional themes to public audiences (e.g., the Sacred Heart, continuous exposure of (and prayer before) the Blessed Sacrament). Such devotions were not in conflict with previous church doctrines; however, they often represented the adaptation and restatement of that doctrine in terms immediately relevant to church members in a particular era.

New orders additionally identified with diverse national and ethnic traditions and aspirations. In Ireland, nationalism and Catholicism had been suppressed, in varying degrees, by the government imposed by Protestant England. But, during the nineteenth century, many new religious orders were created in Ireland. The orders were tolerated by the British partly due to the general lessening of religious restraints in Great Britian.

Because of the Irish orders' declared religious purposes, they were less subject to British control than formal, political organizations. They often served as tacit or explicit means of communicating Irish national values, and, at the same time, improving the status of the Catholic Irish through education. The various ethnic orders, understandably, tended to develop bodies of doctrine that expressed themes unique to their special circumstances. James Joyce, in *A Portrait of the Artist as a Young Man*, portrayed some of these themes in his description of studenthood in a Jesuit school in Ireland. One particularly striking section portayed a dramatic, terrifying sermon delivered to the pupils on the topic of the tortures inflicted on the damned in Hell. [10]

Some of the same themes are reiterated in *Formation of Christian Character*, a book written by an Irish Jesuit priest. The text showed how such education systems relied on adult teachers imbued with a complex mix of pragmatism, determination, insight, and altruism. One section, subtitled "Turning the Soul," provided suggestions for the conduct of relatively rigorous religious exercises at boys' residential schools:

> When the Stations of the Cross with the Stabat Mater [a hymn commemorating the sufferings of the Virgin Mary] are done with a solemn ceremonial, attended by a cross-bearer and acolytes, they are more than welcome; while Benediction of the Blessed Sacrament, with appropriate music before and after, helps to lighten the labor and freshen the spirits of exercitants. The singing of hymns at public service is important as a factor of mass psychology, tending to lessen tension and forestall apathy. But a careful selection of hymns and a skillful organist are essential for the purpose of sustaining devotion. In a school of, say, 250 boys, public exercises should never be less than a half an hour, since it is not practical to transfer boys in large numbers for duties of less duration. [11]

The increases in persons enrolled in orders affected the size of both contemplative and active orders. The active orders were those directly involved in providing charity and religious services to laypersons. The increases had implications for the economic sustenance of orders. As in all previous eras, the sources of support were very diverse. Many active orders provided services to individuals, families and Catholic parishes. In turn, the orders received payments back from some beneficiaries (either individuals or parishes), and sometimes from government agencies on behalf of some beneficiaries (e.g., tuitions, payments to hospitals). Sometimes sliding payment scales were applied. Then, the better-off beneficiaries subsidized the costs of those who were less affluent. Many active orders were engaged in missionary work. In such environments, there was often insufficient local support for order members; then, subsidies were needed. The contributions came from a myriad of sources: funds sometimes came from the central church (i.e., Rome); sometimes they were raised by order members engaged in fund-raising at the home base of the order; and sometimes through area-wide communication and fund-raising networks developed by the church in general, and the order, in particular. The area-wide patterns of fund raising caused many Catholics to be informed about the diverse mission activities they were asked to pray for, and support through contributions.

A sensitive example of the ties between foreign missions and their stay-at-home religious supporters is presented in *Death Comes to the Archbishop*, a novel by Willa Cather. The novel is really a relatively accurate portrayal of the life of Father John Baptist Lamy (1814-1888), the first archbishop of Santa Fe, New Mexico. The archbishop was reared in France. During his American service he made several arduous trips back to his homeland to solicit various forms of support. One part of the novel described his musings about the propriety of Father John Valliant, his colleague, also from France, soliciting special help for their work from sisters in a French convent (e.g., the sewing of garments and altar vestments).

> . . . [D]uring one visit to France, the Bishop came to see his concerns in a new light. When he was visiting Mother Philomene's convent, one of the younger sisters had confided to him what an inspiration it was to them, living in retirement, to work for the far-away missions. She told him how precious it was to read Father Valliant's long letters, letters of which he told of his sister [another nun] in the country, the Indians, the pious Mexican

women, the Spanish martyrs of old. These letters, she said, Mother Philomene read aloud in the evening. The nun took the Bishop to a window that jutted out, and looked up the narrow street, where the wall turned at an angle, cutting off further view. "Look," she said "after the Mother has read us one of those letters from her brother, I come and stand at this alcove and look up our little street with its just one lamp, and just beyond the turn there is New Mexico; all of that he has written us of those red deserts and blue mountains, the great plains and the herds of bison, and the canyons more profound that the deepest mountain gorges. . . ." The Bishop went away believing that it was good for these Sisters to work for Father Joseph.[12]

The economic problems of contemplative orders were different. Female contemplative orders had never engaged in farming; some male orders did, and still do. Many female orders accepted cottage-type production responsibilities, often with church-related purposes (e.g., baking the bread for the sacrament of Holy Eucharist). These responsibilities produced some level of income. Otherwise, these orders were supported by endowments (from contributions by living or deceased Catholics, perhaps relatives of order members), and contributions solicited from Catholics who asked to be remembered in the prayers of the order members, and who were informed of the order via newsletters and other written communications.

Religious Orders in America

The United States of America was an important area of order expansion during the nineteenth century. During that century, increasing proportions of American immigrants came from European countries with Catholic traditions (e.g., Ireland, Italy, Germany). The immigrants often saw their religious beliefs as one means of maintaining ties with their roots, since their native villages and traditional means of livelihood could not be transported to America. But Catholicism was incidentally an international religion, and the United States guaranteed them freedom of worship. As a result, many immigrants probably attached more importance to religious commitments in America than they did in their homelands. But it was difficult to translate this interest into concrete measures in the face of many complex obstacles. There were few institutions in largely Protestant America to train appropriate priests and religious, especially those with the foreign language skills needed to communicate with many immigrants. In their homelands, the adult immigrants had learned their religious beliefs and traditions through socialization in a pervasive, pro-Catholic environment. Such environments could not easily be recreated in a foreign country. And the immigrants often lacked substantial financial resources. A medley of policies and measures evolved to overcome these obstacles.

Homeland religious orders were often stimulated to recruit, train, and support members who themselves emigrated to America to assist immigrants—and some new orders evolved in the homelands with this mission in mind. Catholic schools gradually developed in America, staffed with female and male religious who were sometimes recruited in ethnic homelands. Religious orders also created and served ethnic parishes, and special resources were made available by religious of appropriate ethnic backgrounds. And residents in the homelands were importuned, by citizens and religious leaders, to provide funds to help supply their overseas brethren with appropriate aid. Obviously, all of these measures were immensely assisted by the special structures of religious orders, with their essentially international perspectives—despite their sometimes local roots.

The patterns of support applied in America were also eventually adapted for other immigrant European populations in Argentina, Canada, Australia, and elsewhere. A typical instance of such international support is mentioned in the history of the Sisters of the Immaculate Blessed Virgin Mary (Loreto) in India. In 1840, the archbishop of Calcutta, travelling in Europe, tried to recruit sisters from the mother house of the IBVM's near Dublin to create schools for the children of European Catholics in India. At first the mother superior refused, since she already had too many demands on her resources. The archbishop, in a letter, reported that he ask the mother, "Would you be willing to hold yourself responsible for the souls of the children who are now being deprived of a religious education?"[13] Eventually, the superior, after a brief meditation, agreed to let him address the sisters and ask for volunteers. The whole community volunteered. The archbishop sailed off in high spirits with twelve sisters—average age, eighteen. (His inital hope had been to enlist six sisters.) The immigrant sisters established a community which eventually developed a network of order-maintained schools throughout many parts of India.

The institutions—schools, colleges, hospitals, churches—formed by these orders played complex transitional roles. They first maintained sympathy with the traditions of the homeland—its language, unique patterns of worship, ethnic and national loyalties. They acted as general representatives of their particular ethnic communities, since the order members spoke with special authority and did have significant practical experience. But, despite such reverence for Old World traditions, the institutions did have to relate in various ways to America—a secular and relatively rational, society. As a result, the institutions had to engage in different forms of adaptation: to be subject to professional certification; to learn the political processes of a multireligious, secular democratic society; and to teach students how to succeed in relatively cosmopolitan environments. Inevitably, as generations passed, the institutions' ties to their homelands moderated. They became more deeply rooted in semi-ethnic American culture. Over decades, the proportion of foreign-born and first generation immigrants in "senior" ethnic groups declined. The groups became more Americanized. Similarly, the various ethnic orders underwent an equivalent modification. Those modifications are proceeding to this day.

Lifting the Veil

Twentieth century environments have subjected religious life to relatively high levels of deliberate observation. While seclusion has been a long-term goal of religious life, that aim has often been only imperfectly attained. During some periods in the past, rule observance was often inefficient. Isolation was thus fractured by unauthorized visits of laypersons to religious communities, or by order members who made improper visits to the secular world. By the nineteenth century, however, a relatively uniform level of rigor prevailed affecting order life. As one partly intended consequence, the quantity of information about order life available to nonreligious became more limited; rule observance, in general, simultaneously increased.

By the mid-twentieth century, a series of changes increased the visibility of order life. More secular and semisecular institutions were willing to publish information which the church might prefer to see buried. Growing numbers of order members left orders and reported about the life they had lived.[14] And, there was an enlarging sympathy in the church and in some orders with the value of formal research on the exact nature of religious life.[15]

The research was often carried out by religious themselves, sometimes as part of their responsibilities as graduate students (pursuing doctorates) or as faculty members of academic institutions. Due to these developments, considerable information has been disclosed about religious practices, which, in the recent past, had been kept relatively private. The findings of the research are constrained: they describe order members and religious life in a single era, and in particular orders and situations. Still, even with such qualifications, those findings are relatively consistent with the historic patterns portrayed here: Most orders members come from traditionally religious families. It is not uncommon for them to have order members among their relatives. There is a certain socioeconomic hierarchy of membership: particular orders attract (or pursue) members from higher socioeconomic statuses than others—though no absolute lines of division have been identified (i.e., your parents must be wealthy for you to join this order). Order members retrospectively report that their first strong inclinations to become religious occurred at diverse times in their lives, although a moderate number say the inclination occurred before the age of ten. A high proportion of them had frequent and positive contacts with religious during childhood and adolescence.

One careful American study analyzed the mental health and development of candidates in a women's order which maintained high schools and colleges.[16] The researcher, who obtained a doctorate at the University of Chicago, was a member of the Sisters of the Presentation of the Blessed Virgin Mary (founded in Ireland in 1805). The community (and sisters) that was the subject of her study appeared to be sister members of her order: they were educated in schools administrated by the unnamed order and had the high level of academic training generally associated with the Sisters of the Presentation. The order's formation process extended over eight years. The study concluded that the candidates were "religiously concerned, determined, self-assured, serious and intelligent."[17]

It also described the pattern of psychological development of the postulants and novices during formation. The candidates who persisted became progressively more "shy, serious and silent."[18] The author implied that this outcome was of questionable value; what would the author's (or reader's) conclusion, however, be if we substituted adjectives such as *introspective* or *meditative?* Some of the personality shifts indentified were presumably developmental—the normal effects of chronological maturation. But it wa• evident that formation accentuated this process. The study concluded that formation did not change the candidates' "core personality structure," though it did modify their "ideals." This conclusion is obviously burdened with semantic ambiguity.

An interesting French study, conducted in about 1960, reported the written responses of over 1800 members of female contemplative orders to a series of open-ended questions.[19] The respondents whose replies were quoted were necessarily a selective sample. Still, the replies disclose a striking level of serious, purposeful introspection and systemic concern with mental prayer.

One autobiography of a former female contemplative religious, written in 1950, characterized her motivation to be a contemplative in the following terms:

Most contemplatives enter convents less because
they themselves choose to do so than because they
are chosen by God. These are the real "vocations."
Some spiritual adventure has happened to them:
some vital encounter has taken place between their
souls and God. They know, beyond all possibility of
doubt, that God is not just some vague, remote,
spiritual ideal, but a living Person. They therefore
become possessed by a kind of burning hunger and
thirst for God, which only he himself can satisfy.

To those who have never had this experience, such
an idea will probably seem fantastic. But the fact
remains that you cannot read the lives and writings
of the saints and mystics without repeatedly
coming up against the assertion that, even in this
life, it is possible for the veil to be lifted and for the
human soul to enter into what is, literally, a
conscious, experimental contact with God. And
those who have experinced this contact declare
unanimously that it can only be described as
aforetaste of the bliss of heaven.

This being so, it is not really so very surprising
that when this craving for contact with God
becomes fierce and urgent, as it undoubtedly does
in certain people, they are ready to trample
underfoot the world and everything in it, if by that
means their longing can be satisfied.

It is, of course, for this type of person that
contemplative convents primarily exist. They are
organized, down to the very smallest details, with
one object in view—to provide for those who live in
them the kind of life which will be enable them to
attain their end.

The discipline to which religious subject themselves
is extremely rigorous. God, lovelier than any
dream, is pure Spirit; therefore, if contact is to be
established, the counter-attraction of the senses

must be overcome. You can't be completely
wrapped up in God (and He is a jealous lover),
unless you are unwrapped up in what this world
has to offer you. In convents, this process of
unwrapping is effected by a system of remorseless
separation from everything that is not God.[20]

The considerable increase in members leaving orders
provided researchers with subjects who could respond to
questions contrasting the religious and secular (after leaving the
order). In one study of former sisters, the subjects emphasized
that (a) they felt less commitment to secular jobs than they had
felt toward their order responsiblities (even though the jobs were
in helping activities equivalent to the assignments they had as
sisters); and (b) they had garnered higher levels of support from
their community members while sisters than they did with their
female secular colleagues—in secular work, other females were
implicitly perceived as sexual rivals for male attention.[21] The
latter conclusion suggests that, despite the efforts of orders to
control special friendships, supportive relationships were
typically the norm in religious life.

Not all the reports of members who choose to leave have
been sympathetic. One ex-Franciscan described his order life in
late nineteenth-century England.[22] Among the major themes
portrayed were mediocrity, tedium, and an excessive concern
with trivia. In particular, his community was responsible for
preaching periodic, special services at scattered churches. The
individual members, over time, developed personal, relatively
effective presentations that they routinely repeated to their
scattered audiences. While the approaches usually worked, they
did little to heighten the spiritual life of the community
members. A more recent autobiography of an American ex-
Jesuit presented a mixed evaluation of the constraints,
satisfactions, dedication and evasions that affected his religious
formation and life.[23] He told a story of being discovered by an
order superior, sitting in the stands watching a professional
baseball game—a severe violation of the Rule. He was directed
to publicly confess his breach to the community during dinner
and to invite some appropriate penance. (The tradition of such
confessions was derived from the Chapter of Faults, and was

common in the community.) The precise form of the confession was significant. It had to be truthful. But a cleverly-phrased confession might moderate the ultimate punishment. The malefactor stood up and said, "I accuse myself of publicly recreating in violation of the rules." The confession was a coup. It was truthful. It did not, however, disclose exactly what had been done. It would have been uncharitable for the other community members to publicly press him for specifics. And there was a grudging admiration, felt by all, for a member who had displayed ingenuity. The penance ultimately required was quite mild.

It is obviously difficult to weigh the merits of such mixed judgments about the nature of religious life. For instance, a fair comparison might require us to measure such judgments against the retrospective satisfactions (and frustrations) of a sample of ex-lawyers, public school teachers, or social workers, all of whom choose to leave their occupations.

Another contemporary form of disclosure about religious life is less novel: the relatively accurate description of the activities of prominent and admirable founders or order members. There is a long tradition of such reports. Indeed, one talent of charismatic persons is the ability to dramatize events so as to motivate others. An instance of contemporary dramatization is the narrative of the life of Mother Teresa, the founder of the Congregation of the Missionaries of Charity. That order was insituted in Calcutta, India, in 1960. Since its founding, the order has opened branch units in many countries throughout the world and developed a parallel male order of brothers. Mother Teresa, born in Yugoslavia in 1911, first went to India to be a member of an order of teaching sisters (the IBVM's described earlier in this chapter). Eventually, moved by the terrible plight of the inhabitants of the streets and slums of Calcutta, she determined (with the permission of her order), to dedicate herself to providing charity to these suffering beings. She took a short course in providing simple medical care. Then, while residing in the convent of another order, she walked each day through the streets, providing help to those in immediate need. One of her first concerns was to provide a shelter for dying persons. There they might at least expire with dignity,

surrounded with affection. One observer described the situation
as follows:

> The need for a shelter had become starkly obvious
> when Mother Teresa had found a woman lying on
> the pavement outside one of Calcutta's busiest
> hospitals. She was so spent, so desperately ill, that
> she appeared unmindful of her feet having been
> gnawed away by rats and cockroaches. If my
> memory serves, Mother carried the woman into the
> hospital only to be told that her precarious
> condition and her poverty did not allow her to be
> admitted. Mother Teresa's pleading was to no
> avail, so she set out with her patient for another
> hospital. One can imagine her anguish and despair
> when the woman died on the streets where she had
> been found. At much the same time, an early
> helper of Mother Teresa recalls how, as he and
> Mother once went in search of medicines for her
> pavement dispensary, they saw what Mother
> thought to be a child lying under a tree, again
> outside a city hospital. Returning a while later in
> pouring rain with the medicines, they found a
> pathetically wizened and emaciated man, not a
> child, lying dead in a mess of vomited blood. "Cats
> and dogs are treated better than this," Mother said
> sadly.[24]

Gradually, Mother Teresa recruited a number of young
women students from the school where she formerly taught to
assist her. She stressed that they had to obtain their parents'
consent: she determined not to enroll helpers with ambiguous
motives, nor provoke conflicts with the families concerned. The
enormous dedication and energy the mother displayed, plus her
considerable good judgment, had a great effect on potential
recruits, and on Indian citizens in general. In 1979, Mother
Teresa was awarded the Nobel Peace Prize.

Gradually, the order has enlarged its concerns. (Some of
the sisters are now dedicated to a contemplative life.) Still, in
the order's active work, it has remained focused on serving the

poorest and neediest. Because they began in India, the sisters' dress is the standard garment of lower-class women of Calcutta—even when they serve in other countries. The members observe a rule with relatively rigorous provisions regarding prayer and religious observance. As one of the sisters said, "Mother does not want us to see ourselves as simply social workers." An informative story can be told about the sisters establishing a mission in the desolate slums of the South Bronx in New York City. One of the sisters, interviewed shortly after the mission opened, reported that the poor of Calcutta suffered more material deprivation (lack of food, shelter, medical aid) than the poor in the South Bronx; but the poor in the South Bronx suffered more severe loneliness and despair.[25]

I interviewed a young woman who worked for sometime as a lay volunteer in the Sisters' South Bronx mission. Her most profound recollection was of the sisters' persistent and wholesome cheerfulness.

The Tensions Affecting Active Orders

By the mid-twentieth century, probably more than 80 percent of all order members in the world were enrolled in active orders. Members of active orders were authorized to routinely come in contact with laypersons and secular institutions to meet their diverse responsibilities. Perhaps the most important force affecting order life has been the gradual but steady penetration of active religious life by technical and rational modes of operation. That penetration is the natural by-product of the many outreach responsibilities accepted by active orders. Those responsibilities inevitably subjected order members to divisive tensions. The tensions arose when members were expected to lead relatively traditional religious lives and simultaneously meet their charitable responsibilities in an efficient fashion. One former sister told of the problems generated when her teaching responsibilities were coupled with fundraising activities away from her school:

> My frequent trips to solicit funds for our school
> caused important changes in my attitudes. First,
> towards spiritual exercises. Rather than an

opportunity for union with Christ and a special time for insight, spiritual exercises were burdens I carried through the day until I found spare moments to discharge them. On early morning departures, meditation was made with the feel of automobile wheels moving beneath the seat and the sound of horns and passing cars. There was often no time for spiritual reading until right before bed. I was convinced that even Mother Benedict couldn't have found the time.[26]

Of course, obstacles to the performance of spiritual exercises by religious did not originate with the twentieth century. But it is evident that the more fully orders did accept semisecular responsibilities, the more likely those responsibilities would intrude on traditional patterns of religious life. There was good reason to believe that the overall level of intrusion was rising.

Secular patterns also intruded into religious life due to government and professional regulations affecting their teaching and social service activities. Thus, in America, teachers in schools staffed by religious orders were placed under pressure to conform to state teacher certification requirements. Similarly, high schools conducted by orders were stimulated to satisfy secular accreditation standards, so graduates would be eligible for admission to many colleges. The drive to meet such standards was generated not only by external forces. Catholic families and many orders, on their own motion, thought that meeting the standards was inherently desirable. This concern for improving the professional performance of order members was expressed in the concept of *aggiornamento*--meaning, bringing up to date. The word became current in the church during the 1950s. Some of the spirit of such concerns was expressed by Pope Pius XII (pontificate, 1939-1958) in 1951, in his *Discourse to the Teaching Sisters*:

Many of your schools are being described and praised to us as being very good. But not all. It is our fervent wish that all endeavors become excellent. This presupposes that your teaching sisters are masters of the subjects they expound. See to it, therefore, that they are well trained and that their education corresponds in quality and academic degrees to that demanded by the State.[27]

Meeting state and professional standards had implications for the management of formation. It meant that the socialization of novices had to integrate college training with religious formation. But college training was often partly based on premises different from those prevailing in formation--very few college classes would treat the history presented in the Bible as a practical guide of conduct. Furthermore, the novices' academic classes would probably include lay students, and some might even occur in a secular college. Accreditation for high schools conducted by orders meant that students had to be taught by a variety of properly-certified specialists (e.g., biology teachers, drivers' education teachers). This either added additional encumbrances to the formation process, or increased the pressure for schools to employ lay specialists. All of these developments diminished the quality of the religious message communicated among, to and by order members.

Order members engaged in providing higher education or medical services faced different, but somewhat equivalent, complexities. Some tensions generated by scientific work were nicely illustrated by Kathryn Hulme's novel, *The Nun's Story*.[28] The protagonist was a sister serving as a medical missionary in the Belgian Congo before World War II. To practice charity, she has to display great dedication to the scientific aspects of her work. Gradually, that dedication generated many intellectual distractions for her in her more traditional religious role. (I recall an interesting review of the novel written by a sister who was a member of an active order. The reviewer contended that the book erred in implying that a relatively typical sister would allow her active responsibilities to distract her from her religious life. Considering *The Nun's Story* almost thirty years after this critical review, it seems that Kathryn Hulme made a prescient judgment).

Another element of specialization—either in teaching or the sciences—was the development of a reference group partly comprising laypersons. To stay current in a professional or technical field, practioners must read certain literature, attend occasional professional meetings, and otherwise focus on the concerns of one's intellectual peers. But, for order members, their critical peers are other members of the order. When a second group of peers—fellow specialists, who are typically laypersons—are concurrently identified, a source of conflict is generated. (In earlier eras, when religious specialized in an intellectual endeavor, their intellectual peers would probably be other religious—also working in theology, or homoletics.)

Traditional religious life, especially as it focused on the provision of charity, was poorly structured to resist destructive penetration by technical and rational modes of thought. If charity was the aim, the tenets of obedience and humility apparently required orders to structure their operations to facilitate that purpose. If the new modes of providing charity interfered with norms of order operation, then the norms should be modified. In other words, orders had extensive experience in trying (often successfully) to resist the inroads of lust, sloth, and materialism. But the plea that certain changes should be made to permit the order to be of greater service was very seductive. Furthermore, the norms of order life had already demonstrated remarkable adaptability. Why should one assume that further flexibility could not occur without vitiating traditional order values?

The effects of some of the changes just sketched did not uniformly affect all order members, or even all members of the same cohort receiving a similar exposure. Human beings vary in their levels of adaptability. Thus, some order members might operate in an extremely secular and rational environment and simultaneously maintain high levels of religious observance. But one can plot an imaginary curve. We can see the integrity of formation being continuously eroded and imagine the demands of specialization steadily increasing. Gradually, the severity of such tensions intensifies. Increasing proportions of order members find themselves under growing stress. The degree of stress felt by particular members could be affected by their length of enrollment in traditional religious life, their specific responsibilities, the tradition and contemporary policies of their order, their immediate religious (and secular) peer group, and their own unique personalities. Despite these individual differences, the overall pattern of the curve would be up; eventually, a point would be reached where very few persons would choose to join or stay members.

Values Hostile to Religious Life

The rationalization and desacralization of secular life throughout the world had important effects on religious life. Previously, even when the external world was hostile or indifferent to religious life, that world was still one explicitly related to mystic forces. It was prevaded with beliefs in folk magic, militant Protestantism, or anthropomorphism. Often the persons who opposed the values of order members did not essentially disbelieve in the supernatural. They simply had different supernatural explanations for events than did order members. Conversely, in many modern environments, the assumption is that there are *natural* environmental explanations for all phenomena. These explanations may not now be known to us, but they ultimately can be discovered through the further refinement of science. This hypothesis underlies many elements of modern life. It may be more or less true than the supernatural assumption it replaced. It is surely no more capable of proof. But it has affected the character of many of the responsibilities assumed by religious orders.

Throughout much of the secular world, there has also been a general shift in the values applied in weighing human conduct. This shift has affected order policies. In all societies, except those under communist domination, egalitarian principles have gradually increased in salience. Of course, despite this shift, there are non-communist totalitarian regimes. At this time, however, even those regimes generally hold their authority through the exercise of raw power. They rarely have the legitimacy many authoritarian regimes possessed in earlier eras. The question whether the world is actually more democratic now than fifty years ago will receive perhaps an uncertain reply; but there is no doubt that more people today than in the past see democracy as the right thing.

In practice, the spread of egalitarianism is revealed through measures such as the prolongation and diffusion of formal education; the hostility to traditional (but often noncoercive) forms of authority; the pervasive tendency to regard most forms of distinction and discrimination as invidious; the legitimization of various civil liberties; and the growing belief in the philosophical centrality and inherent morality of the detached, solitary individual. Such concepts may be right or wrong, or good or bad. It is unquestionable that they have displayed increasing popular appeal. Their appeal is larger due to the relationship between such concepts, and the material and institutional changes that have occurred throughout society. For example, consider the invention and distribution of the relatively low-cost home video player. These devices provide individuals with extremely simple means to view pornographic and sadistic materials at low cost in their private homes. It is cumbersome to imagine or apply a system for constraining such perverse viewing. As a result, there is a ready market for the diffusion of philosophic perspectives that propose that (a) public intrusion in such viewing is wrong, and (b) the effects of such viewing will probably be benign. In other words, we invent or buy philosophies that gratify our desire to use novel technologies. Obviously, religious orders that operate in an intellectual milieu pervaded with such values will find themselves—and their members—afflicted with serious conflicts.

Now, we cannot forget that many orders have previously worked closely with delinquent or wrong-doing persons. But many of those orders were performing acts of charity to persons who were admittedly in error—or "lost." There was little suggestion that the malefactors were equal to typical citizens, or that their wrongs were inconsequential. Thus, an order could maintain its traditional values and regard them as superior to those of the persons being helped. But this implies the application of a frank hierarchy of values. This concept is out of harmony with current egalitarian perspectives.

The long-term rise in the division of labor (or specialization) in society also has had important effects. Traditional religious life was familiar with the concept of specialization. St. Benedict's Rule provided for a variety of specially-designated jobs. More basically, divisions of labor have been inherent in all persisting collective life. A significant characteristic of religious life was the ways different orders operated to maintain group cohesion despite the centrifugal tendencies inherent in specialized and subdivided work. Essentially, orders relied on devices such as prolonged formation; strong systems of hierarchy; the daily collective reiteration of the Office, or some appropriate substitute; members living in common residences; the wearing of a uniform; measures to maintain relative isolation from the outside world; and emphasis on the benign exercise of authority.

These factors caused members to strongly identify with each other—even when their specialized responsibilities meant their understanding of each other's secular work was limited. But in contemporary environments, specialization has gone even further. Order members, who are often specialists in essentially secular activities, find themselves strongly identifying with their co-specialists, who may well not be order members, or Catholics, or even religious believers. Furthermore, the level of community in any group is diminished when it compromises too many divergent specialists working towards some remote, common end. Each specialist, due to his excellence, may help the group attain its goal. But, if the elements of specialization become too refined, the task of maintaining harmony can become very cumbersome. In the twentieth century, orders assumed the responsibilities of maintaining modern schools, colleges, hospitals, and social welfare agencies. They were constrained to operate such agencies in ways somewhat parallel to their secular counterparts. The danger of overextended specialization arose. Secular institutions may sometimes be able to manage that danger, in part because their employees are motivated by the desire of economic gain. Even if their a work environment is unpleasant (due, in part, to overspecialization), many secular workers will persist in order to earn a living or support their families. But order members, whose security is assured, will have little reason to enthusiastically persist in their work unless it involves practices highly related to their beliefs.

The Welfare State

The steady spread and growth of the welfare state has had corrosive effects on order life. Formerly, in countries where Catholicism was dominant, or among Catholic ethnic groups (in secular countries), religious orders supported by charitable contributions performed many of the responsibilities currently provided by state institutions, or by religious institutions partly funded by government monies. The services formerly rendered by orders were not as complete or sophisticated as those now coming from the state—but the orders were partially constrained by the lower levels of wealth generally existing in the past. As state-supplied benefits increased, (a) there were fewer incentives for people to look to orders for services, (b) there were fewer incentives for orders rendering services to solicit public engagement and contributions, (c) the forms of services provided were increasingly structured by secular premises, and (d) the rationales for providing services were more frequently articulated in secular and economic terms.

None of the preceding discussions are intended to propose that, as a result of these many changes, the overall quality of services now provided is better than in the past. True, the increase in state funding has undoubtedly increased the overall level of services and benefits distributed. But let us take the matter of religion and education as an example worthy of analysis.

Over the past 100 years, throughout all Western societies, more government funds have gone to support education at all levels, with a diminishing proportion of education costs supported by private persons. These developments have been the major cause for the general enlargement and prolongation of education: the average contemporary young person in Western society has probably received 60 to 110 percent more education than his predecessor of fifty years ago. And surely some persons are better off than their predecessors due to such education. But there is no way of proving what the optimum level of education is, compared to insufficient and excessive amounts. There are signs afloat that there has been a general overinvestment in (at least) higher education.

Vigorous state involvement in education has also undercut the traditional religious role in education. And there are real and substantial costs associated with this disassociation of religion from education. It is probably true that a high school teacher cannot teach physics with an essentially supernatural approach. If students at that same school are being taught social studies, however, it is at least arguable that they may be better prepared for life if they study the Old Testament in a relatively literal sense. For example, I recall sitting in on one Catholic high school religion class where the topic was a comparison of the leadership and talents of David and Saul; the students were enthusiastic and reflective. The fact is, that for the Judeo-Christian tradition, the Bible is our Homer. It is not simple to invent substitutes. And Greek youths did not study Homer as literature. His writings were simply stories about what happened a long time ago.

Finally, if a choice must be made, high school school students will probably be better prepared for life by being taught that premarital sex is sinful, compared to being taught, in sex education, that all sexual experiences are equally valid. Someone may argue that we can maintain the best elements of traditional religious education without simultaneously acquiescing to other objectionable aspects of doctrine. Maybe.

The welfare state resulted from a gradual shift from religious-supplied to government-supplied (or funded) services and benefits. The shift brought about changes in the way many persons perceived their responsibility to help others. At one time, religious motives were critical incentives to persons choosing to supply help, either directly (to relatives and neighbors), or indirectly (through contributions to charitable organizations). Such motives were expressed in a vocabulary replete with terms such as charity, mercy, and pity. Gradually, providing help became more of a government obligation. Then semilegalistic and economic concepts such as obligations, rights, and efficiency became more prevalent as stimulants to contributions (or taxes). The previous religious terminology emphasized relatively integrative themes: the kinship between givers and receivers; the moral benefits earned by generous givers; and the indefinite continuation of a class labelled *the poor*.

The plea of the Islamic beggar, "Alms for the love of Allah," epitomizes those themes. The plea emphasizes that both the beggar and the donor share a common faith. God will reward the donor for his charity. The gift is not particularly supposed to eliminate poverty, but more simply to demonstrate fealty to doctrine. The semilegalistic and economic themes endemic to the welfare state stimulate a more adversarial climate, and the expectation by some givers of dramatically successful effects. Theoretically, a rational system of evaluation might arbitrate the conflicts generated by adversarial approaches. Some evaluation technique might, presumably, finally show that society is better off paying taxes for a particular social service, as compared to individual citizens choosing to spend their money for their personal benefit. But all foreseeable systems of evaluation are relatively imperfect. Thus, the differences generated by the adversarial (and rights-oriented) approach are not really settled by rationality. They are largely determined by the groups voicing the strongest threats, or acting in the most Machiavellian fashion. It is true that the stimulation of guilt among givers was one ordinary tool of charitable fundraising. Effective fundraising was, however, was also facilitated by the virtues and community-building devices practiced by religious fund-raisers (such as Mother Teresa's acts of conspicuous dedication). Thus, exemplary and socially efficacious persons are effective fund-raisers. Such people are usually scarce. That scarcity is a natural cap for charitable fundraising. Furthermore, one may assume that when effective, visionary people ask us for money to help others, giving may hurt less. Visionary people can help us attain a powerful sense of our own virtue—a precious good. As a result, we are pleased to give.

Notes

1. Guibert de Nogent, *An Autobiography*, trans. C. C. Swinton (New York: E. P. Dutton, 1925), p. 60.

2. For specifics about the prevalence of superstition and lax belief, see Jean Delumeau, *Catholicism Between Luther and Voltaire* (Philadelphia: Westminister Press, 1977).

3. For some discussion of these themes, see E. E. Y. Hales, *The Catholic Church in the Modern World* (Garden City, NY: Image Books, Doubleday, 1960); and Owen Chadwick, *The Secularization of the European Mind in the Nineteenth Century* (New York: Cambridge University Press, 1975).

4. Some of the sources underlying the topic of orders in the nineteenth and twentieth centuries include (listed by order): Female orders: Benedictine Sisters (in Kansas), Mary Faith Schuster, *The Meaning of the Mountain* (Baltimore, MD: Helicon, 1963); Sisters of Charity of the Blessed Virgin Mary (Ireland and the United States), Jane Coogan, *The Price of Our Heritage* (Dubuque, IA: St. Carmel Press, 1975); Sisters of the Divine Compassion (New York State), Mary Treasa, *The Fruits of His Compassion* (New York: Pagent Press, 1962); Discalced Carmelite Sisters (in England and France), *In The Silence of Mary* (London: Carmel, Notting Hill, 1964); Sisters of Notre Dame de Namur (France), Sr. Saint Joseph, *The Memoirs of Mother Francis Blin de Bourbon* (Westminister, MD: Christian Classics, 1975); Sisters of Loretto at the Foot of the Cross (United States), Camillus P. Maes, *The Life of Rev. Charles Nerinckx* (Cincinatti, Ohio: Robert Clarke Co., 1888); Sisters of Mercy (United States), Justine Sabourin, *The Amalgamation* (St. Meubrac, ID: Abbey Press, 1976); Sisters of Mercy (Chicago), St. Xavier's College, *Reminiscences of Fifty Years* (Chicago: Fred J. Ringley, 1916); Daughters of St. Paul (Italy and elsewhere), Daughters of St. Paul, *Woman of Faith* (Boston: Daughters of St. Paul, 1965); Sisters of the Presentation of the Blessed Virgin Mary (Ireland), Roland

B. Savage, *A Valiant Dublin Woman* (Dublin: M. H. Gill, 1940). Male orders: Benedictines (United States), Colman Barry, *Worship and Work* (Collegeville, MD: The Liturgical Press, 1980); Redemptorists (United States), Michael J. Curley, *The Provincal Story* (New York: Redemptorist Fathers, 1963); Scalabrians (Italy and elsewhere), March and Mario Francesconi, *John Baptist Scalabrini* (New York: Center for Migration Studies, 1977); Resurrectionists (United States), John Iwicki, *The First Hundred Years* (Rome: Gregorian University Press, 1966).

5. Calculation derived from Oliver Kaspner, *Catholic Religious Orders* (Collegeville, MD: St. John's Abbey Press, 1957).

6. Lancelot C. Sheppard, *Lacordaire* (New York: Macmillan, 1964).

7. For specifics on the Trappist revival, see Louis J. Lekai, *The Cisterians: Ideals and Realities* (Kent, OH: Kent State University Press, 1977), pp. 180-185.

8. Thomas J. Campbell, *The Jesuits* (New York: The Encyclopedia Press, 1921), p. 695.

9. *New Catholic Encyclopedia* (Washington, DC: Catholic University, 1967), vol. 7, p. 907.

10. James Joyce, *A Portrait of the Artist as a Young Man* (New York: Huebsch, 1921).

11. Ernest J. Mackey, *Formation of Christian Character* (Dublin: Clonmore and Reynolds, 1962), p. 25.

12. Willa Cather, *Death Comes to the Archbishop* (New York: Alfred A. Knopf, 1970), p. 181. For a formal biography of Lamy, see Paul Horgan, *Lamy of Santa Fe* (New York: Farrar, Straus and Giroux, 1975).

13. Mother Mary Colmcille, *First the Blade* (Calcutta, India: Firma K. L. Mukhopadhyay, 1968), p. 15.

14. For example of writings by former order members, see Monica Baldwin, *I Leap Over the Wall* (New York: Rinehart and Co., 1950); Nancy Henderson, *Out of the Curtained World* (Garden City, NY: Doubleday, 1972); and Midge Turk, *The Buried Life* (New York: World Publishing, 1971).

15. For examples of research conducted by secular scholars, see Suzanne Campbell-Jones, *In Habit* (New York: Pantheon Books, 1978); Helen Rose Fuchs Baugh, *Out of the Cloister* (Austin, TX: University of Texas Press, 1977); Lucinda San Giovanni, *Ex-Nuns: A Study of Emergent Role Passage* (Norwood, NJ: Ablex, 1978). For research by order members or secular priests, see Joseph H. Fichter, *Religion as an Occupation* (South Bend, IN: University of Notre Dame Press, 1961); and W. W. Meisser, *Group Dynamics in Religious Life* (South Bend, IN: University of Notre Dame Press, 1965).

16. St. Mary George Thompson, "Modifications in Identity: The Socialization Process During a Sister Formation Program" (Ph.D. diss., University of Chicago, 1963), p. 57.

17. Thompson, "Modifications," p. 97.

18. Ibid., p. 99.

19. Bro. Bernard, ed., *Contemplative Nuns Speak* (Baltimore, MD: Helicon Press, 1964).

20. Baldwin, *I Leap*, pp. 7-8.

21. San Giovanni, *Ex-Nuns*, pp. 100, 115.

22. Joseph McCabe, *Life in a Modern Monastery* (London: Grant Richards, 1898).

23. F. E. Peters, *Ours* (New York: Richard Marek, 1981), especially p. 179.

24. Desmond Doig, *Mother Teresa: Her People and Her Work* (New York: Harper and Row, 1976), p. 54.

25. "Mother Teresa's Mission in the Bronx," *New York Times*, 8 Aug. 1980, p. 1.

26. Henderson, *Out of,* p. 95.

27. *New Catholic,* vol. 13, p. 262.

28. Kathryn Hulme, *The Nun's Story* (Boston: Little, Brown, 1956).

Epilogue

Readers are familar with the general principles enunciated by the Vatican II Council (1962-1965) called by Pope John XXIII (pontificate, 1959-1963). An enormous and complex literature has developed interpreting the aims and effects of that council, particularly with regards to religious life. An adequate consideration of the issues would unduly extend the scope of this book. Therefore, only a few general remarks will be uttered, and these will basically focus on developments in the United States. The remarks will largely interpret the council and its effects in a sociological light, compared to its administrative and theological ramifications.

For over a century preceding the council, the church had been confronted with a variety of changes in secular life. These changes had forced the church to accept many adaptations. Despite the adaptations, a considerable discrepancy existed between the institutions of the church (and its orders) and the norms of the secular world. The council was an effort to formally confront these developments, and the church's past and potential adaptations. Undoubtedly, a variety of forms of further adaptation could be proposed or adopted by the church. The council, and/or many people in the church and in religious life, opted for a relatively open acceptance of many policies that had already been accepted by some religious and significant laypersons. And such open acceptance greatly accelerated the previous patterns of tacit and incremental adoption. In a comparatively short period of time—perhaps ten to fifteen years after the council—the acceptance triggered a remarkable number of changes in church and order practices. Formerly, those practices had persisted for many decades and centuries. The changes were accompanied by outbursts of support from many church members. The vocabulary of support was replete with words such as *love, renewal, authenticity, experimental modes,* and *creativity.*

Structurally speaking, the changes might be characterized as diminishing the authority of central entities and inviting new forms of structure and authority to evolve from the bottom. The diminution of central authority was symbolically potrayed by the abandonment of Latin as the language of the Mass (and its replacement by the local vernacular language); the restructuring of the Mass, so the priest no longer looks up to God as the representative of the group; the removal of the communion rail, separating the priest from the congregation; and the lessening of pressures on Catholics for regular Mass attendance and the reception of Confession. Such measures did free individual Catholics and groups of Catholics for creative innovation. It became hard, however, to identify priciples that would guide such groups. It was also difficult to see how separate groups of Catholics could find well-defined bases for cooperation. In practice, the changes caused many church activities to lessen in formerly supernatural focus, and to be affected by prevailing secular currents.

These developments affected all parts of the church: laypersons, the hierarchy, secular priests, and members of religious orders. But, for our purposes, it will be constructive to focus on their effects on religious life. Those effects varied widely among different orders and communities, and among orders located in different countries.[1] Still, certain general patterns of change can be identified: the rigor of order rules was modified; less stress was placed on simple obedience; the requirements for frequent and formal prayer were lessened; provisions for mortification, diet and community dining were tempered or abolished; voting procedures, which previously discriminated in favor of particular classes of order members, were made more egalitarian; formation was often accompanied by proximate academic training, sometimes in partly secular environments; and the tradition of gradual, incremental institutional change was downplayed in favor of more expeditious renewal. Concretely, these changes were reflected by revisions in patterns of conduct such as: order members regularly wearing secular dress; assignments of members to new responsibilities being openedup to volunteers, just like bids in a large firm; increasing numbers of order members taking assignments working largely removed from community observance and control; and many order members living in small groups of three to four members, or even in solitary residences.

An interesting example of the operation, in the United States, of many of the preceding themes can be found in an attractive calendar prepared and distributed nationally on behalf of many Catholic groups to encourage young persons to enter religious or diocesan life.[2] Almost every month of the calendar portrays, via attractive color photographs, the activities of particular order members or diocesan priests. The purpose of the calendar and its text is to stimulate young persons to seriously consider religious vocations. Nine of the calendar's panels involve persons clearly designated as order members. The activities of these persons include: medical surgery; computer operator; lawyer in a legal clinic; author and photographer; manager of a publishing house; and communication director of a group of Franciscans (who had, *inter alia*, written a comic book life of St. Francis). Most of these activities were evidently related to various evangelical or helping themes.

The calendar's text remarks that "a religious vocation opens . . . opportunities for contemporary career situations." Of course, the activities portrayed are unexceptionable, and may well advance the overall goals of the Catholic church. And some of the activities are modern counterparts of activities engaged in by order members in earlier eras. But the activities can now be engaged in by competent persons without joining a religious order; and it is not clear why one should submit to a prolonged religious formation to engage in them or accept obligations to live in a community, and practice poverty, chastity, and obedience. Finally, the typical structures of such work activities do not facilitate order members living in community, sharing common meals, or frequently practicing common worship.

Something of the spirit of these many changes is expressed in the following letter to the editor, written by an American Catholic sister, and published in a secular newspaper in 1985.[3] It represents the sister's interpretation of her order's response to an important official church meeting:

As communications director for the Sisters of Mercy, Province of Chicago, I am concerned that The *Tribune's* account of the recent visit of Jerome Cardinal Hamer, prefect of the Congregation for Religious and Secular Institutes ("Nuns protest visit of Vatican cardinal," Aug. 22) failed to convey the real significance of that event for the church and for the religious congregations themselves.

By choosing to focus on the actions of the persons who leafletted outside the cathedral, *The Tribune* gave its readers the impression that the event was a kind of donnybrook instead of the respectful coming together of religious with church authorities that it was. About 1,600 religious packed Holy Name Cathedral. They represented a wide spectrum of theologies, ministries and lifestyles.

Taking the directives of Vatican II seriously, U.S. religious have engaged in a process of systemic renewal over the past 20 years. This process has led them to a new appreciation of their dignity as adults and of the uniqueness of their American experience as well as a growing awareness of the impact of culture on their world view.

The persons who demonstrated outside the cathedral acted out of these insights, which are shared by many inside the cathedral. As women religious have grown in their understanding and appreciation of themselves as women and of the church as the people of God, their pain at being denied full participation in its life and worship has become more intense.

The uniformity of thought and action that once characterized religious life is a thing of the past. Religious congregations today struggle to deepen their love and respect for one another as they act out of very different insights.

The real significance of Cardinal Hamer's
visit rests in his exposure to this diversity. May it
not be the end, but the beginning of greater
dialogue.

Karen M. Donahue, RSM
Communications Director
Sisters of Mercy
Province of Chicago

Consideration should also be given to patterns of political
activism by order members. These patterns were often
associated with the changes. In particular, some orders, or
order members, became identified with political causes that
most observers would identify as liberal or leftist. This
development warrants some discussion. The church has always
been concerned with secular politics. Sometimes its engagement
has been tacit, sometimes more overt. During most of the
industrial era, its formal sympathies have rarely ranged beyond
slightly left of center. In the post-Vatican II environment, some
factions in the church took positions that brought them into
alignment with secular groups which were distinctly to the left.
Of course, biblical and theological precedents were cited by the
religious involved on behalf of their political positions. But those
supposed precedents had sometimes existed for thousands of
years. The significant issue is that groups arose in the church
that determined to quote those precedents and to apply them in
particular ways.

The changes in the conduct of order members were
accompanied by certain demographic shifts in many (but not all)
orders. Total numbers of members enrolled declined. The
average age of new members increased substantially. Many
order members left their orders for secular life, often with
church consent. The average age of persisting order members
increased considerably. Many remaining order members,
particularly females, withdrew from work in elementary and
secondary teaching in favor of more independent work. In the
United States, these changes were reflected in the following
data: between 1963 (a relatively "high" year) and 1985, the
total number of female order members declined 42 percent, the

number of brothers declined 38 percent, and the number of order priests remained approximately constant.[4]

Many church members, both in and outside of the hierarchy, have objected to some or many of the liberalizing changes that succeeded the council. Some of the objectors have contended that the changes distort the real aims of the council, *per se.* Others argue that if the council had not been called, or if it had taken different positions, church and order life would have gone on as before. These are all highly problematic contentions.

Taking the objectors' positions at their best, the declarations and pronouncements of the council are pervaded with considerable ambiguity. This is understandable. Any documents covering a vast medley of topics, and which must be approved by an enormous number of busy people, brought together for temporary deliberations, will necessarily be relatively general. Furthermore, it is true that some church councils——such as the Council of Trent——have succeeded in articulating relatively coherent positions on elaborate issues. But the Council of Trent, including adjournments, extended over twenty-one years and had twenty-five sessions; Vatican II covered three years and had four sessions. The issues finally settled at Trent had previously been the subject of public controversy in and outside the church for over 400 years. The debates and opinions affecting the conclusions at Trent were wonderfully focussed (to paraphrase Samuel Johnson) by the militant hostility of the Protestant Reformation. Finally, the church assembled at Trent was necessarily a European church; the church assembled at Vatican II was a world church, with the attendant problems of refining a concensus. In sum, considering the constraints surrounding Vatican II, its prospects for developing consistent policies were not very great.

Even if there had been no council, the tensions between modernity and church (and order) life could not be indefinitely suppressed, nor could tacit adaptations persist or increase without controversy. Through one means or another, the tensions had to result in painful disorder. Sincere, dedicated people had made deep investments on both sides of a festering dispute. Some religious had committed themselves to living traditional lives—and maintaining a cautious distance from worldly involvement. Other religious had become extremely enmeshed in semisecular and welfare activities. They saw such activities as the justification for their religious life. These externally-oriented religious members could locate influential allies in many parts of secular and non-Catholic society. (Thus, in America, the purely secular Ford Foundation supplied funds to support various in-church efforts towards aggiornamento and the post-Vatican II restructuring of some orders.)[5] Any effort to clarify principles and policies would inevitably generate strong objections from some order members and enthusiastic approval from others.

None of this is to contend that a church council was the best way of dealing with the problem, or that the council that was held developed the best solutions possible in the time available. The point simply is that profound contradictions were developing in church life. Some form of explosion was increasingly likely. And the final outcomes of that explosion are still to be determined.

Obviously, many Catholics are frustrated with the current situation for diverse reasons. One consolation can be proposed to them. The contradictions between the traditonal church and many elements of modern life in effect mirror contradictions between human nature *per se* and modern life. The church, and particularly its orders, can be perceived as a model of certain basic forms of social organization. These forms may persist because they gratify particular, recurrent, profound human needs and aspirations. Speaking from a secular perspective, there is no guarantee that society will indefinitely evolve in directions congruent with the basic traditions of the Catholic church. But it is theoretically impossible for any persisting society to develop operating principles inherently antithetical to human nature. Such a development may temporarily occur; however, inevitable reactions will lead to a restructuring of that discrepant situation. Perhaps the best way to sum up the vexsome issues generated by the tensions affecting the Catholic church and religious life is to recall the import of an observation by Thomas B. Macauley:

We are confident that the world will never go back to the solar system of Ptolemy; nor is our confidence in the least shaken by the circumstance, that even so great a man as Bacon rejected the theory of Galileo with scorn; for Bacon had not all the means of arriving at a sound conclusion which are within our reach. . . . But when we reflect that Sir Thomas More [an extremely thoughtful man] was ready to die for the doctrine of transubstantiation, we cannot but feel some doubt whether the doctrine of transubstantiation may not triumph over all opposition.[6]

Surely, Catholic religious life has engaged the energies of many notable persons. Their implicit conclusions about the best way to lead our lives can never be subject to definitive assessment. Those conclusions may still have the vitality to affect the patterns of future Christians.

Notes

1.   The topic of the current status of religious life, especially as related to the effects of Vatican II, is complex, volatile and controversial. For these reasons, it will only be summarily covered in this book. One recent helpful source is John M. Lozano, "Trends in Religious Life Today," *Review for Religious* 42, no. 4 (July/August 1983): 481-504.

2.   *Catholic Family Appointment Calendar, 1986* (Schiller Park, IL: J. S. Paluch, National Vocational Awareness Division, 1986).

3.   Sister Karen N. Donahue, "The Visit of Cardinal Hamer," *Chicago Tribune*, Letters to the Editor, 18 Sept. 1985, p. 18.

4.   *Official Catholic Register, 1963* (Wilmette, IL: P. J. Kennedy and Sons, 1963), General Summary, p. 1; and *Official Catholic Register, 1985* (Wilmette, IL: P. J. Kenedy and Sons, 1985), General Summary, p. 1.

5.   For specifics about Ford Foundation grants to assist change in religious life, see Midge Turk, *The Buried Life* (New York: World Publishing, 1971), p. 77; and Reginald Neuwein, *Catholic Schools in Action* (South Bend, IN: University of Notre Dame Press, 1966), p. 9.

6.   Thomas B. Macauley, *Works*, vol. 9, "Review of Ranke's *History of the Popes*," (London: Longmans, Green & Co., 1898), p. 292.